INDIAN LAW/ RACE LAW

INDIAN LAW/ RACE LAW

A Five-Hundred-Year History

JAMES E. FALKOWSKI

PRAEGER

New York
Westport, Connecticut
London

Library of Congress Cataloging-in-Publication Data

Falkowski, James E.
Indian law/race law : a five-hundred-year history / James E. Falkowski.
p. cm.
Includes bibliographical references and index.
ISBN 0-275-94318-6 (alk. paper)
1. Indians—Legal status, laws, etc.—History. 2. Indians of North America—Legal status, laws, etc.—History. 3. Indians of North America—Treaties—History. 4. Human rights—Western Hemisphere—History. I. Title.
KDZ480.F35 1992
346.701'3—dc20
[347.0613] 91-46995

British Library Cataloguing in Publication Data is available.

Library of Congress Catalog Card Number: 91-46995
ISBN: 0-275-94318-6

First published in 1992

Praeger Publishers, One Madison Avenue, New York, NY 10010
An imprint of Greenwood Publishing Group, Inc.

Printed in the United States of America

The paper used in this book complies with the Permanent Paper Standard issued by the National Information Standards Organization (Z39.48-1984).

P

In order to keep this title in print and available to the academic community, this edition was produced using digital reprint technology in a relatively short print run. This would not have been attainable using traditional methods. Although the cover has been changed from its original appearance, the text remains the same and all materials and methods used still conform to the highest book-making standards.

Copyright Acknowledgments

The author and publisher gratefully acknowledge permission to use extracts from the following copyrighted materials.

Davenport, Frances Gardiner, and Charles Paul Paullin, eds. European Treaties Bearing on the United States and Its Dependencies. Carnegie Institution of Washington. Gloucester, MA: P. Smith, 1967. Reprinted by permission.

Hanke, Lewis. The "Requerimiento" and Its Interpreters, Revista De Historia De America, vol. 1, no. 1, at 25 (1938).

MacNutt, Francis Augustus. Bartholomew de Las Casas: His Life, His Apostolate, and His Writings. New York: G. P. Putnam's Sons, 1909.

Wheaton, Henry. Elements of International Law. 1866. Reprint. Reprinted by permission of Oceana Publications.

Cohen, Felix S., Original Indian Title 32 Minn. L. Rev. 28 (1947).

Las Casas, Bartolome de. Bartolome de Las Casas: A Selection of His Writings. Copyright © 1971 by Alfred A. Knopf, Inc. Reprinted by permission of Alfred A. Knopf, Inc.

Victoria, Franciscus de. De Indis Et De Ivre Belli Reflectiones. Ed. E. Nys, trans. J. P. Bate. In J. B. Scott, ed., The Classics of International Law. 1917. Reprint. New York: Oceana, 1964.

Cohen, Felix S. The Legal Conscience. Ed. L. K. Cohen. New Haven, CT: Yale University Press, 1960. Reprinted by permission of Yale University Press.

Our interest in Indian self-government today is not the interest of sentimentalists or antiquarians. We have a vital concern with Indian self-government because the Indian is to America what the Jew was to the Russian Czars and Hitler's Germany. . . . The issue is not only an issue of Indian rights; it is the much larger one of whether American liberty can be preserved. If we fight only for our *own* liberty because it is our own, are we any better than the dog who fights for his bone? We must believe in liberty itself to defend it effectively. What is my own divides me from my fellow man. Liberty, which is the other side of the shield of tolerance, is a social affair that unites me with my fellow man. If we fight for civil liberties for our side, we show that we believe not in civil liberties but in our side. But when those of us who never were Indians and never expect to be Indians fight for the cause of Indian self-government, we are fighting for something that is not limited by the accidents of race and creed and birth; we are fighting for what Las Casas and Vitoria and Pope Paul III called the integrity or salvation of our own souls. We are fighting for what Jefferson called the basic rights of man. We are fighting for the last best hope of earth. And these are causes that should carry us through many defeats.

—Felix S. Cohen, 1907–1953[1]

Contents

Preface

I have been studying Indian law for about half my forty years. My first memory of native peoples was as a child, driving through the Allegany Indian reservation west of Salamanca, New York. I vividly recall seeing the shell-shocked faces of the soon-to-be-removed Seneca Indians on the front steps of their homes, which were surrounded by land that looked as if it had been carpet bombed to make way for the flood waters of the Kinzua Dam. It was many years later that I learned we broke a treaty with these people, not for flood control for Pittsburgh but to take the last Six Nations Confederacy lands in Pennsylvania and place one of their traditional religious centers under five hundred feet of water.

I began to pursue my academic interests in Indian law under the guidance of Helen DiPota at Erie Community College. After transferring to the University of Buffalo, I took as many courses as I could from the three best teachers (other than my parents) that I ever had: Oren Lyons, Howard Berman, and Johnny Mohawk. Mr. Lyons taught me about the theocratic indigenous government and religion that he represented. Mr. Berman taught me how to do original research. Mr. Mohawk taught me that the most complicated ideas in the universe can be broken down into easy-to-understand concepts, and vice versa.

After a brief respite from my academic career into a more concrete career, I followed my fate of pursuing the law. I attended the University of California at Davis, where I learned only how to pass the bar. In an attempt to preserve my values, I coauthored a law review article that instinctively expressed many of the international human rights principles about which I was soon to learn more.

At the University of Essex (England), I gained international experience under the direction of Malcolm Shaw. My research was assisted by a project for Davis Weisbrodt while he was at Amnesty International. My dissertation at Essex focused on the international human rights of American Indians and coincided with the first chapters of the United Nations' *Study of the Problem of Discrimination against Indigenous Populations* and the founding of the Working Group on Indigenous Populations.

After beginning my professional career, first as a public defender and later as a district attorney, I followed the developments made by the working group with great interest. It has made substantial progress, but it still has not reached the top of the mountain. With the five-hundredth anniversary of legalized discrimination against the indigenous peoples of the Western Hemishphere, participants in the international legal system are pretending to listen to indigenous peoples for the first time, although they are still unwilling to make the fundamental changes necessary to remove the institutionalized discrimination against them. This book is not as eloquent as I would like, but it is the truth as I see it.

INDIAN LAW/ RACE LAW

Introduction

Indian law is race law.[2] This book is an attempt to illustrate that fact. The human rights of the indigenous peoples of the Western Hemisphere have been constantly violated since their lands were first invaded by European colonizers.[3] The Indian peoples have been subject to discrimination, ethnocide, and genocide.[4] Over the last five hundred years, the violations of their rights to exist, own land, and be self-governing have become institutionalized.[5]

The legal system of the European colonizers, as adopted by the European settler population, has developed special legal doctrines that only apply to the indigenous peoples and that legalize the "erosion" of the rights of the "vanishing race."[6] However, Indian peoples are not vanishing, nor is the process of the erosion of their rights a natural one.[7] Only recently has there been a reexamination of the pervasive racial prejudice inherent in the special legal doctrines that are used to place America's indigenous peoples into their legally anomalous situation.[8]

This book will trace the treatment of the indigenous peoples of the Western Hemisphere by the Christian-European "international" legal system to place current law into historical perspective. It will focus on the rights of Indian nations in their treaty relationship with the United States, although references to other indigenous peoples will be freely made. It will attempt to dispel some of the prevalent myths that were developed by the overseas European settler population to disregard the inherent and inalienable right of indigenous peoples to self-determination.

Indian Law/Race Law will demonstrate how two systems of law—one applying to "civilized" peoples, and the other applying to the so-called "backwards races"—were devised and justified. It will explain the beginnings of this dual system of law in the Western Hemisphere which began with Columbus's so-called "discovery" of America and the papal bull Inter Caetera in 1493. It will outline the expansion of international law to include more of the so-called "backward races," but will also reveal how the indigenous peoples of the Western Hemisphere remain excluded. It will conclude that although the recent steps toward the international recognition of the problem of discrimination against indigenous peoples by the United Nations should be encouraged, care must be taken to end the institutionalized violations of the human rights of indigenous peoples.

NOTES

1. F. S. Cohen, The Legal Conscience 313–14 (L. Cohen ed. 1960): Cohen has been referred to as the "Blackstone of Indian law"; R. Strickland, Genocide-at-Law: An Historic and Contemporary View of the Native American Experience, 34 U. Kan. L. Rev. 713, 740 (1986); *see also* Biography of Felix S. Cohen, 9 Rutgers L. Rev. 345 (1954).

2. "The law affecting land rights of indigenous peoples in the United States is racially discriminatory, and manifestly offends fundamental human rights widely recognized in international law": Indian Law Resource Center, United States Denial of Indian Property Rights: A Study in Lawless Power and Racial Discrimination, in Rethinking Indian Law 25 (National Lawyers Guild Committee on Native American Struggles ed. 1982); *see also* W. R. Jacobs, Dispossessing the American Indian: Indians and Whites on the Colonial Frontier (1972).

3. This is often expressed as the "discovery" of an inhabited land: F. Jennings, The Invasion of America: Indians, Colonialism, and the Cant of Conquest 39 (1975).

4. R. Sanders, Lost Tribes and Promised Lands: The Origins of American Racism (1978); J. Stewart and P. Wiley, Cultural Genocide, Penthouse, June 1981, at 80; R. Weston, Racism in United States Imperialism (1972); R. Dunbar Ortiz, Indians of the Americas: Human Rights and Self-determination (1984).

5. G. Alfredsson, International Law, International Organizations, and Indigenous Peoples, 36 J. Int'l. L., Spring/Summer 1982, 1, at 113; U.N. Doc. E/CN.4/Sub.2/NGO/98.

The American Indian's most valued possession is his land. From the moment English settlers debarked at Jamestown, Virginia, white men took Indian land. Two billion acres were taken from the time of the American Revolution until the end of the nineteenth century. By 1970, all Indian land acquired by white men had a value of $560 billion. Yet, a century earlier, the lands' original inhabitants had been paid only one tenth its value. Poverty and subservience have forever followed. "When the Indian was dispossessed of his land, he lost all hope of finding any niche in civilized society except that of servant or slave." [footnotes omitted]

L. Landman, International Protection for American Indian Land Rights 5 B.U. Int'l L.J. 59 (1987).

6. B. W. Dippie, The Vanishing American: White Attitudes and U.S. Indian Policy (1982); D. McNickle, Native American Tribalism (1973); R. Horsman, Race and Manifest Destiny: The Origins of American Racial Anglo-Saxonism, III, ch. 10, at 189 (1981).

7.

> Contrary to the insistently repeated theories, indigenous populations are not in the process of physical disappearance but are indeed now increasing in absolute figures in almost all the countries concerned. In two cases they are also increasing as a percentage of the population of the country in which they live.

U.N. Doc.E/CN.4/Sub.2/476, at 2.

8. The American and English Encyclopedia of Law 213 (D. S. Garland & L. P. McGehee eds. 1889); W. Washburn, The Moral and Legal Justification for Dispossessing the Indians, Seventeenth-Century America: Essays in Colonial History (J. Smith ed. 1959); W. Jacobs, Dispossessing the American Indian 148 (1972); J. Clinebell & J. Thompson, Sovereignty and Self-Determination: The Rights of Native Americans Under International Law, 27 Buf. L. Rev. 669, 670 (1978).

1

The Early Development of International Law and the "Discovery" of the Western Hemisphere

International law reflects a constant tension between existing law and the rules that ought to govern relations among states.[1] Historically it reflects a double standard, with one set of rules that apply to Christian-European states and another set that applies to the so-called "backward races."[2] Although international law is evolving toward the recognition of the rights of all peoples, remnants of this double standard remain firmly entrenched in the body of existing international law.

What has come to be known as international law was originally called the European Law of Nations or, even more accurately, the public law of Christian Nations.[3] The major premise of the European Law of Nations was that, absent an agreement to the contrary, war was the basic state of international relations—even among Christian-European states.[4] The European Law of Nations had its beginnings in the microscopic city-states system of ancient Greece and Italy.[5] During the Roman Empire, the emperor was the single source of authority. After the fall of the Roman Empire, the Catholic Church became the dominant influence in the development of international law.

Although international treaties were an important source of international law, the popes—claiming a line of succession back to Saint Peter—also played a central role in the development of international law. Citing their divine spiritual mission, the popes claimed supreme arbitral power over all Christian princes in temporal matters. On occasion, a pope would either issue a bull (a formal authoritative statement) or would otherwise mediate disputes between Christian princes. These papal actions were backed with sanctions that proved to be effective at the time: interdiction (denial of communion or other sacraments) or excommunication.[6]

For hundreds of years, international law was confined exclusively to relations among Christian-European states. Gradually, the test of civilization—in a narrow, Western sense—replaced the test of Christianity as the condition for recognition as a member of the Family of Nations.[7] This transformation was fairly recent. Turkey became the first non-Christian state to be received into the Family of Nations in 1856, although its territorial sovereignty remained subject to restrictions until after World War I.[8] Contemporary international law claims to cover relations between all sovereign states, but as will be seen, the historical exclusion of some non–Christian, "noncivilized" states persists to this day.

The expansion of the European Law of Nations throughout the rest of the world only followed the expansion of European trade and colonization throughout the rest of the world. The primary purpose of the European Law of Nations was to assist in the process of European expansion. It was intended to advance the Christian, capitalist, imperialist interests of the colonizing European powers, and it showed little or no concern for the rights of non-European peoples.[9]

A number of historical antecedents laid the foundation for the dynamic period of European expansion that began in the fifteenth century. During the early Middle Ages, Europe was largely self-contained and self-sufficient. In the seventh century, Europe was more concerned with resisting the invasions of the proselytizing, colonizing Muslims than with expansion. The Muslims believed that they were commissioned by their God to bring the Islamic value system into the world through holy war.[10]

This period of European self-containment ended in the eleventh century with the Christians' own holy war—the Crusades. Although the Crusades had the primary purpose of expelling the Muslims from their occupation of Jerusalem, it also had the incidental effect of creating a demand for trade goods from the Far East, from which overland trade routes passed through the Mongol Empire to various ports in the Middle East. The major sea routes passed through the Indian Ocean and the Red Sea to Alexandria, Egypt. With the fall of the Mongol Empire in the early fifteenth century, the overland trade routes were closed and Venice obtained a monopoly over the trade from Alexandria.[11]

This Venetian monopoly led other European nations to seek new trade routes to the Far East. By this time, translations of the works of Ptolemy, the second-century Alexandrian astronomer and geographer, were available in Europe. Through exposure to these works, a growing number of Europeans believed that the world was round and that the best way to reach the East was to sail West. Yet others believed that the best sea route to the East was to sail around Africa. Both these routes were attempted.

The exploration of the coast of Africa was mainly a Portuguese concern in the fifteenth century, although the Castilians had already occupied the Canary Islands (off northwest Africa). In 1452 Pope Nicholas V granted to King Alfonso of Portugal "general and indefinite powers to search out and conquer all pagans, enslave them and appropriate their lands and goods."[12] In 1455 and 1456 Pope Nicholas V gave Portugal the exclusive right to trade and acquire territory in the region lying south of Cape Bojador (western Africa), through and beyond Guinea "all of the way to the Indians."[13] Despite these papal grants, Castile made a rather dubious claim to Guinea based on earlier possession by their ancestors, the Visigothic kings.[14]

In 1469 the marriage of Ferdinand of Aragon to Isabella of Castile led the couple to achieve leadership in the expansion of Europe. With their marriage, almost all of what is now Spain became united, with the exception of Granada, which was occupied by the Moors. In 1479 Portugal and Castile negotiated a treaty that cleared up many of their disputes. Under this agreement, Alfonso V of Portugal renounced his claims to the crown of Castile and recognized the Castilian possession of the Azores (west of Portugal), Cape Verde Islands (off West Africa), Madeira (north of the Canaries), and Guinea.[15] The Portuguese then continued their southward explorations along the coast of Africa, while the Spanish turned their attention in other directions.

Ferdinand and Isabella of Spain were devout Catholics. They wanted to create a strong and unified nation, and they believed that the Muslims and Jews were a threat to this goal. In 1480 Ferdinand and Isabella established the Spanish Inquisition, which lasted over three hundred years. The Inquisition was a special court that imprisoned or killed all persons suspected of not following Roman Catholic teachings.[16]

The year 1492 was a big year for Spain. In that year Spanish forces conquered Granada, the last center of Moorish control in Spain, and the last of the Spanish Jews were either converted, killed, enslaved, or driven from the country. This was also the year that Columbus returned from his first voyage to the West, convinced that he had discovered a new route to India. On his way back to Spain, Columbus was forced by storms to land in Portugal, whereupon the king of Portugal claimed Columbus's discovery for himself. The Portuguese king believed that Columbus's discovery was within the bounds of Guinea.[17] Although the Portuguese had rounded the Cape of Good Hope (South Africa) by this time, it would still be another six years before Vasco da Gama reached India via this route and returned to Portugal.[18]

Upon learning of the discovery made by Columbus, Ferdinand and Isabella sent a messenger to Rome. As fate would have it, the settlement of this dispute fell into the hands of Pope Alexander VI, who was a native of Valencia (Spain) and a friend of King Ferdinand.[19] Pope Alexander VI was one of the most degenerate and corrupt of the Borgia popes and had a reputation for his crimes and vices.[20] He issued a series of bulls that were highly favorable to Spain. These bulls marked the zenith of the pope's assertion of temporal authority over all Christian princes.

In the bull Inter Caetera of May 3, 1493, Pope Alexander VI "granted to the rulers of Spain all of the world not already possessed by Christian states, so that the Abandoned heathen could be drawn to embrace the Catholic faith and be trained in good morals."[21] Under this bull, the Spanish claimed sovereignty over the land and seas west of a line drawn through the Atlantic Ocean from pole to pole one hundred leagues west of the Azores.[22] The complete text of this very important bull, also known as the Bull of Donation, follows:

Alexander, bishop, servant of the servants of God, to the illustrious sovereigns, our very dear son in Christ, Ferdinand, king, and our very dear daughter in Christ, Isabella, queen of Castile, Leon, Aragon, and Granada, health and apostolic benediction. Among other works well pleasing to the Divine Majesty and cherished of our heart, this assuredly ranks highest, that in our times especially the Catholic faith and the Christian religion be exalted and everywhere increased and spread, that the health of souls be cared for and that barbarous nations be overthrown and brought to the faith itself. Wherefore inasmuch as by the favor of divine clemency, we, though of insufficient merits, have been called to this Holy See of Peter, recognizing that as true Catholic kings and princes, such as we have known you always to be, and as your illustrious deeds already known to almost the whole world declare, you not only eagerly desire but with every effort, zeal, and diligence, without regard to hardships, expenses, dangers, with the shedding even of your blood, are laboring to that end; recognizing also that you have long since dedicated to this purpose your whole soul and all your endeavors—as witnessed in these times with so much glory to the Divine Name in your recovery of the kingdom of Granada from the yoke of the Saracens—we therefore are rightly led, and hold it as our duty, to grant you even of our own accord and in your favor those things, whereby with effort each day more hearty you may be enabled for the honor of God himself and the spread of the Christian rule to carry forward your holy and praiseworthy purpose so pleasing to immortal God. We have indeed learned that you, who for a long time had intended to seek out and discover certain lands and islands remote and unknown and not hitherto discovered by others, to the end that you might bring to the worship of our Redeemer and profession of the Catholic faith their residents and inhabitants, having been up to the present time greatly engaged in the siege and recovery of the kingdom itself of Granada, were unable to accomplish this holy and praiseworthy purpose; but the said kingdom having at length been regained, as was pleasing to the Lord, you, with the wish to fulfill your desire, chose our beloved son Christopher Columbus, whom you furnished with ships and men equipped for like designs, not without the greatest hardships, dangers, and expenses, to make diligent quest for these remote and unknown countries through the sea, where hitherto no one had sailed; and they at length, with divine aid and with the utmost diligence sailing in the ocean sea, through western waters, as is said, toward the Indians, discovered certain very remote islands and even mainlands, that hitherto had not been discovered by others; and therein dwell very many peoples living in peace, and, as reported, going unclothed, and not eating flesh, Moreover, as your aforesaid envoys are of the opinion, these very peoples living in the said islands and countries believe in one God, the Creator in heaven, and seem sufficiently disposed to embrace the Catholic faith and be trained in good morals. And it is hoped that, were they instructed, the name of the Savior, our Lord Jesus Christ, would easily be introduced into the said countries and islands. Also, on one of the chief of these aforesaid islands the above-mentioned Christopher has already caused to be put together and built a fortress fairly equipped, wherein he has stationed as garrison certain Christians, companions of his, who are to make search for other remote and unknown islands and countries. In the islands and countries already discovered are found gold, spices, and very many other precious things of divers kinds and qualities. Wherefore, after earnest consideration of all matters, as becomes Catholic kings and princes, and especially of the rise and spread of the Catholic faith, as was the fashion of your ancestors, kings of renowned memory, you have purposed with the favor of divine clemency to bring under your sway the said countries and islands with their residents and inhabitants, and to bring them to the Catholic faith. Hence, heartily commending in the Lord this your holy and praiseworthy purpose, and desirous that it be duly accomplished, and that the name of our Savior be carried into those regions, we exhort you very earnestly in the Lord and by your reception of holy baptism, whereby you are bound to our apostolic commands, and by the bowels of the mercy of our Lord Jesus Christ, enjoin strictly, that inasmuch as with eager zeal for the true faith you design to equip and despatch this expedition, you purpose also, as is your duty, to lead the peoples dwelling in those islands to embrace the Christian profession; nor at any time let dangers or hardships deter you therefrom, with the stout hope and trust in your hearts that Almighty God will further your undertakings. And, in order that you may enter upon so great an undertaking with greater readiness and heartiness endowed with the benefit of our apostolic favor, we, of our own accord, not at your instance nor the request of anyone else in your regard, but of our own sole largess and certain knowledge and out of the fullness of our apostolic power, by the authority of Almighty God conferred upon us in blessed Peter and of the vicarship of Jesus Christ which we hold on earth, do by tenor of these presents give, grant, and assign forever to you and your heirs and successors, kings of Castile and Leon, all and singular the aforesaid countries and islands thus unknown and hitherto discovered by your envoys and to be discovered hereafter, provided however they at no time have been in the actual temporal possession of any Christian owner, together with all their dominions, cities, camps, places, and villages, and all rights, jurisdictions, and appurtenances of the same. And we invest you and your aforementioned heirs and successors with them, and make, appoint, and depute you lords of them with full and free power, authority, and jurisdiction of every kind, with this proviso however, that by this our gift, grant, assignment, and investiture no right acquired by any Christian prince is hereby to be understood to be withdrawn or taken away. Moreover we command you in virtue of holy obedience, that, employing all due diligence in the premises, as you also promise—nor do we doubt that you will act in accordance with your devoted loyalty and royal greatness of spirit—you should appoint to the aforesaid countries and islands worthy and God-fearing, learned, skilled, and experienced men to instruct the aforesaid inhabitants and residents in the Catholic faith, and to train them in good morals. And under penalty of excommunication *late sententie* to be incurred *ipso facto*, should any thus contravene, we strictly forbid all persons of no matter what rank, estate, degree, order, or condition, to dare, without your special permit or that of your aforesaid heirs and successors, to go for the sake of trade or any other reason whatever to the said islands and countries after they have been discovered and found by your envoys or persons sent out for that purpose. And inasmuch as some kings of Portugal, likewise by apostolic grant made to them, have similarly discovered and taken possession of islands in the regions of Africa, Guinea, and the Gold Mine, and elsewhere, and divers privileges, favors, liberties, immunities, exemptions, and indults have been granted to them by the Apostolic See, we through similar accord, authority, knowledge, and fullness of apostolic power, by a gift of special favor, do grant to you and your aforesaid heirs and successors, that in the islands and countries thus discovered and to be discovered by you, you may and rightly can use, employ, and enjoy freely and legally, in all things and through all things, just as if they had been especially granted to you and your aforesaid heirs and successors, all and singular these favors, privileges, exemptions, liberties, faculties, immunities, and indults, the terms of all of which we wish to be understood as being sufficiently expressed and inserted, as if they were inserted word for word in these presents. Moreover we similarly extend and enlarge them in all things and through all things to you and your aforesaid heirs and successors, apostolic constitutions and ordinances as well as all those things that have been granted in the letters set forth above or other things whatsoever to the contrary notwithstanding. We trust in Him from whom empires and governments and all good things proceed, that should you with the Lord's guidance pursue this holy and praiseworthy undertaking, in a short while your hardships and endeavors will attain the most felicitous result, to the happiness and glory of all Christendom. But inasmuch as it would be difficult to have these present letters sent to all places where desirable, we wish, and with similar accord and knowledge do decree that to copies of them, signed by the hand of a notary public commissioned therefor and sealed with the seal of any ecclesiastical officer or ecclesiastical court, the same respect is to be shown in court and outside as well as anywhere else, as would be given to these presents should they be exhibited or shown. Let no one, therefore, infringe, or with rash boldness contravene this our exhortation, requisition, gift, grant, assignment, investiture, deed, constitution, deputation, mandate, inhibition, indult, extension, enlargement, will, and decree. Should anyone presume to do so, be it known to him that he will incur the wrath of Almighty God and of the blessed apostles Peter and Paul. Given in Rome, at St. Peter's, on the third day of May in the year one thousand four hundred and ninety-three of the incarnation of our Lord, in the first year of our pontificate.

Gratis by order of our most holy lord the Pope.[23]

It has been said that "of all the crimes of Borgia, this bull was the greatest."[24]

Inter Caetera was based on the "omni-insular doctrine," which was founded on the Donation of Constantine—a famous eighth-century forgery.[25] According to the Donation of Constantine, the Roman emperor gave the pope dominion over "various islands." Pope Urban applied this doctrine for the first time in 1091 when he gave the Archipelago of Lipari (off west Italy) to a local abbot and Corsica to the bishop of Pisa.[26] Other popes later granted dominion over various other islands in exchange for the payment of feudal tribute. A number of different areas—including England, Ireland, Scandinavia, and the Canary Islands—became feudatory to the Holy See.[27]

Along with this purported grant of land from Pope Alexander VI, the Spanish were also given the duty to convert the Indians to Catholicism. To carry out this duty, the Spanish believed that a "just war" could be waged against the Indians if they refused to convert to Catholicism or to acknowledge the authority of the Spanish monarch.[28] However, before hostilities could legally be commenced, one formality had to be observed. The following document, called the Requirement, had to be read to the Indians:

On the part of the King, Don Fernando, and of Dona Juana, his daughter, Queen of Castile and Leon, subduers of the barbarous nations, we their servants notify and make known to you, as best we can, that the Lord our God, Living and Eternal, created the Heaven and the Earth, and one man and one woman, of whom you and I, and all the men of the world, were and are descendants, and all those who come after us. But, on account of the multitude which has sprung from this man and woman in the five thousand years since the world was created, it was necessary that some men should go one way and some another, and that they should be divided into many kingdoms and provinces, for in one alone they could not be sustained.

Of all these nations God our Lord gave charge to one man, called St. Peter, that he should be Lord and Superior of all the men in the world, that all should obey him, and that he should be head of the whole human race, wherever men should live, and under whatever law, sect, or belief they should be; and he gave him the world for his kingdom and jurisdiction.

And he commanded him to place his seat in Rome, as the spot most fitting to rule the world from; but also he permitted him to have his seat in any other part of the world, and to judge and govern all Christians, Moors, Jews, Gentiles, and all other sects. This man was called Pope, as if to say, Admirable Great Father and governor of men. The men who lived in that time obeyed that St. Peter, and took him for Lord, King, and Superior of the universe; so also have they regarded the others who after him have been elected to the Pontificate, and so it has been continued even until now, and will continue until the end of the world.

One of these Pontiffs, who succeeded that St. Peter as Lord of the world, in the dignity and seat which I have before mentioned, made donation of these isles and Terra-firma to the aforesaid King and Queen and to their successors, our lords, with all that there are in these territories, as is contained in certain writings which passed upon the subject as aforesaid, which you can see if you wish.

So their Highnesses are kings and lords of these islands and land of Terra-firma by virtue of this donation; and some islands, and indeed almost all those to whom this has been notified, have received and served their Highnesses, as lords and kings, in the way that subjects ought to do, with good will, without any resistance, immediately, without delay, when they were informed of the aforesaid facts. And also they received and obeyed the priests whom their Highnesses sent to preach to them and to teach them our Holy Faith; and all these, of their own free will, without any reward or condition, have become Christians, and are so, and their Highness have joyfully and benignantly received them, and also have commanded them to be treated as their subjects and vassals; and you too are held and obliged to do the same. Therefore as best we can, we ask and require you that you consider what we have said to you, and that you take the time that shall be necessary to understand and deliberate upon it, and that you acknowledge the Church as the Ruler and Superior of the whole world and the high priest called Pope, and in his name the King and Queen Dona Juana our lords, in his place, as superiors and lords and kings of these islands and this Terra-firma by virtue of said donation, and that you consent and give place that these religious fathers should declare and preach to you the aforesaid.

If you do so, you will do well, and that which you are obliged to do to their Highnesses, and we in their name shall receive you in all love and charity, and shall leave you your wives, and your children, and your lands, free without servitude, that you may do with them and with yourselves freely that which you like and think best, and they shall not compel you to turn Christians, unless you yourselves, when informed of the truth, should wish to be converted to our Holy Catholic Faith, as almost all the inhabitants of the rest of the islands have done. And besides this, their Highnesses award you many privileges and exceptions and will grant you many benefits.

But if you do not do this, and wickedly and intentionally delay to do so, I certify to you that, with the help of God, we shall forcibly enter into your country and shall made [*sic*] war against you in all ways and manners that we can, and shall subject you to the yoke and obedience of the Church and of their Highnesses; we shall take you and your wives and your children, and shall make slaves of them, and as such shall sell and dispose of them as their Highnesses may command; and we shall take away your goods, and shall do all the harm and damage that we can, as to vassals who do not obey, and refuse to receive their lord, and resist and contradict him; and we protest that the deaths and losses which shall accrue from this are your fault, and not that of the Highnesses, or ours, nor of these cavaliers who come with us. And that we have said this to you and made this Requisition, we request the notary here present to give us his testimony in writing, and we ask the rest who are present that they should be witnesses of this Requisition.[29]

The Spanish read the Requirement routinely, if not religiously, before beginning an invasion. However, it was often read when or where no one could hear it or in Spanish or some other language that the Indians who were being addressed did not understand.[30] When told of the Bull of Donation and the Requirement, the Peruvian Inca remarked that the pope "must be crazy to talk of giving away countries which do not belong to him."[31]

The Requirement was based on the doctrine of papal sovereignty, which was first formulated in the thirteenth century. According to this doctrine, the earth was divided into a Christian world and a heathen world. Before the birth of Christ, heathen peoples possessed their own temporal authority based on natural law. However, after the birth of Christ, all the spiritual and temporal authority held by heathen peoples passed to Christ, who became the temporal and spiritual lord over the entire earth. This authority passed to Christ's successors—first to St. Peter, and then to the other popes. Based on this authority, the pope could extinguish all the rights that non-Christians obtained prior to the division of the world into Christian and heathen. Thus, the European Law of Nations viewed the natural rights of heathen peoples to be subordinate to the authority of the pope, who could then delegate this authority to other Christian princes.[32]

The Requirement basically extended the Spanish Inquisition to include the indigenous peoples of the Western Hemisphere. Despite the widespread conversion of large numbers of Indians, many others were either killed or enslaved by the Spaniards. In a matter of decades, the systematic genocide committed by Spain against the Indians had exterminated almost the entire native population of the Caribbean. The Indian population of Mexico fell from about 30 million in 1492 to about 1.5 million in 1650.[33] Indeed, it was only after the decimation of the native slave population that the African slave trade to the Western Hemisphere grew in popularity.[34]

Portugal contested the division of the Western Hemisphere that had been made by Pope Alexander VI. This dispute came to a head when Alexander VI issued another bull revoking earlier papal grants that seemed, in 1492, to have given Portugal a claim to lands not actually possessed by that country. Negotiations to settle this dispute only started after the king of Portugal began to prepare for war. This disagreement was finally settled in 1494 by the Treaty of Torsedillas. A new line of demarcation was drawn from pole to pole, 370 leagues (approximately 1,300 miles) west of the Cape Verde Islands.[35] Everything east of the line pertained to Portugal, and everything west of the line pertained to Spain.

Thus, Spain initially claimed the right to exclude everyone from the Western Hemisphere (both land and sea), based on the Bull of Donation. The one exception was Portugal, which had acquired rights to Brazil under the Treaty of Torsedillas. However, the papal claim to grant to particular Christian nations the sole right to acquire dominion over non-Christian countries broke down under the refusal of the English, French, and Dutch to acquiesce in this division of the world.[36] With the collapse of the validity of the Bull of Donation, the Europeans created a state of total lawlessness in the Western Hemisphere. There was a constant state of warfare and/or piracy whenever ships from rival countries met.

The first rule of European customary international law that arose out of this state of chaos was the doctrine of two spheres.[37] According to this doctrine, Europe was recognized as having its own system of international law which did not apply in the Western Hemisphere. The only rule that did apply was that might makes right; in other words, "No law beyond the line."[38] However, hostilities that occurred west of the line would not be a good cause to commence hostilities east of the line. Consequently, the piracy and plundering that persisted in the Western Hemisphere did not disturb the relative tranquility of Europe.

The second rule of customary international law that arose has become known as the doctrine of discovery. Any discussion of this doctrine should begin with a criticism of the use of the word "discovery" to apply to the finding of land that had been inhabited by human beings since time immemorial. Correctly speaking, it is only proper to refer to the discovery of something that has no previous owner. The use of the word "discovery" is appropriate only in the limited sense of finding something previously unknown to the Europeans, and not the more usual sense of finding something previously without an owner. These two distinct meanings of the word "discovery" should not be confused, although they often are.[39]

Regardless, the doctrine of discovery began as a simple rule of colonial economics. A constant state of warfare threatened the profitability of all colonial enterprises. A rule was needed that would minimize expense and maximize profits, and the doctrine of discovery met this need.[40]

After the demise of the Spanish claim to exclusive dominion over the entire Western Hemisphere, based on the Bull of Donation, merely sighting or landing on a particular portion of territory was not sufficient to give title. Such acts were only sufficient to give an inchoate title or a right to occupy that had to be perfected by actual possession—defined as permanent settlement and cultivation of the soil—within a reasonable time after the initial sighting.[41] Even though a problem remained as to the extent of the hinterlands that went with such settlements, the doctrine of discovery proved to be fairly effective.[42] Although disputes did arise and extravagant claims continued to be made, conflicting claims were often settled by agreement and only rarely by the use of force. Hence, the doctrine fulfilled its primary purpose of reducing expenses and thereby facilitated European expansion.

A brief review of the claims made by the English, French, and Spanish rulers demonstrates the role played by the doctrine of discovery in the colonization of eastern North America. In 1498, Henry VII of Britain commissioned John Cabot to conquer, occupy, and possess the lands of the "Heathens and Infidels" and to acquire title and jurisdiction over them.[43] Cabot enforced this commission by sailing along the East Coast from 56 to 38 degrees north latitude. Based on Cabot's voyage, Britain claimed all the territory from the Gulf of Mexico to the most northern regions and all the way west, even though its first permanent settlement was not made until 1607 at Jamestown, Virginia.

Despite the fact that the Spanish had been the first to discover the Mississippi River in 1540, France claimed the entire watershed of this river upon the establishment of a settlement at the mouth of the Mississippi in the early eighteenth century. The French ceded Louisiana to Spain, and the western boundary of England's possessions was fixed along the middle of the Mississippi River. Later, Spain receded its claims to this territory back to France. Finally, in 1803 the United States government purchased Louisiana from France.[44]

Florida was first discovered by the Spanish in 1513, but it was first settled by French Protestant Huguenots. Spain destroyed that colony in 1565, more because of its religion than its nationality, and established its own colony in St. Augustine. In 1763, England received Florida in return for Havana, Cuba. After the Revolutionary War, Florida was returned to Spain; it was finally ceded to the United States in 1819.[45]

A valid claim of discovery brought with it two main benefits. First, it gave the discovering European nation an exclusive area within which it was left free to pursue its colonizing activity, thus preempting the colonizing activity of other European countries. This resulted in a monopoly of trade and an exclusive proselytizing zone. Under the Spanish arrangement, the Crown granted certain merchants the right to carry on trade in exchange for 20 percent of the profits. The Spanish also sent numerous Dominican and Franciscan missionaries to convert the Indians to Roman Catholicism.[46]

The second benefit obtained by discovery was the right of the discovering European nation to obtain the land from the indigenous people, either by purchase or by conquest. Although the British Crown generally purchased the land from the Indians by treaty, the usual method employed by Spain was conquest. The rules of conquest that the European Law of Nations applied to the Western Hemisphere were different from the rules of conquest applied in Europe.[47] In Europe the only just wars were those to redress a wrong actually suffered, and necessitated reparations. In the Western Hemisphere, all wars against the "infidel heathen" were considered just. Genocidal wars of extermination against the indigenous peoples, or their enslavement, were perfectly legal.[48] The European Law of Nations considered the treatment of the indigenous peoples to be a matter exclusively within the domestic jurisdiction of the discovering European nation. Thus, the indigenous peoples of the Western Hemisphere had no human rights that the white man was bound to respect.

NOTES

1.

> Regarding the general relation of natural law to international law, later eighteenth-century and nineteenth-century writers were practically unanimous in the positivist doctrine that the only source of international law lay in treaties and in the actual practice of States. . . . The wars of the twentieth century and the Nazi abominations led to a reaction against positivism and a feeling even among international lawyers that a thing is not justified merely because it exists, and that some attempt should be made to establish the principles of what international law ought to be. . . . The Nuremberg trials also introduced the charge of "crimes against humanity" which could apply to things done by the German leaders to German subjects in Germany, an assertion of the supremacy of international law over national law, and of an international law based not on existing practice but on moral principle. This idea, influential in the Mandate provisions of the Covenant of the League of Nations and the Trusteeship provisions of the Charter of the United Nations, has also inspired the Declaration of Human Rights (1948) and the setting up of the European Commission and Court of Human Rights.

J. D. Tooke, The Just War in Aquinas and Grotius 232–33 (1965).

2. M. F. Lindley, The Acquisition and Government of Backward Territory in International Law, Being a Treatise on the Law and Practice Relating to Colonial Expansion (1926); *see also* A. Snow, The Question of Aborigines in the Law and Practice of Nations (1972).

3. L. Oppenheim, International Law 48 (1955); *see also* J. L. Kunz, The Changing Law of Nations 13–45 (1968).

4. L. Oppenheim, 2 International Law, 144 (1955).

5. *Id.* at 74–76; *see also* New Approaches to International Relations (Morton A. Kaplan ed. 1968); E. Sjoquist, Sicily and the Greeks: Studies in the Interrelationship between the Indigenous Populations and the Greek Colonists (1973).

6. M. Savelle, The Origins of American Diplomacy: The International History of Angloamerica 1492–1763 at 194–99 (1967); *see also* European Treaties Bearing on the History of the United States and Its Dependencies to 1648, at 11 (F. G. Davenport & C. P. Paullin eds. 1967); R. A. Williams, Jr., The Medieval and Renaissance Origins of the Status of the American Indian in Western Legal Thought, 57 So. Cal. L. Rev. 1, 18 nn. 53–57 (1983); R. A. Williams, Jr., The American Indian in Western Legal Thought: The Discourses of Conquest (1990: This article and book contain excellent footnotes for anyone interested in further research.)

7. M. Smith, The Development of International Law 208 (1928); *see also* B. Roling, International Law in an Expanded World (1960).

8. H. Wood, The Treaty of Paris and Turkey's Status in International Law, 37 Am. J. Int'l. L. 262, 272–74 (1943). "Three stages can be clearly distinguished in the history of international law, the period of the 'Christian Nations' (c. 1648–1856), the period of the 'Civilized Nations' (c. 1856–1945), and the period of the 'Peace-loving Nations,' which began with the U.N. Charter": B. Roling, International Law in an Expanded World, at xv (1960).

9. L. Henkin, How Nations Behave: Law and Foreign Policy 121 (1979).

10. 6 Encyclopedia of Public International Law: International Law, Islamic 227–33 (1983).

11. M. Savelle, The Foundations of American Civilization: A History of Colonial America 8–22 (1942).

12. *Id.* at 12.

13. *Id.* at 39.

14. *Id.* at 10.

15. *Id.* at 34.

16. R. Sanders, Lost Tribes and Promised Lands: The Origins of American Racism 72 (1978); *see also* H. Kamen, The Spanish Inquisition (1965); H. Lea, A History of the Inquisition in Spain (1966).

17. European Treaties, *supra* note 6, at 9, 35; *see also* M. Savelle, Origins, *supra* note 6, at 7.

18. H. E. Bolton, The Colonization of North America 1492–1783, at 5 (1935).

19. European Treaties, *supra* note 6, at 56.

20. Alexander VI bought his position as the pope. Two of the most notorious of his many children were Lucretia and Cesare. Alexander VI was a party to Cesare's plans to murder numerous cardinals, whose property was inherited by Alexander VI; then, the newly created positions for cardinals were sold at high prices. This money was spent on occasions such as the time when Alexander, Lucretia and Cesare watched an infamous ballet performed in the Vatican by fifty Roman courtesans. The papal revenues noticeably increased in the years after Columbus's voyage, and Pope Alexander VI completed the gilded ceiling in Santa Maria Maggiore in Rome with the first gold brought from America. H. Kuhner, Encyclopedia of the Papacy 134–37 (1958); M. Malachi, Rich Church Poor Church 127 (1984); *see also* J. McCabe, Crises in the History of the Papacy 240 (1916); R. A. Williams, Jr., Medieval Origins, *supra* note 6, at 33.

21. F. Jennings, The Invasion of America: Indians, Colonialism, and the Cant of Conquest 5 (1975).

22. M. Savelle, Empires to Nations 139 (1974).

23. European Treaties, *supra* note 6, at 61–63.

24. H. Fertig, The Pope 216 (1975).

25. According to the Donation of Constantine,

> Before departing to Constantinople, the Emperor Constantine has handed over to his contemporary pope, Silvester, large, though unspecified provinces and regions in Italy and in the Western hemisphere as well as all islands, in addition to the Lateran palace which was to be the official papal residence.

W. Ullmann, A Short History of the Papacy in the Middle Ages 77 (1972). *See also* R. A. Williams, Jr., Medieval Origins, *supra* note 6, at 16–17.

26. *See* M. F. Lindley, *supra* note 2, at 124–28.

27. *See* R. A. Williams, Jr., Medieval Origins, *supra* note 6, at 21–25, and notes cited therein.

28. R. Berkhofer, The White Man's Indian 123 (1978), cited in R. A. Williams, Jr., Medieval Origins, *supra* note 6, at 74 n. 325.

29. L. Hanke, The "Requerimiento" and its Interpreters, Revista De Historia De America, vol. 1, no. 1, at 26–28 (1938). Hanke noted, "[T]his remarkable proclamation offers many vulnerable spots to the barbs of cynics, and the use made of it by the Spaniards affords consummate proof of the hypocritical religiosity in the Spanish character to persons who already see it there": Hanke, *supra*, at 28.

See also C. MacLachlan, Spain's Empire in the New World: The Role of Ideas in Institutional and Social Change 30–31 (1988).

30. J. H. Parry, The Spanish Theory of Empire in the Sixteenth Century (1940); *see also* L. Hanke, The Spanish Struggle for Justice in the Conquest of America 34 (1949).

31. M. F. Lindley, Backward Territory, *supra* note 2, at 127.

32. J. H. Parry, *supra* note 30, at 13; *see also* R. A. Williams, Jr., Medieval Origins, *supra* note 6, at 11–20; S. Zavala, New Viewpoints on the Spanish Colonization of America (1943).

33. H. F. Dobyns, Estimating Aboriginal American Population: An Appraisal of Techniques with a New Hemispheric Estimate, 7 Current Anthropology 395–416 (1966); and H. F. Dobyns, Reply, 440–44 (1966). "The idea that social scientists hold of the size of the aboriginal population of the Americas directly affects their interpretation of New World civilizations and cultures": Dobyns, *supra*, at 415. Dobyns postulates a conservative hemisphere-wide depopulation ratio of 20 to 1. Immediately prior to 1492, he estimated the indigenous population of the Western Hemisphere to be about 90 million persons, which translates to a nadir population of about 4.5 million, or a net decline of over 85 million.

34. J. Friede & B. Keen, Bartolome de Las Casas in History: Toward an Understanding of the Man and His Work 166 (1971).

35. European Treaties, *supra* note 6, at 79, 84–85.

36. M. Savelle, The Foundations of American Civilization: A History of Colonial America 53 (1947); *see also* M. Savelle, Empires to Nations: Expansion in America 137–38 (1974); European Treaties, *supra* note 6, at 7.

37. M. Savelle, Origins, *supra* note 6, at 210–15; European Treaties, *supra* note 6, at 220.

38. M. Savelle, Empires to Nations, *supra* note 36, at 141; *see also* W. Washburn, Red Man's Land/White Man's Law: A Study of the Past and Present Status of the American Indian 32 (1971).

39. Even though it is not true, whites reasoned that they owned the land because they were a race of cultivators, while the Indians merely roamed over the land like herds of wild animals. *See* L. B. Priest, Uncle Sam's Stepchildren: The Reformation of United States Indian Policy 1865–1887, at 189 (1942); *see also* F. Jennings, *supra* note 21, at 39; R. Preiswerk & D. Perrot, Ethnocentrism and History: Africa, Asia and Indian America in Western Textbooks 108 (1978).

40. European Treaties, *supra* note 6, at 290–92, 329–32, 353–60.

41. *Id.* at 119.

42. The Collected Papers of John Westlake on Public International Law 169–72 (L. Oppenheim ed. 1914).

43. F. Jennings, *supra* note 21, at 5.

44. *See, generally*, H. E. Bolton, The Colonization of North America 1492–1783 (1935); *see also* N. Hordern, God, Gold and Glory, Indian Labor in the Spanish Indies (1966).

45. J. Leitch Wright, Jr., Anglo–Spanish Rivalry in North America (1971).

46. H. E. Bolton, The Mission as a Frontier Institution in the Spanish-American Colonies (1962).

47. A. P. Sereni, The Italian Conception of International Law (1943), ch. 5, at 85–117.

48. "Peoples outside of European Christian civilization hardly came within its sphere at all. They could be massacred and their villages pillaged without regard to the law of war": Q. Wright, Mandates under the League of Nations 7 (1968). *See also* 8 Encyclopedia of Public International Law 48 (1985); European Treaties, *supra* note 6, at 17 n. 37.

2

Status and Rights of the Indigenous Peoples of the Western Hemisphere and the Origins of the "Sacred Trust of Civilization"

SPANISH PERSPECTIVE

The status and rights of the indigenous peoples of the Western Hemisphere soon became an issue of endless debate. This issue was not of much concern to the conquistadors, who thought they were on a last great Crusade to convert the infidel heathen to Christianity. The conquistadors devised two main systems for dealing with Indian peoples: slavery and the *encomiendo* system. Slavery was viewed as a mitigation of the death sentence that could be imposed on Indians who either refused to convert to Christianity or submit to the authority of the Spanish monarch.[1]

The encomiendo system was a feudal system whereby a plot of land and a group of Indians were turned over to a conquistador as a reward for his services to the Spanish Crown.[2] The Indians would be kept in a village so that the conquistador, or *encomiendero*, could Christianize them and collect the annual tribute that the Indians owed to the king of Spain. Since the Indians were almost always unable to pay this tribute, the encomiendero would be allowed to extract it through forced labor. The Indians were often forced to work in mines that were owned by the Spanish. This legal fiction allowed the encomiendero to reduce the Indians to a status of de facto slavery.

In contrast to the conquistadors, the Spanish missionaries and theologians were vitally concerned with the moral issues raised by the activities of their country. Francisco de Victoria, a well-known Dominican professor at the University of Salamanca, was one of the first to address these issues. He is even considered by some to be the father of international law as a result of his writings on relations between Christian-European and Indian nations.[3]

In a series of lectures delivered in 1532, Victoria repudiated all the arguments put forth by the Spanish conquistadors to justify their domination of the Indians. Victoria addressed the question of

> whether the aborigines in question were true owners in both private and public law before the arrival of the Spaniards; that is, whether they were true owners of private property and possessions and also whether there were among them any who were the true princes and overlords of others.[4]

Victoria rejected the arguments that Indians were precluded from being true owners by reason of unbelief, heresy, unsoundness of mind, or any other mortal sin. He concluded that

> the aborigines undoubtedly had true dominion in both public and private matters, just like Christians, and that neither their princes nor private persons could be despoiled of their property on the ground of their not being true owners. It would be harsh to deny to those, who have never done any wrong, what we grant to Saracens and Jews, who are the persistent enemies of Christianity.[5]

"Implicit in the argument [of Victoria] is the doctrine that certain basic rights inhere in men *as men*, not by reason of their race, creed, or color, but by reason of their humanity."[6]

In refutation of those who asserted that Indians were slaves by nature because of their incapability for self-government, Victoria contended that the Indians constituted sovereign nations and had dominion over their land.[7] The doctrine of the sovereign equality of states was derived from the writings of Victoria.[8] According to this doctrine, just as all men are created equal, so too were all states, and they all possess certain fundamental rights. Among the fundamental rights of states are the right to exist and the right to legal equality.[9] Ironically, however, Indian nations have never been recognized as equal members of the Family of Nations.

Victoria also rejected the temporal authority of the pope to give away the land of Indians as Pope Alexander VI had purported to do in the Bull of Donation. At best, Victoria believed that the pope could give the Spanish government the exclusive right to regulate spiritual matters between Christian states. He said that "a division of the New World by the Pope could serve only as an allocation of zones for trading and proselytizing purposes, not as a distribution of land."[10] Victoria even rejected the validity of the doctrine of discovery because he thought that this title "in and by itself gives no support to a seizure [of the land] of the aborigines any more than if it had been they who had discovered us."[11] Victoria believed that only vacant land could be claimed by discovery, not land that was owned and occupied by Indians.[12] Perhaps the most important contribution that Victoria made to the development of modern international law was his formulation of the trusteeship concept of colonialism. He addressed the assertion that although Indians were not natural slaves, they needed to be ruled and governed by other nations; and that it was good for them to be subject to others, just as sons need to be subject to their parents until they come of age.[13] Victoria expressed this trust relationship in the following equivocal language:

There is another title which can indeed not be asserted, but brought up for discussion, and some think it a lawful one. I dare not affirm it at all, nor do I entirely condemn it. It is this: Although the aborigines in question are . . . not wholly unintelligent, yet they are little short of that condition, and so are unfit to found or administer a lawful State up to the standard required by human and civil claims. Accordingly they have no proper laws nor magistrates, and are not even capable of controlling their family affairs; they are without any literature or arts, not only the liberal arts, but the mechanical arts also; they have no careful agriculture and no artisans; and they lack many other conveniences, yea necessaries, of human life. It might, therefore, be maintained that in their own interests the sovereigns of Spain might undertake the administration of their country, providing them with prefects and governors for their towns, and might even give them new lords, so long as this was clearly for their benefit. I say there would be some force in this contention; for if they were all wanting in intelligence, there is no doubt that this would not only be a permissible, but also a highly proper, course to take; nay, our sovereigns would be bound to take it, just as if the natives were infants. The same principle seems to apply here to them as to people of defective intelligence; and indeed they are no whit or little better than such so far as self-government is concerned, or even than the wild beasts, for their food is not more pleasant and hardly better than that of beasts. Therefore their governance should in the same way be entrusted to people of intelligence. There is clear confirmation hereof, for if by some accident of fortune all their adults were to perish and there were to be left boys and youths in enjoyment, indeed, of a certain amount of reason, but of tender years and under the age of puberty, our sovereigns would certainly be justified in taking charge of them and governing them so long as they were in that condition. Now, this being admitted, it appears undeniable that the same could be done in the case of their barbarian parents, if they be supposed to be of that dullness of mind which is attributed to them by those who have been among them and which is reported to be more marked among them than even among the boys and youths of other nations. And surely this might be founded on the precept of charity, they being our neighbors and we being bound to look after their welfare. Let this, however, as I have already said, but put forward without dogmatism and *subject to the limitation that any such interposition be for the welfare and in the interests of the Indians and not merely for the profit of the Spaniards*. For this is the respect in which all the danger to soul and salvation lie. And herein some help might be gotten from the consideration, referred to above, that some are by nature slaves, for all the barbarians in question are of that type and so they may in part be governed as slaves are.

Now, it seems to follow from all this discussion that, if there be no force in any of the titles which have been put forward, so that the native Indians neither gave cause for just war nor wished for Spanish rulers, etc., all the travel to, and trade with, those parts should be stopped, to the great loss of the Spaniards and also to the grave hurt of the royal treasury (a thing intolerable).[14]

In this passage, Victoria, who was obviously laboring under a number of erroneous assumptions, placed distinct limitations on the exercise of this trust by the "advanced" Spanish over the "backward" Indians. The interests of the Indians were to be of paramount importance, which is analogous to the common law trust duty that a guardian has the obligation to exercise a trust in the best interest of the beneficiaries and to preserve the trust's assets. Victoria also envisioned the duration and purpose of the trust to be limited. It was to last only as long as the Indians were "unfit to found or administer a lawful State up to the standard required by civil and human claims."[15] This implies the fundamental purpose of the trust—to develop self-government.

Victoria's ideas were given papal support by Pope Paul III. Pope Paul III began the Counter-Reformation, which was a protest against the corruption of the medieval Church.[16] In 1537 he issued three bulls concerning the treatment of Indians. The first transferred jurisdiction over the spiritual upbringing of the Indians from the Spanish Holy Office to the bishops. The second was a strong condemnation of Indian slavery. The third, the celebrated Sublimis Deus, follows:

Paul III Pope To all faithful Christians to whom this writing may come, health in Christ our Lord and the apostolic benediction.

The sublime God so loved the human race that He created man in such wise that he might participate, not only in the good that other creatures enjoy, but endowed him with capacity to attain to the inaccessible and invisible Supreme Good and behold it face to face; and since man, according to the testimony of the sacred scriptures, has been created to enjoy eternal life and happiness, which none may obtain save through faith in our Lord Jesus Christ, it is necessary that he should possess the nature and faculties enabling him to receive that faith; and that whoever is thus endowed should be capable of receiving that same faith. Nor is it credible that any one should possess so little understanding as to desire the faith and yet be destitute of the most necessary faculty to enable him to receive it. Hence Christ, who is the Truth itself, that has never failed and can never fail, said to the preachers of the faith whom He chose for that office "Go ye and teach all nations." He said all, without exception, for all are capable of receiving the doctrines of the faith.

The enemy of the human race, who opposes all good deeds in order to bring men to destruction, beholding and envying this, invented a means never before heard of, by which he might hinder the preaching of God's word of Salvation to the people: he inspired his satellites who, to please him, have not hesitated to publish abroad that the Indians of the West and the South, and other people of whom We have recent knowledge should be treated as dumb brutes created for our service, pretending that they are incapable of receiving the catholic faith.

We, who, though unworthy, exercise on earth the power of our Lord and seek with all our might to bring those sheep of His flock who are outside, into the fold committed to our charge, consider, however, that the Indians are truly men and that they are not only capable of understanding the catholic faith but, according to our information, they desire exceedingly to receive it. Desiring to provide ample remedy for these evils, we define and declare by these our letters, or by any translation thereof signed by any notary public and sealed with the seal of any ecclesiastical dignitary, to which the same credit shall be given as to the originals, that, notwithstanding whatever may have been or may be said to the contrary, the said Indians and all other people who may later be discovered by Christians, are by no means to be deprived of their liberty or the possession of their property, even though they be outside the faith of Jesus Christ; and that they may and should, freely and legitimately, enjoy their liberty and the possession of their property; nor should they be in any way enslaved; should the contrary happen, it shall be null and of no effect.

By virtue of our apostolic authority We define and declare by these present letters, or by any translation thereof signed by any notary public and sealed with the seal of any ecclesiastical dignitary, which shall thus command the same obedience as the originals, that the said Indians and other peoples should be converted to the faith of Jesus Christ by preaching the word of God and by the example of good and holy living.

Given in Rome in the year of our Lord 1537. The fourth of June and of our Pontificate, the third year.[17]

Sublimis Deus had the effect of revoking Inter Caetera insofar as it purported to give the Spanish monarchy title to the Indians' land, although Spain continued to have the duty to convert the Indians to Roman Catholicism. Sublimis Deus has been called a declaration of human rights because it recognized the right of Indians to own land regardless of their race, religion, degree of civilization, or any other circumstance.[18]

In 1550 an important debate over the nature of Indian rights took place in Valladolid, Spain. This debate was arranged by Charles V of Spain to settle the issue of whether it was lawful to wage war on the Indians before preaching the gospel to them so that afterwards they might be more easily instructed in the faith.[19] Unfortunately, Victoria had died four years earlier, or he certainly would have been called on to express his views. The two debaters selected by Charles V were Juan Gines de Sepulveda and the Dominican Friar Bartholome de Las Casas. These two men came from very different backgrounds.

Sepulveda never set foot in the Western Hemisphere, and, in the words of Las Casas, he "was entirely ignorant of the affairs of the Indies."[20] Sepulveda's only qualification to debate the rights of the Indians was his academic knowledge of the theories of Aristotle. He had just completed a Latin translation of Aristotle's *Politics*. Sepulveda believed in Aristotle's "natural slave theory" which stated that some men are "from the hour of their birth . . . marked out for subjection, others for rule."[21] Aristotle's ideal state consisted of a small aristocracy of Greek citizens born to a life of virtue and free of manual labor, who ruled over a large non-Greek population.[22]

Las Casas, on the other hand, had extensive firsthand knowledge of the Indians. He spent about half his ninety-two years in the Western Hemisphere. As a young man, he took part in the conquest of Cuba, and he received an encomiendo as a reward for his efforts. After over a decade of willing participation in the activities of the conquistadors, Las Casas renounced his encomienda in 1514 and took up the cause of Indian rights. He entered the Dominican order and began to lobby the Council of the Indies for reform. He was instrumental in the passage of the New Laws which attempted to protect the Indians by bringing the encomiendo system to an end.[23] In 1544 Las Casas was named the bishop of Chiapas in Guatemala to implement these laws. He risked being burned at the stake by the Inquisition when he also threatened to excommunicate Spanish slaveholders who would not free their Indian slaves and make restitution to them.[24] After several uprisings against these reforms by the Spanish ruling class, the New Laws were repealed. Las Casas, then in his seventies, returned to Spain and renewed his efforts on behalf of the Indians before the Spanish court and the Council of the Indies.

Las Casas was not an Aristotelian. He described Aristotle as "a gentile burning in hell, whose philosophy should be accepted only when it proved consistent with Christian doctrine."[25] Not only were the backgrounds of Las Casas and Sepulveda very different, but their views on the nature of Indian rights were very different as well. Sepulveda believed that Aristotle's "natural slave theory" was applicable to the Indians. Indians were seen as "inferior to the Spaniards just as children are to adults, women to men, and, indeed, one might even say, as apes to men."[26] Sepulveda viewed war against the Indians to be both lawful and expedient as an indispensable preliminary to teaching the faith: "In order that they might learn from the missionaries, and prepare themselves for entry into the Church, it was necessary to place them under civilized government and tutelage, with or without their consent."[27] According to him:

These inferior people "require, by their own nature and in their own interests, to be placed under the authority of civilized and virtuous princes or nations, so that they may learn, from the might, wisdom, and law of their conquerors, to practice better morals, worthier customs and a more civilized way of life. . . . [The] mere fact that the Indians lived under some form of government by no means proved that they were equal to Spaniards. It simply showed that they were not monkeys and did not entirely lack reason."[28]

Therefore, Sepulveda reasoned, a war against the Indians would be just if they did not recognize the Spaniards as their natural superiors.[29] As further support of the lawfulness of war against the Indians, Sepulveda interpreted the Bull of Donation as authorizing war against the Indians if they refused to submit to the religion and jurisdiction of the Spaniards.[30] One author has noted that almost "all of the arguments ever cited in favour of imperialism were used by Sepulveda":

> Natural law, which in Sepulveda's thought coincided on the one hand with divine law . . . and on the other with the law of nations, gave to the Spaniards a well-defined chain of rights of conquest and colonisation in the New World. . . .
>
> All Christian and civilized nations enjoyed these rights and owed these duties. The special rights and duties of Spain in the New World arose from three causes: the natural superiority of the Spaniards over the other European nations; the right of the first discoverer to occupy land (such as the Indies) which had no legitimate ruler; and the decree of the Pope, at once a spiritual commission to convert the heathen, and a temporal grant of legally unoccupied territory. . . . The logic of Sepulveda's arguments was undeniable—their principle defect was that they tended to prove too much. Many of his contemporaries and most historians since his time regarded him as an apologist for naked slavery. . . . Certainly he wrote in ignorance of colonial conditions and used purely theoretical arguments to support a system which lent itself in practice to appalling abuses.[31]

The essence of Sepulveda's argument was that native peoples were not fully human beings, they could not own land, they could not form governments, and they were incapable of adapting to the "civilized arts."[32]

Las Casas, on the other hand, rejected the application of Aristotle's "natural slave theory" to Indians. Rather, he believed in the natural equality of all humankind:

> All the nations of the world are men, . . . all have understanding and volition, all have the five exterior senses and four interior senses, and are moved by the objects of these, all take satisfaction in goodness and feel pleasure with happy and delicious things, all regret and abhor evil.[33]

The third word of this quotation is also translated as "peoples" or "races."[34] This passage anticipated the language contained in the Universal Declaration of Human Rights, which states: "All human beings are born free and equal in dignity and rights."

On a collective level, Las Casas recognized that the Indians had an inherent right and capacity for self-government:

To the sixth supposition of Your Fathership [the pope], which states that the Spaniards are necessary for the Indians and for their good way of life, especially for their religion, I say . . . would to God that, in temporal affairs, Spain had been as well governed as the Indies and had such a good way of life!

Where throughout the inhabited world were there greater populations . . . than in the Indies? The great City of Mexico . . . had over 200,000 residents; and in Tlascala, Mechuacan, Tepeaca, Tezcuco, and an infinite number of other cities in New Spain and Guatemala, in the city of Cuzco, and in all parts of the Indies, . . . there were many millions of people. . . . When we entered there . . . would we have found such great unions of peoples in their towns and cities if they had lacked the order of a good way of life, peace, concord, and justice? No republic or city can be preserved or can last, nor can a multitude of men live together, without the said virtues, as is apparent from [Aristotle] the Philosopher's *Ethics and Politics*, and as is manifest to every prudent man.

Therefore, Father, the Indians have no need of Spaniards for their good way of life; thus, to say . . . that the Indians need them for that—what else is this but an excuse and feigned pretext to rob and oppress the Indians, to keep them in servitude, and to hold them in encomiendas and under Spanish despotism? Truly, I say to Your Fathership that to . . . restore the Indians to their human and temporal good way of life, not a single Spaniard would have to remain in the Indies. For who has disturbed, disordered, and completely annihilated the good way of life of the Indians—insofar as pagans are capable of a good way of life—but the Spaniards? . . . I affirm before Jesus Christ that it would be necessary, and the best thing imaginable, to cast them all out, except for a few chosen ones, so that the Indians could receive the faith.[35]

He also found, "All men who are self-governing, under whatsoever form are sovereign" and "the law of nations and natural law apply to Christians and gentiles alike, and to all people of any sect, law, condition, or colour without any distinction whatsoever."[36] Thus, Las Casas anticipated the expansion of the circle of the Family of Nations to include all peoples of all nations, including the Indian nations.

Las Casas rejected the notion that a just war could be fought against the Indians to convert them to Christianity. He proposed peaceful persuasion as the only legitimate way to convert anybody—including the Indians—and asserted that unbelievers could not lawfully be forced to hear the gospel:

The one and only method of teaching men the true religion was established by Divine Providence for the whole world, and for all times: that is, by persuading the understanding through reason, and by gently attracting or exhorting the will. This method should be common to all men throughout, without any distinction made for sects, errors, or corrupt customs.

This conclusion will be proved in many ways: by arguments drawn from reason; by examples of the ancient Fathers; by the rule and manner of preaching which Christ instituted for all times; by the practices of the Apostles; by quotations from holy teachers; by the most ancient traditions of the Church and by her numerous ecclesiastical decrees. . . .

A method contrary to the one we have been defending would be the following: that . . . the pagans should first be subjected, whether they wished to be or not, to the rule of the Christian people, and that once they were subjected, organized preaching would follow. . . .

But since no pagan, above all no pagan kings, would wish voluntarily to submit to the rule of a Christian people, or of any prince, it would certainly be necessary to come to a war. . . . War also fills every place with highwaymen, thieves, ravishers, fires, and murders. Indeed, what is war but general murder and robbery among many?[37]

Neither, in Las Casas's opinion, did the Bull of Donation authorize war against the Indians. He interpreted the use of the word "inducere" in the bull as specifically negating the use of force. Las Casas rejected a holy war against the Indians as "iniquitous and Mahometan."[38] Additionally, Las Casas argued that the Bull of Donation was superseded by Sublimis Deus, and the latter clearly opposed the use of force against the Indians.

This debate was not settled in the sixteenth century and, as will be seen, it is by no means settled today. Both sides of this debate can be found in legal decisions that form the body of law that currently applies to the Indian people. Over the years, writers on international law have fluctuated between the two positions first addressed by Las Casas and Sepulveda. Two of the most well known writers on the subject were Hugo Grotius and Emmerich Vattel. A review of their writings is in order since they have been so influential and since their writings form one of the links between the earlier writers and current law.

Grotius denied that any rights could be claimed over the Indians or their land on the basis of the doctrine of discovery.[39] According to Grotius, the doctrine of discovery was applicable only to vacant land, and it was inapplicable to land occupied by Indians who "now have and always have had their own kings, their own governments, their own lands, and their own legal systems."[40] Further, no rights could be claimed over Indians because of their religion, character, or perceived lack of civilization:

Vitoria then is right in saying that the Spaniards have no more legal right over the East Indians because of their religion, than the East Indians would have had over the Spaniards if they had happened to be the first foreigners to come to Spain. Nor are the East Indians stupid and unthinking; on the contrary they are intelligent and shrewd, so that a pretext for subduing them on the ground of their character could not be sustained. Such a pretext on its very face is an injustice. Plutarch said long ago that the civilizing of barbarians had been made a pretext for aggression, which is to say that a greedy longing for the property of another often hides itself behind such a pretext. And not that well-known pretext of forcing nations into a higher state of civilization against their will, the pretext once seized by the Greeks and by Alexander the Great, is considered by all theologians, especially those of Spain, to be unjust and unholy.[41]

Grotius, like Victoria and St. Thomas Aquinas before him, also denied the right of the pope over temporal matters and dismissed Alexander VI's bull as "empty ostentation."[42] Grotius supported Pope Paul III's policy in favor of restoring to the Indians the "liberty of which they had been robbed in the name of religion."[43]

Vattel, in contrast to Grotius, believed that the doctrine of discovery was applicable not only to vacant land but also to some of the territory occupied by "wandering tribes of men continuing to possess it in common."[44] Vattel addressed the "celebrated question, to which the discovery of the New World has principally given rise . . . [of] whether a nation may lawfully take possession of some part of a vast country, in which there are none but erratic nations whose scanty population is incapable of occupying the whole."[45] As a result of what Vattel perceived as a "natural obligation to cultivate the earth":

Those nations can not exclusively appropriate to themselves more land than they have occasion for, or more than they are able to settle and cultivate. Their unsettled habitation in those immense regions cannot be accounted a true and legal possession; and the people of Europe, too closely pent up at home, finding land of which they made no actual and constant use, were lawfully entitled to take possession of it, and settle it with colonies. The earth, as we have already observed, belongs to mankind in general, and was designed to furnish them with subsistence: If each nation had, from the beginning, resolved to appropriate to itself a vast country, that the people might live only by hunting, fishing, and wild fruits, our globe would not be sufficient to maintain a tenth part of its present inhabitants. We do not, therefore, deviate from the views of nature, in confining the Indians within narrower limits.[46]

Thus, Vattel legitimated the colonization of America. Once such colonies were established, their territory was considered to be an integral part of the mother country.

ENGLISH PERSPECTIVE

The English settlements in North America were made in negation of the validity of the Spanish claims made under the Bull of Donation. Queen Elizabeth I did not recognize the Spanish title by donation from the "bishop of Rome," and limited Spanish claims to areas of "actual possession."[47] According to Sir William Blackstone, the English perfected the inchoate title it obtained by discovery "by right of Conquest and driving out the natives (with what natural justice I shall not at present inquire) or by treaties."[48] The English generally obtained land from the Indians by treaties rather than the more usual means of conquest employed by the Spanish. The treaties made by the English led to dividing lines being drawn between the land in English possession and the land that remained in the possession of the various Indian nations.

In an attempt to limit white settlement to the eastern seaboard and to keep the loyalty of their Indian allies, the English issued the Proclamation of 1763. This proclamation prohibited individuals from purchasing land from the Indians and prohibited whites from settling west of a line that ran roughly along the crest of the Appalachian Mountains.[49] It also recognized the right of the Indians to the undisturbed possession of the land west of this line.

After the American Revolution, which was caused in part by this proclamation, the English government made one last initiative with respect to the development of a new policy toward the American Indians. In an attempt to avoid an area of potential conflict, the British proposed the creation of an independent Indian buffer zone along the entire frontier between Canada and the American states.[50] This would have ended the seemingly endless problems that arose between the British and the Americans when Indian land was wrongfully expropriated. However, the American government rejected this proposal as an unwarranted interference with its right to obtain this land from the Indians by purchase or conquest as a successor in interest to British claims made under the doctrine of discovery.[51]

The next step in the development of the trusteeship concept first addressed by Victoria was taken by Edmund Burke. Burke, the famous Whig parliamentarian, expanded on Victoria's trusteeship notion in his explanation of the nature of the relationship between the British and the Asian Indians. Speaking before the House of Commons in 1783, Burke expressed the trusteeship concept of colonialism as follows:

> All political power which is set over men, and . . . all privilege claimed or exercised in the exclusion of them, being wholly artificial, and for so much a derogation from the natural equality of mankind at large, ought to be in some way or other exercised ultimately for their benefit.
>
> If this is true with regard to every species of political dominion, and every description of commercial privilege, none of which can be original self-derived rights, or grants for the benefit of the holders, then such rights or privileges, or whatever else you choose to call them, are all, in the strictest sense, a trust; and it is of the very essence of every trust to be rendered accountable; and even totally to cease, when it substantially varies from the purpose for which alone it could have a lawful existence.[52]

Although Burke's ideas may seem to be out of character for a British conservative, they really were not. Burke, who revered the customs and institutions of England, was equally concerned with the unnecessary disruptions of the customs and institutions of India that were made by the East India Company. His thought also "went beyond the idea of a national trust to that of a collective responsibility of the whole community of civilized nations."[53] Burke recognized that "justice and morality are universal and not 'geographical': 'The laws of morality are the same everywhere.' "[54]

Burke did not content himself with statements of theory. In 1788 he brought impeachment proceedings against the governor-general of India, Warren Hastings. Burke charged Hastings not only with graft and corruption, but also with a breach of the "sacred trust" of Parliament and with subverting the natural rights and liberties of the people of India.[55] Burke's largely symbolic impeachment effort against Hastings was successful, even though Hastings was ultimately acquitted after a seven-year trial in the House of Lords. Burke remained convinced that Hastings had infringed on a higher morality—the natural rights of the people of India—even if his deeds could not be punished under the positive law of nations or the domestic law of England. More important, the idea of the colonial trust gained general acceptance throughout the British Empire.

Another step in the development of the trusteeship concept of colonialism was made by Lord Lugard. Lugard held a variety of positions in numerous British colonies during his long career. He not only elaborated on the theory of colonialism, he also put his words into practice. In 1893, Lugard introduced a system of indirect rule in Uganda whereby colonial administration was carried out through tribal institutions.[56]

The dual mandate was another of Lugard's developments.[57] Under the dual mandate, the administering power recognized a trust for the world at large and a trust for the native peoples. The trust for the world at large was a recognition of the Open Door policy, which broke up the colonial powers' monopoly of trade and gave other nations access to raw materials. The trust for the native peoples—the real heart of the system—recognized that the interests of the native peoples are paramount and that the trust was to be exercised for their benefit.

Other English writers on the theory of international law argued both for and against the rights of the so-called "backwards races." Writing in 1879, Robert Phillimore disagreed with the exclusion of the "backwards races" from the circle of the Family of Nations. After reviewing the work of earlier writers, Phillimore concluded:

> [T]he *principles* of international justice do govern, or *ought* to govern, the dealings of the Christian with the Infidel Community. They are binding, for instance, upon Great Britain, in her intercourse with the native powers of India; upon France, with those of Africa; upon Russia, in her relations with Persia or America; upon the United States of North America, in their intercourse with the Native Indians.
>
> The violation of these principles is indeed sometimes urged in support of an

opposite opinion, but to no purpose; for it is clear that the occasional vicious practice cannot affect the reality of the permanent duty.[58]

John Westlake, on the other hand, argued in 1914 for the continued exclusion of the so-called "backwards races" from the Family of Nations. He rationalized this result by quoting J. B. Martens Ferrao of Portugal:

[I]n savage tribes . . . we must recognize all natural rights. Natural rights are born with man; they constitute his personality, which the want of cultivation does not extinguish. *But* international rights cannot be recognized in those tribes, for want of the capacity for government (capacite dirigeante). Being nomads or nearly such, they have no international character. For the same reason they have no constituted sovereignty, that being no doubt a political right derived from civilization, and therefore having civilization at its base and the condition of its existence. Modern international law is a result of civilization.[59]

Westlake's position raises the related issue of how international law regarded treaties made with such "savage tribes." Although the negotiation of a bilateral treaty supposedly is an act of recognition of both parties as sovereign nations and imposes international rights and responsibilities on both, in reality, treaties with such peoples have an inferior status. Westlake explained this status as follows:

[N]o document in which such natives are made to cede the sovereignty over any territory can be exhibited as an international title, although an arrangement with them, giving evidence that they have been treated with humanity and consideration, may be valuable as obviating possible objections to what would otherwise be a good international title to sovereignty. And this is reasonable. A stream cannot rise higher than its source, and the right to establish the full system of civilized government, which in these cases is the essence of sovereignty, cannot be based on the consent of those who at the utmost know but a few of the needs which such a government is intended to meet.[60]

Consequently, so-called "civilized" peoples did not need to keep the promises that they made to so-called "uncivilized peoples," or even to recognize their very existence. Although international law applied the new test of civilization—in a narrow, Western sense—rather than the old test of Christianity, much the same result was reached. Thus, international law at this time continued to regard the treatment of such indigenous peoples as a matter exclusively within the domestic jurisdiction of the "civilized," Christian, colonizing country.

BEGINNING OF INTERNATIONAL ACCOUNTABILITY FOR THE PROTECTION OF INDIGENOUS PEOPLES

In the half-century before World War I, international law began to break down the traditional barriers that shielded colonizing countries from censure for the mistreatment of native peoples. The growth of humanitarian concern for peoples under colonial rule on a national level, on the part of people like Burke, led to a growth of concern for these peoples on an international level. European colonization created the conditions necessary for the Industrial Revolution to occur by expanding markets and the availability of raw materials. By the late nineteenth century, the race for control of markets and raw materials had led to the exhaustion of areas that could be colonized.[61] Increasing competition for natural resources led to the conclusion of bilateral agreements between colonial powers for the reciprocal application of the Open Door policy. The expansion of these bilateral agreements into multinational agreements marked the beginning of concerted international action in the area of colonial policy.

The earliest attempt at international regulation of the treatment of native peoples dealt with the slave trade. On a domestic level, Britain led the way by abolishing the slave trade in 1807. In 1885 the General Act of the Berlin Conference, which was only applicable to the Congo Basin, recognized that the slave trade was forbidden by "the principles of international law as recognized by the signatory powers."[62] The Brussels Conference of 1890 saw the extension of both the subject matter and the geographic area under international scrutiny. The General Act of Brussels regulated not only the slave trade but also the importation of arms and trade spirits throughout all the territories in Africa under European control. From this time forward, the welfare of colonial peoples was unquestionably a matter of international concern, and further expansion in their welfare occurred through the progressive removal of the subject matter and geographic barriers placed on the application of such provisions.

The internationalization of the trusteeship concept of colonialism followed the internationalization of the protection of indigenous peoples. John Locke and Jean-Jacques Rousseau provided the theoretical foundation for the concept of the sacred trust of civilization with their development of social contract theory, which was based on natural rights and the equality of all human beings.[63] The American Revolution, which was referred to by the British as the American War of Secession, built on this theory of natural rights, which flatly rejected any imposition of government from above. The Declaration of Independence asserted, "Governments are instituted among Men, deriving their just powers from the consent of the governed." In his first draft of the declaration, Thomas Jefferson redundantly avowed these natural rights to be "inherent and unalienable."[64]

Initially, these theories of natural equality were applied exclusively to peoples of European stock. However, these natural rights theories and notions of equality inevitably came to impact as well on colonialism and peoples of non-European stock.[65] A moral justification had to be found for the imposition of rule by one people over another in violation of the natural right of all peoples to govern themselves. The Europeans justified their domination of other peoples by claiming that they were "backward" and incapable of self-government and had to be placed under the protection of an advanced nation. The advanced nation then had the obligation to develop the self-governing institutions of the native peoples. These ideas provided the theoretical foundation on which the further internationalization of the trusteeship concept of colonialism was built in the aftermath of World War I.

NOTES

1. L. B. Simpson, The Encomiendo in New Spain: The Beginnings of Spanish Mexico (1950); *see also* J. H. Parry, The Spanish Theory of Empire in the Sixteenth Century 8 (1940); K. Sale, The Conquest of Paradise: Christopher Columbus and the Columbian Legacy (1990); E. Korth, Spanish Policy in Colonial Chile: The Struggle for Social Justice 1535–1700 (1968).

2. W. Hagan, American Indians 8 (1974); *see also* R. A. Williams, Jr., The Medieval and Renaissance Origins of the Status of the American Indian in Western Legal Thought, 57 So. Cal. L. Rev. 1, 36–40 (1983); J. H. Parry, *supra* note 1, at 67.

3. F. S. Cohen, Original Indian Title, 32 Minn. L. Rev. 28, 44 (1947).

4. F. de Victoria, De Indis et de Ivre Belli Relectiones [Reflections on the Indians and the Law of War] (E. Nys, ed., J. Bate trans.) in J. B. Scott, The Classics of International Law 120 (1917).

5. *Id.* at 128.

6. F. S. Cohen, *supra* note 3, at 44; *see also* L. Hanke, The Spanish Struggle for Justice in the Conquest of America (1949).

7. F. de Victoria, *supra* note 4, at 115.

8. J. H. Parry, *supra* note 1, at 21.

9. P. H. Kooijmans, The Doctrine of the Legal Equality of States 57 (1964).

10. F. S. Cohen, *supra* note 3, at 44.

11. F. de Victoria, *supra* note 4, at 139.

12. *Id.*

13. L. Hanke, Aristotle and the American Indians: A Study in Race Prejudice in the Modern World 47 (1959).

14. F. de Victoria, *supra* note 4, at 160–61. Emphasis added.

15. *Id.*

16. J. McCabe, Crisis in the History of the Papacy 310 (1916).

17. F. A. MacNott, Bartholemew de Las Casas 427–31 (1909); *see also* J. H. Parry, *supra* note 1, at 28.

18. F. S. Cohen, *supra* note 3, at 45; *cf.* J. H. Parry, *supra* note 1, at 29.

19. L. Hanke, Aristotle, *supra* note 13, at 38.

20. *Id.* at 31.

21. W. W. Washburn, Red Man's Land/White Man's Law: A Study of the Past and Present Status of the American Indian 15 (1971).

22. L. Hanke, Aristotle, *supra* note 13, at 98; Aristotle advised Alexander the Great "to treat Greeks as members of the family, the *Barbarians* as animals": Legal Consequences for States of the Continued Presence of South Africa in Na-

mibia (South West Africa) Notwithstanding Security Council Resolution 276 (1970), Order No. 1 of 26 January 1971, I.C.J. Reports 1971, at 3, 77 (1971). *See also* L. Hanke, Bartolome de Las Casas: Bookman-Scholar and Propagandist 39 (1952).

23. R. Sanders, Lost Tribes and Promised Lands: The Origins of American Racism 164 (1978); *see also* J. H. Parry, *supra* note 1, at 30.

24. J. F. Bannon, Indian Labor in the Spanish Indies: Was There Another Solution? (1966); *see also* Bartolome De Las Casas, The Devastation of the Indies: A Brief Account (Herma Briffault trans. 1974); H. R. Wagner, The Life and Writings of Bartolome de Las Casas 186 (1967).

25. L. Hanke, Aristotle, *supra* note 13, at 56.

26. 10 The New Encyclopedia Britannica, 685 (1974); *see also* L. Hanke, All Mankind Is One: A Study of the Disputation between Bartolome de Las Casas and Juan Gines de Sepulveda in 1550 on the Intellectual and Religious Capacity of the American Indians 80 (1974).

27. J. H. Parry, *supra* note 1, at 37.

28. L. Hanke, Aristotle, *supra* note 13, at 47–48.

29. *Id.* at 69.

30. *Id.* at 40; *see also* L. Hanke, All Mankind Is One, *supra* note 26, at 86.

31. J. H. Parry, *supra* note 1, at 38–40.

32. J. Mohawk, A Message for the Work Ahead, 12 Akwesasne Notes, no. 5, at 21 (Winter 1980).

33. L. Hanke, Bartolome de Las Casas: An Interpretation of His Life and Writings 82 (1951).

34. L. Hanke, Aristotle, *supra* note 13, at 111; Bartolome de Las Casas 200 (G. Sanderlin trans. & ed. 1971).

35. Bartolome de Las Casas 195–96 (G. Sanderlin trans. & ed. 1971).

36. L. Hanke, Aristotle, *supra* note 13, at 112–13.

37. Bartolome de Las Casas, *supra* note 35, at 158–62; *see also* L. Hanke, Aristotle, *supra* note 13, at 28; L. Hanke, Bartolome de Las Casas: Bookman-Scholar and Propagandist, *supra* note 22, at 10.

38. Marcel Brion, Bartolome de Las Casas, "Father of the Indians" 179 (1929).

39. H. Grotius, The Freedom of the Seas 13 (R. Magoffin trans. 1916).

40. *Id.* at 11.

41. *Id.* at 13–14.

42. *Id.* at 45.

43. *Id.* at 20–21.

44. E. Vattel, The Law of Nations 97 (J. Chitty ed. 1867).

45. *Id.* at 99.

46. *Id.* at 100.

47. The Collected Papers of John Westlake on International Law 160 (L. Oppenheim ed. 1914); Encyclopedia of Public International Law: History of the Law of Nations: Ancient Times to 1648, at 153–54 (1985).

48. Cited in M. F. Lindley, The Acquisition and Government of Backward Territory in International Law, Being a Treatise on the Law and Practice Relating to Colonial Expansion 14–15 (1926).

49. R. N. Clinton, The Proclamation of 1763: Colonial Prelude to Two Centuries of Federal-State Conflict over Management of Indian Affairs, 69 B.U.L. Rev. 329 (March 1989); *see also* W. R. Jacobs, Dispossessing the American Indian: Indians

and Whites on the Colonial Frontier 94–103 (1972); H. D. Hall, Mandates, Dependencies, and Trusteeship 97 (1948); E. Robinson & H. Quinney, The Infested Blanket: Canada's Constitution—Genocide at Law 5–6 (1985); K. Narrey, The Royal Proclamation of 7 October 1763, The Common Law and Native Rights to Land within the Territory Granted to the Hudson's Bay Company, 38 Sask. L. Rev. 123 (1974).

50. G. R. Mellor, British Imperial Trusteeship 1783–1850, at 374 (1951).

51. W. Jacobs, Dispossessing the American Indian, Indians and Whites on the Colonial Frontier 97–100 (1972); in 1776 nearly all the estimated 2.5 million citizens of the United States lived within two hundred miles of the Atlantic seaboard. P. White, This Land is Ours—How Are We Using It? 150 National Geographic, no. 1, at 40 (July 1976).

52. T. C. Hansard, 23 Parliamentary History, cols. 1316–17 (1783); cited in C. E. Toussaint, The Trusteeship System of the United Nations 6 (1956).

53. H. D. Hall, Mandates, Dependencies and Trusteeship 99 (1948).

54. *Id.*; E. Burke, Speech on Opening the Articles of Impeachment, 15 February 1788, in 4 Speeches, 312–13; cited in F. O'Gorman, Edmund Burke: His Political Philosophy 103 (1973).

55. E. Burke, *supra* note 54, at 7.

56. British Information Services, Towards Self-Government in the British Colonies 38 (Jan. 1950).

57. F. Lugard, The Dual Mandate in British Tropical Africa (1923).

58. R. Phillimore, 1 Commentaries upon International Law 60–61 (1854; repr. 1985).

59. The Collected Papers of John Westlake on Public International Law 148 (L. Oppenheim ed. 1914). Emphasis added.

60. *Id.* at 146.

61. R. F. Betts, The "Scramble" for Africa; Causes and Dimensions of Empire (1966).

62. E. Sady, The United Nations and Dependent Peoples 15 (1956); *see also* R. L. Barsh, Indigenous North America and Contemporary International Law, 62 Ore. L. Rev. 73, at 74 (1983).

63. E. Sady, The United Nations and Dependent Peoples 5 (1956); *see also* R. A. Williams, Jr., *supra* note 2, at 3 n. 4.

64. The Papers of Thomas Jefferson (J. P. Boyd ed. 1950).

65. Q. Wright, Mandates under the League of Nations 14 (1968).

3

The League of Nations and the "Sacred Trust of Civilization"

After World War I, the trusteeship concept of colonialism became a matter of international concern. However, this was only a small part of the internationalization of the underlying principle on which the trusteeship concept is based—the self-determination of peoples.[1] The Soviet Union recognized the principle of self-determination in the Decree of Peace of November 8, 1917, which forbid the annexation of small or weak peoples without their voluntary and express consent.[2] The principle of self-determination was later declared to be a right by the Soviets and was incorporated into the constitution of the Soviet Union in 1918.[3]

President Woodrow Wilson of the United States became the leading advocate of the internationalization of the principle of self-determination of peoples through the vehicle of the League of Nations. Even before the U.S. entry into World War I, Wilson sought to establish a new world order based on consent rather than conquest.[4] Wilson's campaign was a crusade for the internationalization of the ideals of American democracy. He believed that World War I would be the "war to end war" only if there was a "peace without victory." Wilson said:

> No peace can last, or ought to last, which does not recognize and accept the principle that governments derive all their just powers from the consent of the governed. . . . I speak of this, not because of any desire to exalt an abstract political principle which has always been held very dear by those who have sought to build up liberty

in America, but for the same reason that I have spoken of the other conditions of peace which seem to me clearly indispensable—because I wish frankly to uncover realities. Any peace which does not recognize and accept this principle will inevitably be upset.[5]

After America's entry into World War I, Wilson enumerated his famous Fourteen Points which were expanded on in subsequent addresses and which he regarded as essential to a lasting peace. All these points revolved around the central principle of self-determination. They included provisions for the establishment of a "general association of nations . . . formed under specific covenants for the purpose of affording mutual guarantees of political independence and territorial integrity to great and small states alike" and for the "free, open-minded, and absolutely impartial adjustment of all colonial claims."[6]

The Treaty of Versailles, which contained the Covenant of the League of Nations, contained two manifestations of the principle of self-determination: national self-determination and the sacred trust of civilization.[7] Although national self-determination had the most immediate impact, time has shown that the decolonization provisions laid the foundation for revolutionary change in the way that the European Law of Nations viewed most—if not all—of the so-called "backwards races."

The bulk of the Treaty of Versailles dealt with national self-determination—the redrawing of the boundary lines of Europe along ethnic frontiers. Although this was purportedly done in conformity with the principle of self-determination, numerous exceptions were made. The national aspirations of some peoples were respected. This included the recognition of large states such as Poland, Czechoslovakia, and Yugoslavia, and small states such as Monaco, Liechtenstein, Andorra, and San Marino. The national aspirations of other peoples were ignored. These included the Armenians, Azerbaijanis, Koreans, Ukrainians, Ruthenians, White Russians, Georgians, Kurds, and Montenegrans. In yet other cases, the principle of national self-determination was compromised in favor of economics, defensible borders, or historical ties—all euphemisms for the vestiges of the spoils system of former times.[8]

The most important of these exceptions dealt with Germany's borders. In violation of the principle of self-determination, an "inalienable independence" was forced on Austria, whose population at the time would have preferred to be incorporated into Germany. Three million Germans were placed under Czech rule and over a million Germans were placed under the rule of the Polish.[9] These exceptions to the application of the principle of self-determination sowed the seeds of World War II. Indeed, it was Hitler's professed view that World War II was due entirely to the inequities of the Treaty of Versailles.[10]

MANDATE SYSTEM

The second manifestation of the principle of self-determination in the Treaty of Versailles was the sacred trust of civilization, which was contained in the Mandate system and the Native Inhabitants clause of the League of Nations Covenant.[11] These provisions marked the first attempt to make advanced nations accountable on an international level for the treatment of the native populations under their colonial control. In theory, these provisions were universal in nature. In practice, however, they were applied on a very limited scale.

The Mandate system was confined in scope to fourteen former Turkish and German territories.[12] The Class A mandates consisted of areas formerly belonging to the Turkish Empire that were provisionally recognized as independent nations "subject to the rendering of administrative advice and assistance by a Mandatory until such time as they are able to stand alone."[13] The Class A mandates were Syria, Lebanon, Iraq, Palestine, and Transjordan.

The Class B mandates were kept administratively separate from existing colonies but were administered as colonies by the mandatory power. The Class B mandates included Tanganyika, Ruanda-Urundi, Togoland, and the Cameroons. The last two territories were each divided between two mandatory powers—France and Great Britain. The Class C mandates,

> owing to the sparseness of their population, or their small size, or their remoteness from the centres of civilization, or their geographical contiguity to the territory of the Mandatory, and other circumstances, can be best administered under the laws of the Mandatory as integral portions of its territory . . . [subject to a list of safeguards] in the interests of the indigenous population.[14]

The Class C mandates included South-West Africa, Yap and other former German North Pacific Islands, German New Guinea and certain adjacent South Pacific islands, Nauru, and Western Samoa.

The league failed to establish mandates in some former Turkish territories. For example, Wilson's fourth draft of the covenant listed Armenia and Kurdistan as former Turkish territories to be placed under mandate.[15] The Armenian mandate was rejected by the Unites States Senate and then forgotten.[16] The rights of the Kurdish people were also forgotten, and Kurdistan was divided up between Turkey and the mandates of Iraq and Syria.[17]

NATIVE INHABITANTS CLAUSE

Under the Native inhabitants clause, members undertook "to secure just treatment of native inhabitants of territories under their control."[18] "Article 23(b) was the outcome of the same general trend that produced the mandate system, the trend since the late eighteenth century towards concerted international action regarding indigenous peoples."[19] Although no league body ever defined the words "just treatment," it has been suggested that they were "in fact clearly enough defined by the general principles and safeguards of Article 22."[20]

There was never any question of the universal application of Article 23(b). It "was invoked without protest as the legal basis for investigations conducted by the League in 1931 into the inhuman treatment meted out by the Liberian government to the nomadic tribes inhabiting its desert interior."[21] Liberia was warned that the failure to honor its obligations under Article 23(b) warranted its expulsion from the league.[22] However, this situation did not result in any recommendation being taken by the assembly.[23]

There were seven clauses in Article 23. Six of these clauses became technical organs, but Article 23(b) did not. Nonetheless, this provision, like the other international trust provisions, was a recognition of the inadequacy of domestic trust relationships which were often totally lacking in accountability.[24]

These decolonization provisions laid the foundation for the expansion of the European Law of Nations far beyond the borders of Europe, even though the circle of the Family of Nations remained relatively small. The League of Nations had between forty-two and sixty-three members which were mostly European:

> Among the League's original members, there were only five Asian countries (China, India, Japan, Thailand, and Iran) and two African countries (Liberia and the Union of South Africa), and it added only three Asian countries (Afghanistan, Iraq, and Turkey) and two African countries (Egypt and Ethiopia) before it was dissolved in 1946. Of the mandated territories under the League's control, only Iraq, Lebanon, and Syria achieved independence during its lifetime.[25]

Although this was a major step forward in international relations, the league remained basically a regional organization.

The league deviated from the concept of universal membership in a number of important cases. First, the league "was originally conceived as an international organization of only 'democratic states.' "[26] It was believed that the admission of nondemocratic states would compromise the effectiveness of the league. The Allied and Associated Powers, which controlled the league, eventually abandoned this democratic limitation on membership.

Second, the league did not admit small states, a policy that ran counter to the principle of the sovereign equality of states. This size limitation was also contrary to the historical roots of the European Law of Nations, which grew out of the relations between the two thousand microscopic city-states during the days of the Roman Empire. Three "ministates" applied for league membership: San Marino, Monaco, and Liechtenstein.[27] Liechtenstein, however, was the only ministate that pursued its application for membership. Although Liechtenstein's application was ultimately denied, size per se was claimed to be irrelevant to the decision. (At this time, Liechtenstein was about 157 square kilometers, and the population was between ten and eleven thousand.) The reason given for denying Liechtenstein membership was that the country had "chosen to depute to others some of the attributes of sovereignty."[28] However, since other states had surrendered even more attributes of sovereignty to other states and still were admitted to full membership, the real reason was, in fact, size, and not limitations on Liechtenstein's sovereignty. This bias of the league has been carried over to the United Nations, although to a lesser extent.

Third, at least two attempts by indigenous representatives to gain access to the League of Nations were summarily rejected. In the 1920s the Maori religious leader Ratana and the Six Nations Confederacy Chief Deskaheh tried to petition the league for the redress of grievances:

> In 1922 Deskaheh presented a petition to the Dutch ambassador to the United States, asking that it be forwarded to the League of Nations. Deskaheh spent much of 1923 and 1924 in Geneva meeting diplomats and arguing the Iroquois case. The governments of the United Kingdom and Canada went to some lengths to prevent the questions from being discussed within the League. The Netherlands did forward the petition to the secretary-general, asking that it be communicated to the council of the League. When that initiative had been successfully stalled, four League members (Ireland, Panama, Persia, and Estonia) revived the question by writing to the president of the League's assembly and asking for an advisory opinion from the Permanent Court of International Justice as to whether the Iroquois Confederacy was a state. In December 1923 the Persian member of the League's council asked that the matter be put on the agenda of the council. Each of these three attempts to have the petition considered was stopped by diplomatic intervention. The government of Canada prepared a reply to the Iroquois allegations, which was published in the official journal of the League.
>
> While Deskaheh was still in Europe, the Canadian government dissolved the traditional council at the Six Nations Reserve and established a new elected band-council system. Since the confederacy supporters refused to participate in the new system, this had the effect of depriving Deskaheh of his right to speak for the confederacy, at least according to Canadian law.[29]

NOTES

1. U. Umozurike, Self-Determination in International Law (1972).
2. G. Starushenko, The Principle of National Self-Determination in Soviet Foreign Policy 88 (1963).
3. S. Finer, Five Constitutions 165 (1979).

4. H. Grimal, Decolonization: The British, French, Dutch, and Belgian Empires 1919–1963, at 12 (1965).

5. War and Peace: Presidential Messages, Addresses, and Public Papers (1917–1924) 411 (R. S. Baker & W. E. Dodd eds. 1927).

6. *Id.* at xxxv, 161.

7. The Treaty of Versailles and After; Annotations of the text of the Treaty (D. Myers ed. 1968).

8. M. Pomerance, The United States and Self-Determination: Perspectives on the Wilsonian Conception, 70 Am. J. Int'l. L. 1, 8 (1976).

9.

> German opinion remained deeply shocked by the fact that over a million Germans were still to fall under Polish rule; to most Germans this seemed unnatural, however reasonable it might be for Germans to rule over Poles, for, as the German observations on the draft treaty put it, "as regards economic, social and cultural importance the German population is far superior to the Polish and Cassubian population."

R. Parker, Europe 1919–1945, at 14 (1967).

10. P. Birdsell, Versailles Twenty Years After 4 (1962); *see also* P. Hastings, Between the Wars 17 (1968).

> The connecting link between genocidal settler societies of the eighteenth and nineteenth centuries and twentieth-century genocide can be discerned in Adolf Hitler's *Lebensraum* program. As a young man, Hitler saw the settlement of the New World and the concomitant elimination of North America's Indian population by white European settlers as a model to be followed by Germany on the European continent. . . . Hitler was keenly aware of Germany's population problems. He was determined that there would be no surplus German population even if a significant portion of Germany's Slavic neighbors were exterminated to provide "living space" for German settlers adjacent to the homeland. Put differently, Hitler proposed to repeat in Europe . . . the exploitative colonialism practiced by other Europeans overseas. In Hitler's eyes the Slavs were destined to become Europe's Indians.

R. Rubenstein: Afterword to Genocide and the Modern Age 287–88 (I. Wallimann & M. Dobkowski eds. 1987).

11. Q. Wright, Mandates under the League of Nations (1948).

12. H. D. Hall, Mandates, Dependencies, and Trusteeship 44 (1948).

13. Q. Wright, *supra* note 11, at 591.

14. *Id.* at 591–92.

15. H. D. Hall, *supra* note 12, at 37.

16. T. Bailey, Woodrow Wilson and the Lost Peace 170–71 (1944).

17. L. Buchheit, Secession: The Legitimacy of Self-Determination 153–62 (1978).

18. League of Nations Covenant Art. 23(b), Native Inhabitants clause; *see* Appendix 1.

19. H. D. Hall, *supra* note 12, at 223.

20. *Id.* at 226.

21. G. Bennett, Aboriginal Rights in International Law 10 (1978); *see also* J. L. Kunz, Chapter XI of the United Nations Charter in Action, 48 Am. J. Int'l. L. 109 (1954).

22. *Id.*

23. H. D. Hall, *supra* note 12, at 224–26.

24. E. Sady, The United Nations and Dependent Peoples (1956); *see also* P. Wohlgemuth Blair, The Ministate Dilemma 49 (1967).

25. 12 The New Encyclopedia Britannica 852–53 (1974).

> The changing participation in the big international congresses clearly illustrated the growth of the community of states. In the Congo Conference of Berlin in 1885, at which Europe acted as legislator for the African world, 14 countries participated, all European with the exception of the United States. The First Peace Conference held in The Hague in 1899 united 27 countries (20 from Europe, the U.S. and Mexico from America, China, Japan, Persia and Siam from Asia); the Second Peace Conference of 1907 brought together 43 countries (21 European, 18 American and 4 Asian). The League of Nations of 1919 numbered between 42 and 63 countries. The United Nations began with 51 members (14 European, 22 American, 12 Afro-Asian, and Australia, New Zealand and South Africa) and now—October 1960—has 98 members (27 European, 22 American, 46 Afro-Asian, and Australia, New Zealand, and South Africa), while Asian and African countries are candidates for membership.

B. Roling, International Law in an Expanded World 5 (1960). *See also* M. Hudson, Membership in the League of Nations, 18 Am. J. Int'l. L. 436 (1924); J. Crawford, The Creation of States in International Law (1979).

26. R. A. Akindele, The Organization and Promotion of World Peace; A Study of Universal-Regional Relationships 4 (1976); W. Schiffer, The Legal Community of Mankind: A Critical Analysis of the Modern Concept of World Organization (1954).

27. J. Dugard, Recognition and the United Nations 70–71 (1987).

28. M. Gunter, Liechtenstein and the League of Nations: A Precedent for the United Nations Ministate Problem? 68 Am. J. Int'l. L. 496, 498 (1974). "Significantly, in the many U.N. debates . . . infinitesimal smallness has never been seen as a reason to deny self-determination to a population": T. M. Franck & P. Hoffman, The Right of Self-Determination in Very Small Places, 8 N.Y.U.J. Int'l. L. & Pol. 331, 383 (1975–76). *See also* Liechtenstein, History, and Institutions of the Principality 58–66 (1970). The smallest mandate was Nauru with a population of three thousand: E. Sady, The United Nations and Dependent Peoples 3 (1956).

29. D. Sanders, "Aboriginal Rights: The Search for Recognition in International Law" in The Quest for Justice: Aboriginal Peoples and Aboriginal Rights 299–300 (M. Boldt, J. Long & L. Little Bear eds. 1985); *see also* R. Veatch, Canada and the League of Nations, ch. 7 (1975); Conditions of Admission of a State to Membership in the United Nations (Article 4 of the Charter), Advisory Opinion of May 28, 1948, I.C.J. (1948); L. Mandell, Indian Nations: Not Minorities, 27 C. de D. 101, at 116–17 (1986); *see also* D. Bonaparte, A Line Drawn in Blood: The US/Canadian Border and the Mohawks of Akwesasne, 23 Akwesasne Notes, no. 1, at 3 (Spring 1991).

4

The United Nations and the "Sacred Trust of Civilization"

After World War II, the trusteeship concept of colonialism was applied in a greatly expanded manner when compared to the earlier actions of the League of Nations. However, it was, once again, only a small part of the internationalization of the underlying principle on which the trusteeship concept is based—the self-determination of peoples. The Preamble to the Charter of the United Nations states:

WE THE PEOPLES OF THE UNITED NATIONS determined to save succeeding generations from the scourge of war, which twice in our lifetime has brought untold sorrow to mankind, and to reaffirm faith in fundamental human rights, in the dignity and worth of the human person, in the equal rights of men and women and of nations large and small, and to establish conditions under which justice and respect for the obligations arising from treaties and other sources of international law can be maintained . . .

Articles 1 and 55 of the charter are based on the principle of "equal rights and self-determination of peoples." Article 1 states that the purpose of the United Nations is:

to maintain international peace and security . . . and to bring about by peaceful means . . . adjustment or settlement of international disputes . . . and to develop friendly relations among nations based on respect for the principle of equal rights and self-determination of peoples . . . and in promoting and encouraging respect for human rights and for fundamental freedoms for all without distinction as to race, sex, language, or religion; and to be a centre for harmonizing the actions of nations in the attainment of these common ends.

The boundary lines of Europe were once again redrawn based on the principle of national self-determination. However, these territorial adjustments were relatively minor. The great shift in emphasis under the United Nations was the application, on an unprecedented scale, of the principle of self-determination through the principles of international trust.

However, the United Nations continued to exclude the indigenous peoples of the Western Hemisphere from the application of these principles of international trust. At the founding conference of the United Nations in San Francisco, the Six Nations Confederacy unsuccessfully sought recognition.[1] This left the only potential for recognition of the indigenous peoples of the Western Hemisphere within the international trust principles of the United Nations, but, as will be seen, this potential has still not been realized.

TRUSTEESHIP SYSTEM

Under the United Nations Charter, the "sacred trust" was embodied in the Trusteeship system and the Non-Self-Governing Territories provision. The Trusteeship system, which is contained in chapters XII and XIII of the charter, was the direct successor of the League's Mandate system. This system was intended to apply to the following three categories of territories: "a. territories now held under mandate; b. territories which may be detached from enemy states as a result of the Second World War; and c. territories voluntarily placed under the system by states responsible for their administration." The Trusteeship system applied to a territory only after the administering power had entered into a trust agreement. A total of eleven territories, all within the first two categories, have been placed within the Trusteeship system.[2]

NON-SELF-GOVERNING TERRITORIES PROVISION

The Non-Self-Governing Territories provision is contained in Chapter XI of the charter, and is the direct successor of the Native Inhabitants clause of the League of Nations. Members assumed the obligations under this provision upon the acceptance of membership to the United Nations. The Non-Self-Governing Territories provision was intended to apply automatically to all "territories whose peoples have not yet attained a full measure of self-government." Members undertook to recognize the principle that the interests of the inhabitants of these territories are paramount, and accept as the sacred trust the obligation to promote to the utmost . . . the well-being of the inhabitants of these territories, and to this end . . . to ensure, with due respect for the culture of the peoples concerned, their political, economic, social, and educational advancement, their just treatment, and their protection against abuses . . . to develop self-government.[3]

Both the Trusteeship system and the Non-Self-Governing Territories provision were a recognition of the need to treat the welfare of dependent peoples as a matter of not only local but also international concern.[4]

In 1946 the secretary-general of the United Nations sent a letter to each member nation requesting its opinion on factors to be taken into account in determining which were the territories referred to in Chapter XI and an enumeration of the non-self-governing territories subject to its jurisdiction.[5] Out of only twenty-two replies received from members, only ten commented on these two questions. Moreover, only eight members voluntarily enumerated territories on which they would transmit information.[6] These eight members enumerated only seventy-four overseas colonies and did not include information on all territories occupied by native peoples that were not self-governing.[7]

The question of which territories fell within the scope of Chapter XI was then referred to a subcommittee.[8] The United States stated that Chapter XI would "appear to apply to any territories administered by a Member of the United Nations which do not enjoy the same measure of self-government as the metropolitan area of that Member."[9] Belgium, France, and the Netherlands contended that members were obligated under Chapter XI to transmit information on areas inhabited by natives or tribal groups under their jurisdiction.

This view has not been seriously considered, despite the fact that there are some areas actually designated and administered as "territories" that fit the definition of non-self-governing territories as proposed by the United States, and whose only distinguishing feature is their [geographical] contiguity to the administering states.[10]

BELGIAN THESIS

The Belgian government gave a number of reasons for its conviction that native peoples with a "backward culture" should be protected under the United Nations Charter.[11] It viewed the history, spirit, and meaning of the charter to require a universal application of the "sacred trust." Moreover, it submitted a list of indigenous peoples that lived in non-self-governing territories in almost every area of the world, including Africa, Asia, North and South America, Australia, and a number of Pacific Islands.[12] Belgium perceived the issue as involving the exploitation of people at a lower stage of civilization by those on a higher stage of civilization and as having nothing to do with geography:

During the last few years, the debates concerning the non-self-governing territories have taken a form which is not in keeping with the spirit of co-operation that the Members of the United Nations pledged themselves to maintain among themselves. . . . [M]ore than half the States represented in this Assembly are in that position. . . . By way of example, [one] might mention, among others, the authority responsible for the Scheduled Tribes in India or the Service for the Protection of Indians in Brazil. There can be no doubt that these great countries and the services they have set up realize the difficulties of such a "sacred trust," the patience and perseverance which it requires—above all in the case of peoples living in tropical forests or almost impenetrable jungle. . . . We are familiar with these problems too, because we have been trying to solve them in the Belgian Congo for generations.[13]

Belgium also maintained that since all native peoples with a "backward culture" were protected under the league, they should also be protected under the United Nations:

All backwards peoples whose advancement is in the hands of representatives of a more highly developed race have the same rights: they are entitled to the same protection. Under the League of Nations they received it; why should we deprive them of it in the United Nations? To claim that only some of them ought to receive the rights proclaimed in principle in the Charter would be unfair to all the rest. . . . What is the mission of civilization entrusted by the Chapter to Member States which administer non-self-governing territories? It consists, in accordance with the principle that the interests of the inhabitants are paramount, of the duty of encouraging their political, economic and social advancement and of developing their capacity for self-government. . . . These obligations are in fact essentially humanitarian and there is no inherent reason why they should be restricted to colonies only.(1) They were enunciated long ago and are to be found both in domestic(2) and in international law.(3) It is not surprising that they should have found expression when the first international organization was set up.

The provisions of Chapters XI, XII and XIII of the Charter of the United Nations are based on similar provisions contained in the Covenant of the League of Nations, as is shown by numerous common features. . . .

There is no reason why these provisions should have been given restricted scope in the Charter when they were given general scope in the Covenant. It is not Members who, like the Belgian Government, maintain that Chapter XI is of general scope, and are trying to introduce a new principle; on the contrary, it is those who wish to impose on Chapter XI narrow limits which were never entertained in connection with the Covenant of the League of Nations. . . . Most of these territories belong to States which before becoming Members of the United Nations were Members of the League of Nations. Was it their intention in adopting Chapter XI of the Charter to free themselves from the obligation they had assumed under the Covenant to treat the indigenous peoples justly? If so, none of them expressed that intention at the San Francisco Conference. In any event, how could they have justified it? . . . Such a policy amounts to establishing among Member States bearing the same responsibilities a system which, because of its discriminatory nature, must doom to certain failure all efforts to develop international safeguards for indigenous peoples. . . .

> Is it in the interests of these peoples that some of them are today not recognized as warranting the protection which they formerly enjoyed? Is not that a case, to use a simile which has come into current usage here, of turning back the pages of history?[14]

Neither did the Belgian government view its position as a threat to state sovereignty since the "only question is whether we treat them properly, and whether we are doing our best to improve their situation."[15] It felt that it would also be erroneous to consider such people to be minorities, since they lived in "clearly defined 'territories.' "[16] Further, although the language in Chapter XI is somewhat more ambiguous than Article 23(b), to limit the application of the Non-Self-Governing Territories provision to overseas colonies is clearly an unduly restrictive interpretation of the language:

> Far from defending a restrictive interpretation we declare ourselves in favor of a wide interpretation in conformity with the humanitarian spirit which should dominate our Organization. Far from wishing to weaken the principle of the priority of the interests of the population we wish to strengthen it.[17]

The Belgians observed that colonialism could occur overland as well as overseas. This was easily demonstrated by pointing out that upon "becoming independent, the former European colonies in America were faced with the same problems with regard to the backward aborigines as the previous regimes."[18] The Belgian government insisted that there was no doubt that it could "place the States of America, from the moment when they acquired their independence, in the category of those who follow the continental colonization policy."[19]

The Belgian government attacked the "myth of salt water colonialism," noting:

> In remote areas within the borders of the States so constituted, however, there are backwards peoples, of different race and culture. Civilization is henceforth transmitted to these peoples by territorial contiguity, but the basic problems involved remain unchanged; the fact that the work of civilization is now effected [*sic*] by territorial contiguity does not make them any simpler. In tropical areas, stretches of land are obstacles far harder to surmount than stretches of sea. This has always been true; for centuries, virgin forests and jungle have been barriers impassable to civilization, whereas the seas and oceans have from the remotest antiquity made contacts possible and even facilitated them. With the development of sea and air communications they are now speedily crossed.[20]

Thus, "backward peoples" who faced the same problems should receive the same protection, and it would be arbitrary and discriminatory to deny them this protection because of such geographic criteria.[21]

Despite the force of its logic, the Belgian thesis was rejected in the face of strong opposition from the Latin American countries.[22] In 1960, United Nations Resolution 1541 was passed, which strengthened the geographic limitation placed on the application of the Non-Self-Governing Territories provision. It states that "there is an obligation to transmit information in respect of territory that is geographically separate and is distinct ethnically and/or culturally from the country administering it."[23] This was "clearly intended to exclude from the scope of Chapter XI indigenous peoples in independent countries, although indigenous peoples occupy territories that are geographically separate by any reasonable interpretation of that term."[24] According to one author:

> Firstly it is strongly arguable that indigenous groups who are isolated from the rest of the nation by vast tracts of unoccupied land, as for example are the Eskimos of Northern Canada, must on any rational basis be regarded as "geographically separate." Secondly, there are many island communities which, although not normally described as colonial peoples, are nevertheless "geographically separate" from the mainland.[25]

In this way, the United Nations has confined the application of the Non-Self-Governing Territories provision to seventy-four narrowly defined "geographically separate" non-self-governing territories and not to all non-self-governing territories, as originally intended.[26] The United Nations uses a mythological geographic barrier to limit the application of these universal human rights principles. Once again, the indigenous peoples of the Western Hemisphere had no international human rights that the white man was bound to respect.

INTERNATIONAL LABOUR OFFICE CONVENTIONS

After indigenous peoples in geographically adjacent non-self-governing territories were excluded from the "sacred trust" protection of the Non-Self-Governing Territories provision, the only international concern for the plight of indigenous peoples was action taken by the UN International Labour Office (ILO). The ILO, unlike other United Nations bodies, is composed of equal representations of governments, trade unions, and employees' associations. Since 1921 the ILO has carried out various studies on indigenous workers. In 1953, it published a comprehensive reference book entitled *Indigenous Peoples: Living and Working Conditions of Aboriginal Populations in Independent Countries*.[27] During these early years, ILO activity was limited almost exclusively to the framing of international labor standards.[28]

Convention 107 of 1957 and Recommendation 104

A drastic change occurred in 1957 when the ILO adopted Convention 107, Concerning the Protection and Integration of Indigenous and Other Tribal and Semi-Tribal Populations in Independent Countries, and Recommendation 104.[29] These instruments cover not only labor standards but also general international standards intended to protect tribal populations while facilitating their progressive integration into their respective national communities.[30] They were developed as a result of the gross exploitation of indigenous laborers that resulted from the international legal system, depriving many of them of their land and natural resources, and "they had nowhere to go."[31] Although the convention sets standards, it also delegates "primary responsibility" for developing those standards to the individual states that ratify it.[32] The convention was intended to apply to Africa, Asia, and the Americas, but it has been ratified by only twenty-seven states, with the vast majority from Latin America.[33]

The convention is subject to criticism on a number of grounds. It has been totally rejected by numerous Indian groups,[34] one of which rejected the document for the following reasons:

> We believe that this Convention, elaborated by oppressive governments, was meant to legalize the colonial oppression of the Indian peoples, given the following facts:
> (a) It was made by Governments without the participation of representatives of the Indian peoples,
> (b) It does not consider in its articles the right to self-determination,
> (c) It seeks integration and assimilation, with total lack of respect for the dignity of every people and its right to freedom,
> (d) Its aim is the destruction of our culture, of our traditions and of our language,
> (e) The mentioned Convention is contradictory in its different articles, allowing for wide interpretations and vague definitions.[35]

A closer examination of the convention reveals the validity of such criticism.

Perhaps the most interesting aspect of the convention is the "balance" it strikes between protection and integration. Whenever there is a conflict, integration receives priority over protection. Two examples are contained in Articles 7(2) and 12(1). Under Article 7(2), the customs and institutions of indigenous populations are protected, but only where "these are not incompatible with . . . the objectives of integration programmes." Under Article 12(1), indigenous populations "shall not be removed without their free consent from their habitual territories *except* . . . in the interest of national economic development" (emphasis added). In practice, this provision legalizes taking the land of indigenous populations without their consent.[36] It takes the control of their land out of the hands of the indigenous populations and puts it into the hands of the nonindigenous populations—the states that drafted the convention. Both these provisions also appear to contradict the provisions forbidding artificial or coercive assimilation.[37] Additionally, the ultimate goal of the convention is clearly the complete integration and assimilation of indigenous populations, as the protection measures can only be temporary.[38]

The priority that the convention gives to individual and collective rights also contrasts sharply with the Non-Self-Governing Territories provision. Under the convention, as noted above, the right of tribal populations to self-government by their own institutions is subordinate to "the national legal system or the objectives of integration programmes." In return for the loss of the tribal populations' collective right of self-government, the convention substitutes the development of individual rights and equal citizenship.[39] Many Indians reject this substitution of rights:

> To speak of equality of citizenship, in the Indian view, means to treat Indians only as individuals by ignoring and suppressing the group rights they possess as peoples. It is to recommend, they believe, a termination of Indian government, the confiscation of tribal property rights and as a consequence, the disappearance of many of the distinctive elements of native cultures. The survival of Indians as peoples with a unique political and cultural identity is the goal of the Indian rights movement, and, while some characterize that as separatism, Indians tend to see this only as continuation of their traditional existence. The radical step, in their view, is a political and cultural assimilation that can come about only when non-Indian America tries to coerce Indians into surrendering their rights.[40]

The convention's substitution of rights contrasts with the Non-Self-Governing Territories provision, under which there is an absolute and unqualified obligation to develop self-government.[41] Under the convention, with regard to the economic development of "areas inhabited by these populations," the interests of the indigenous populations are given a "high priority."[42] In practice, this "high priority" places the interests of the indigenous populations below the interests of the nonindigenous population of the country in which they are located.[43] In terms of controlling their land, it places them in a nondominant position, meaning that their interests are only of secondary importance. This contrasts sharply with the Non-Self-Governing Territories provision, under which the interests of the inhabitants are paramount.

Convention 169 of 1989

Due to criticism of ILO Convention 107's "integrationist approach, the lack of Indigenous Populations' input and its nonconformity with the contemporary views of Indigenous Populations," it was revised in 1989. The new convention, titled Convention 169, Concerning Indigenous and Tribal Peoples in Independent Countries,[44] was revised with the stated purpose of removing the assimilationist orientation of the old convention, Convention 107. However, it is unclear how it removes the absorption or incorporation of indigenous peoples since it only recognizes the rights of indigenous peoples "within the framework of the States in which they live" and places numerous restrictions on their right to own land and be self-governing. Thus, it appears that the new convention is subject to many of the same criticisms of the old convention, and it has in fact been condemned by indigenous peoples.[45]

The new convention strikes a "balance" between protection and integration that is similar to that in the old convention, with the minor difference that indigenous peoples must be consulted before things are done without their consent. Under Article 6, governments are required to

> consult the peoples concerned . . . whenever consideration is being given to legislative or administrative measures which may affect them directly. . . . The consultations carried out in application of this Convention shall be undertaken, in good faith and in a form appropriate to the circumstances, with the objective of achieving agreement or consent to the proposed measures.

This section is of fundamental importance in establishing the rights of indigenous peoples. Either they have a right to make decisions that affect their lives, or somebody else does. This new convention resembles the old convention in that the indigenous peoples' consent is not required when governments decide to take their land or resources or restrict their self-government.

The language contained in Article 6 of the new convention is a shocking departure from the previous drafts of the text. Under the first draft of the revision, governments would have been required to "seek the consent" of indigenous peoples before taking any actions affecting them. The language was then changed to, "obtain the informed consent . . . [of the indigenous peoples as] . . . freely expressed through their own institutions." When this language was rejected, Norway proposed the language, "consult fully with a view to obtaining their consent." When this proposal was also rejected,

> the ILO secretariat recommended to the second meeting of the conference committee that a paragraph be added requiring that consultations be carried out "in good faith *with the objective* of achieving agreement or consent." A number of governments, including Canada, Bolivia, Argentina, Ecuador, and India, opposed any reference to "agreement or consent," while the United States, U.S.S.R., Australia, Denmark, and Portugal joined with the Workers in supporting it. After the secretariat explained that the intended effect was not to *require* agreement "but rather to express an objective for the consultations," the reference to consent was adopted by a narrow vote.[46]

Consequently, although this language on consultation is an improvement over the old convention, which did not even require consultation, it still does not recognize the fundamental principle of requiring the consent of the governed.

Another example of the deficiency of the new convention lies in the provisions that deal with recognizing the rights of indigenous peoples to their land. The members of the ILO again decided that the rights of indigenous peoples to own land are subject to a number of restrictions. Moreover, the ILO again authorized the forced removal of indigenous peoples from their land. Although the language was revised to talk about obtaining the consent of the indigenous peoples, their consent still does not need to be obtained. In this regard, the convention states:

> 1. Subject to the following paragraphs of this Article, the peoples concerned shall not be removed from the lands which they occupy.
>
> 2. Where the relocation of these peoples is considered necessary as an exceptional measure, such relocation shall take place only with their free and informed consent. Where their consent cannot be obtained, such relocation shall take place only following appropriate procedures established by national laws and regulations, including public inquiries where appropriate, which provide the opportunity for effective representation of the peoples concerned.

The use of the word "consent" in this article is intellectually dishonest. The consent of the indigenous peoples does not have to be obtained. What this article really means is that the peoples involved just need to be given a little procedural due process—notice and an opportunity to be heard—before their land is taken without their consent.

Another astonishing limitation that the new convention places on the right of indigenous peoples to own land is contained in Article 15, which does not recognize the right of indigenous peoples to ownership of mineral or subsurface resources or other resources pertaining to land. This provision is totally at odds with the principle of sovereignty over natural resources or any legitimate recognition of the inherent rights of all peoples over land.[47] This provision is a clear continuation of the limitations placed by international law on the ownership of land by the "backwards races." This limitation is apparently based on classic Aristotelian doctrine, the doctrine of discovery, and the racist limitations placed on the ownership rights of the indigenous peoples of the Western Hemisphere to own land, which have not changed in five hundred years.[48]

Yet another restriction placed on the right of indigenous peoples to own land is contained in Article 7. According to this article, the homelands of indigenous peoples can be taken for economic development projects after states conduct studies that "assess the social, spiritual, cultural and environmental impact on them of the planned development activities." This provision again illustrates a major weakness of leaving the development of the human rights of indigenous peoples to the ILO. It would seem that all parties that are ILO members—governments, employers' associations, and even trade unions—are primarily interested in exploiting the indigenous peoples' land and resources and only have a secondary interest in the rights of the indigenous peoples.

Two of the more interesting aspects of the new convention are the way in which it revises the definition of indigenous peoples in Article 1 and the way in which it handles the issue of self-determination. The new convention's definition of indigenous peoples contains one subtle revision that deletes the only reference to the sacred trust of civilization contained in the old convention. The old convention refers to "[m]embers of tribal or semi-tribal populations in independent countries whose social and economic conditions are at a *less advanced stage* than the stage reached by the other sections of the national community." This reference to people at a less advanced stage of civilization would imply that the Non-Self-Governing Territories provision should apply to indigenous peoples, with the further implication that they do have a right of self-determination.

Additionally, according to Article 1 of the new convention, it applies to

> peoples in independent countries who are regarded as indigenous on account of their descent from the populations which inhabited the country, at the time of conquest or *colonization* or the establishment of present state boundaries and who, irrespective of their legal status, retain some or all of their own social, economic, cultural and political institutions.

Since the new convention, by definition, applies to colonized peoples, it would logically seem to follow that they must be decolonized under accepted norms of international law, most notably, the "Declaration on the Granting of Independence to Colonial Countries and Peoples."[49] This means the application of the Non-Self-Governing Territories provision.

The other part of the definition, which states that the convention applies to peoples who were conquered, leads to a similar conclusion. The doctrine of conquest only applies to territories that were incorporated into the conquering nation. Many indigenous nations were not only not incorporated into the particular "conquering" European nation, they also concluded formal peace treaties at the end of the hostilities that defined the respective rights of the parties. Thus, it would appear that many Indian nations were never incorporated into their conquerers; so the doctrine of conquest should not be applied to deny them their rights as defined by treaty. Additionally, as will be seen, the doctrine of conquest as it has been applied to indigenous peoples is, in reality, often the mythological expansion of discovery into conquest.[50] In addition, the doctrine of discovery was merely an agreement by the European powers to divide the land of the indigenous peoples among themselves and to leave the indigenous peoples at the mercy of the discovering European power in its colonization of the formers' homeland.

Yet another interesting aspect of the definition is the use of the word "peoples" in the new convention rather than the word "populations" which was used in the old convention. This semantic difference is important because the human rights conventions grant all "peoples" a right to self-determination, while "indigenous populations" have no rights other than those contained in the old ILO convention. However, the new convention attempts to circumvent the inevitability of this conclusion by the use of the following disclaimer language which was intended to be neutral: "The use of the term "peoples" in this Convention shall not be construed as having any implications as regards the rights which may attach to the term under international law." Only a lawyer would assert that this language is neutral. Clearly it is the intention of the new convention to deny indigenous peoples their right to self-determination since it only recognizes their rights "within the framework of the States in which they live."

The entire dispute between calling this group, which has historically been labeled a "backward race" by international law, either "indigenous populations" or "indigenous peoples" has taken up an enormous amount of time on the part of lawyers and United Nations representatives. The most historically accurate definition that one could give many of the groups of indigenous people in the Western Hemisphere would be "Indian nation." However, the use of that term would once again lead to the inescapable conclusion that Indian nations have a right of self-determination, unless international law continues its historical exclusion of this so-called "backward race" from recognition as a member of the Family of Nations.

This analysis would lead to a further contradiction that is contained in the new convention's definition and applies to peoples. These peoples occupy territories, which are not self-governing because of the restrictions placed on their self-government by Articles 2, 6, 7, 8, 9, 10, 12, 14, 15, 16, 17, 19, and 20.[51] Therefore, the new convention defines indigenous peoples as peoples without a right to self-determination and non-self-governing territories that are outside the protection of the Non-Self-Governing Territories provision. However, the old convention, which entered into force on June 2, 1959, and has been ratified by twenty-four states, remains as the only international instrument that specifically applies to indigenous peoples and is in effect.[52]

WORKING GROUP ON INDIGENOUS POPULATIONS

For most of its history, as we have seen, the United Nations has had a very hostile attitude toward the rights of indigenous peoples. After they were excluded from membership and excluded from the protection of the international trust provisions, the old, assimilationist ILO Convention was the only contact that indigenous peoples had with the international legal system—and basically, nothing was done under the old ILO Convention. In 1949 Bolivia unsuccessfully attempted to establish an organization to study the situation of the aboriginal population of the American continent, and again nothing was done for over two decades.[53]

During this same period of time, the United Nations was busy formulating a number of other specialized human rights documents. Among the most important were the Genocide Convention in 1948, the Universal Declaration of Human Rights in 1949, the International Convention on the Elimination of All Forms of Racial Discrimination in 1965, the two International Covenants on Human Rights in 1966, and the Declaration on the Granting of Independence to Colonial Countries and Territories in 1960.

With the emergence of new African and Asian states in the early 1960s and the passage of the Declaration on the Granting of Independence to Colonial Countries and Territories, there arose another opportunity for the United Nations to address the problems being faced by indigenous peoples. However, old and new UN members alike once again turned their backs on the indigenous peoples of the Western Hemisphere by limiting the application of the sacred trust principles to overseas colonies and taking no steps to remove this geographic limitation.[54]

The recent efforts to recognize the rights of indigenous peoples grew out of the UN Decade to Combat Racism in the 1970s. A 1970 study on racial discrimination called for a complete and comprehensive study of discrimination against indigenous peoples. In 1971, Resolution 1580(L) authorized the Sub-Commission on the Prevention of Discrimination and Protection of Minorities to make a study of discrimination against indigenous populations and to suggest both national and international measures to eliminate such discrimination.

To focus further attention on the discrimination that the international legal system has perpetrated on indigenous peoples, various indigenous organizations have attended a number of international conferences, both inside and outside the United Nations system.[55] In 1977, the first United Nations Non-Governmental Organizations Conference on Discrimination against Indigenous Peoples of the Americas was held in Geneva. This Conference was sponsored by the Non-Governmental Organization (NGO) Sub-Committee on Racism, Racial Discrimination, Apartheid and Decolonization of the Special NGO Committee on Human Rights.[56] The final report of this conference emphasized "the right of indigenous peoples and nations to have authority over their own affairs" and contained a Draft Declaration submitted by Indian participants.[57] This Draft Declaration of Principles for the Defence of the Indigenous Nations and Peoples of the Western Hemisphere called for the recognition of indigenous nations as equal to United Nations members, of indigenous treaties as equal to United Nations members, and of the sovereign right of indigenous peoples over their land and natural resources as equal to United Nations members; moreover, it rejected any rights based on the doctrine of discovery.[58]

In 1978 the World Conference to Combat Racism and Racial Discrimination endorsed

> the right of indigenous peoples to maintain their traditional structure of economy and culture, including their own language, and also recognize[d] the special relationship of indigenous peoples to their land and stresse[d] that their land, land rights and natural resources should not be taken away from them.[59]

A 1981 NGO Conference on Indigenous Peoples and the Land, in concert with the special rapporteur of the Study of the Problem of Discrimination against Indigenous Populations, called for the establishment of a permanent working group on indigenous populations so that indigenous nations and peoples could submit their complaints and make their demands known.[60]

In 1983, Special Rapporteur Jose R. Martinez Cobo (with the assistance of Willemsen Diaz) completed his multivolume report, *Study of the Problem of Discrimination against Indigenous Populations*. The sub-commission called it "a reference work of definitive usefulness' and directed the Working Group on Indigenous Populations to rely on it in their standard-setting activities.[61] Cobo stated "that the report should be regarded as an appeal to the international community to take heed of the painful discrimination practiced against indigenous peoples, one of the largest but weakest sectors of the world's population."[62] The study was based on only thirty-seven countries because of the lack of sufficient information or cooperation from other countries.[63] The special rapporteur formulated the following definition of indigenous populations:

> Indigenous communities, peoples and nations are those which, having a historical continuity with pre-invasion and pre-colonial societies that developed on their territories, consider themselves distinct from other sectors of the societies now prevailing in those territories, or parts of them. They form at present non-dominant sectors of society and are determined to preserve, develop and transmit to future generations their ancestral territories, and their ethnic identity; as the basis of their continued existence as peoples, in accordance with their own cultural patterns, social institutions and legal systems.[64]

This definition has been widely accepted.

The special rapporteur concluded that although "[i]ndigenous peoples have a natural and inalienable right to keep the territories they possess and to claim the land of which they have been deprived[,] . . . [l]arge-scale violations of the rights of indigenous populations to their land and its resources have occurred systematically for many centuries."[65] The special rapporteur also made some important conclusions on the issues of political rights and self-determination:

263. Another aspect which must be considered, albeit in a preliminary manner, is the self-determination and autonomy demanded by indigenous groups, peoples and nations.

264. It has been stressed that indigenous peoples, by their very existence, have the natural and original right to live freely on their own territories.

265. It is beginning to be acknowledged that indigenous peoples have their own national identity based on historical realities that transcend mere solidarity *vis-à-vis* discrimination and exploitation.

266. Respect for the forms of autonomy called for by indigenous peoples is the necessary condition for guaranteeing and ensuring these rights.

267. The specific forms of internal organization of these peoples are an inherent part of their cultural and legal heritage, which has contributed to their cohesion and to the maintenance of their social and cultural tradition.

268. Respect and support for the internal organization of indigenous peoples and their cultural expressions constitute an essential consideration for any arrangement aimed at securing appropriate participation by indigenous communities in all affairs which affect them. Consequently, Governments must abandon their policies of intervening in the organization and development of indigenous peoples, and must grant them autonomy, together with the capacity for controlling the relevant economic processes in whatever way they themselves consider to be in keeping with their interests and needs.

269. Self-determination, in its many forms, is thus a basic pre-condition if indigenous peoples are to be able to enjoy their fundamental rights and determine their future, while at the same time preserving, developing and passing on their specific ethnic identity to future generations.[66]

In 1982, a permanent five-member Working Group on Indigenous Populations was established. "The creation of this Working Group thus completed the sequence of actions begun 34 years earlier by the Bolivian initiative of 1948 . . . regarding the creation of a sub-commission which would concern itself with the problems of indigenous populations."[67] The working group consists of five independent experts chosen from the group of international law experts sitting on the United Nations Sub-Commission on Prevention of Discrimination and Protection of Minorities, with the usual geographic distribution of one member from each region. The working group is below the sub-commission, which is below the Commission on Human Rights, which is below the Economic and Social Council, which is below the General Assembly. The mandate of the working group is to

(a) Review developments pertaining to the promotion and protection of human rights and fundamental freedoms of indigenous populations, including information requested by the Secretary-General annually from Governments, specialized agencies, regional intergovernmental organizations and non-governmental organizations in consultative status, particularly those of indigenous peoples, to analyze such materials, and to submit its conclusions to the Sub-Commission, bearing in mind the report of the Special Rapporteur of the Sub-Commission.

(b) Give special attention to the evolution of standards concerning the rights of indigenous populations, taking account of both the similarities and the differences in the situation and aspirations of indigenous populations throughout the world.[68]

One of the unique aspects of the working group is its rule of procedure, established under the Chairmanship of Asbjorn Eide, which allows oral and written interventions from all indigenous organizations that wish to participate. This contrasts with the usual United Nations requirement of limiting such participation to states, intergovernmental agencies, and accredited nongovernmental organizations.[69] This rule has resulted in a dramatic increase in participation by indigenous peoples. At the first meeting in 1982, only a dozen American Indians participated.[70] However, at the ninth session in 1991, almost five hundred people from all over the world attended.

Another development, which was aimed at increasing indigenous participation, was the creation of a Voluntary Fund for Indigenous Populations in 1985, which

provides financial assistance to representatives of indigenous communities and organizations to enable them to attend sessions of the Working Group. . . . The Fund is administered by the United Nations Secretary-General with the advice of a five-member Board of Trustees, which meets annually to review applications for assistance. . . . In 1988 and 1989, the Fund provided travel grants to 27 and 39 indigenous representatives respectively from over 20 countries.[71]

Although these developments are usually viewed as positive, they also have a negative side. Although indigenous input is being accepted for the first time in the history of the United Nations, the working group "is the fifth and lowest level of discussion on human rights questions in the UN."[72] Some of the indigenous speakers represent indigenous nations or confederacies of indigenous nations that are in a treaty relationship with United Nations members. Rather than feeling grateful that they are allowed to speak before the working group, these speakers may consider it an insult that they are not recognized on an equal basis with United Nations members.

Additionally, since the indigenous organizations have not been credentialed, they are unable to address other United Nations bodies and are unable to speak at the United Nations Headquarters in New York. So far this has resulted in their exclusion from the United Nations Conference on Environment and Development (ECO '92) to be held in Brazil in 1992 and has also resulted in Spain blocking 1992 as the Year of Indigenous Peoples without any formal indigenous input.[73] Since the United Nations has designated 1993 as the Year of Indigenous Peoples, indigenous organizations still have to rely on other, credentialed NGOs to communicate with New York about events during this year.[74] The selection process of the voluntary fund also necessarily results in an element of control over which indigenous views are expressed.

The working group originally met for five days a year prior to the meeting of the sub-commission that receives their annual report. During its early years, the working group spent most of its time on the first part of its mandate—reviewing developments. In response to concern that the working group was uncritically compiling data, the Sub-Commission on Prevention of Discrimination and Protection of Minorities adopted a resolution in 1985 that

> endors[ed] the Plan of Action adopted by the Working Group for its future work . . . as well as its decision to emphasize in its forthcoming sessions the part of its mandate related to standard-setting activities, with the aim of producing, in due course, a draft declaration on indigenous rights which may be proclaimed by the General Assembly.[75]

Since that time, there has been a dramatic shift in emphasis to the standard-setting aspect of the working group's mandate. In 1985, the working group proposed seven "relatively 'noncontroversial' principles and drafted them in a deliberately preliminary manner."[76] These principles have evolved each year and can be found in the annual reports of the working group.

The process of refining these principles was aided by two developments. First, beginning in 1990, the working group's usual one-week session was extended to two weeks, with the first week focusing on drafting language and the second week on reviewing recent developments. However, there has been a problem with the lack of translation facilities so that the many Spanish-speaking indigenous participants were excluded from the first-week drafting process.[77]

The second development was the division of the drafting process into "three informal and open-ended drafting groups . . . with the basic aim of facilitating and accelerating the work on the draft Universal Declaration on the Rights of Indigenous Peoples."[78] The drafts are then circulated among the interested parties, who are allowed to comment on revisions. Then, the five members of the working group have a closed meeting in which they make the final decision on changes to the draft declaration. Consequently, although indigenous peoples have gained some input for the first time, they have no vote and no right to even observe the final deliberations by the members of the working group.[79]

Nevertheless, two areas that can and must be improved in the current version of the draft declaration are its provision on self-determination and its lack of a provision dealing with treaties. The first and most important area of the draft declaration that needs improvement is the provision on self-determination, which necessarily involves the element of self-determination over natural resources. The relevant provisions in the current version of the Universal Declaration on the Rights of Indigenous Peoples follow:

> Operative paragraph 1
>
> Indigenous peoples have the right to self-determination, in accordance with international law. By virtue of this right, they freely determine their relationship with the States in which they live, in a spirit of co-existence with other citizens, and freely pursue their economic, social, cultural and spiritual development in conditions of freedom and dignity. . . .
>
> Operative paragraph (to be numbered)
>
> Nothing in this Declaration may be interpreted as implying for any State, group or individual any right to engage in any activity or to perform any act contrary to the Charter of the United Nations or to the Declaration of Principles of International Law on Friendly Relations and Co-operation among States in Accordance with the Charter of the United Nations. . . .
>
> Operative paragraph 15
>
> Indigenous peoples have the collective and individual right to own, control, and use the lands and territories they have traditionally occupied or otherwise used. This includes the right to the full recognition of their own laws and customs, land-tenure systems and institutions for the management of resources, and the right to effective State measures to prevent any interference with or encroachment upon these rights.
>
> Operative paragraph (to be numbered)
>
> In no case may any of the indigenous peoples be deprived of their means of subsistence.[80]

The language in these provisions consists of a butchered patchwork of the self-determination provisions in the Human Rights Covenants. The language in operative paragraph 1 was clearly intended to limit the right of indigenous peoples to internal self-determination (self-government within the states in which they live—also referred to as autonomy), while not recognizing their right to external self-determination (the right to be recognized as an equal member state of the United Nations).

The next operative paragraph cited, referring to the Declaration of Principles of International Law on Friendly Relations, is an implied reference to protecting the right of United Nations member states to "territorial integrity," which (according to United Nations member states) overrides the right of indigenous peoples to external self-determination.[81] Operative paragraph 15 purports to protect the right of indigenous peoples to own land, but because it is not explicit about subsurface natural resources, it also implicitly preserves the status quo, which does not recognize the right of indigenous peoples to own subsurface natural resources.[82] The last cited paragraph, concerning the right of indigenous peoples to subsistence, is the only sentence in the current draft declaration that makes the rights of indigenous peoples equal to those of all other peoples.

These provisions do not recognize the human rights of indigenous peoples. Rather, they limit their human rights, so that the United Nations member states retain control over indigenous peoples and their land. This can be demonstrated by comparing these provisions with those proposed by the drafting groups. Drafting Group Two, headed by Danilo Türk, proposed the following language for paragraph 1:

> Indigenous peoples have the right to self-determination, by virtue of which they may freely determine their political status, pursue their own economic, social, and religious and cultural development, and determine their own institutions.[83]

This paragraph recognizes the right of indigenous peoples to internal and external self-determination and closely follows the language in the first two sentences of paragraph 1 of the Human Rights Covenants.

Drafting Group One, headed by Miguel Alfonso Martinez, proposed the following language regarding the right to own land:

> The right to effective ownership, [original title,] possession, use, conservation, and control of renewable and non-renewable surface and *subsurface* resources pertaining to the lands and other territories traditionally occupied or otherwise used by them, including flora and fauna, fresh and sea water and sea ice.[84]

This paragraph explicitly recognizes the right of indigenous peoples to self-determination over subsurface natural resources. This is necessary in light of domestic law, which does not recognize original Indian title, and ILO Convention 169, which does not recognize the right of indigenous peoples to subsurface natural resources.

Although the exact workings of the secret deliberations of the working group are unknown, Erica-Irene Daes of Greece, the current Chair and Asbjorn Eide's replacement, seems to be the dominant personality. Her basic position on the right of indigenous peoples was put in writing in a law review article published in 1986:[85] "In any case, I expressly would like to state that in my opinion the interpretation of the term 'self-determination' specifically excludes the right of 'secession.' "[86] The version of Drafting Group Three, which she headed, specifically recommends limiting the right of self-determination of indigenous peoples to only "autonomy."[87] Thus, her views on this issue have not changed.

Her position on subsurface natural resources has changed, however. In her 1986 law review article, Chair Daes stated, "The land rights of indigenous populations include surface and *sub-surface* rights, full right to interior and coastal waters and right to adequate and exclusive economic zones within the limits of international law."[88] The proposed language of her drafting group in 1989 included the following rights: "The right of collective and individual ownership possession and use of the lands or resources which they have traditionally occupied or used [and] . . . [t]he right to reclaim land and *surface* resources."[89] Therefore, her position became clearly less favorable to indigenous peoples. This is no minor change. The subsurface resources on the land belonging to indigenous peoples are worth billions of dollars. Consequently, the change in the chair's language results in a massive transfer of wealth from indigenous peoples to United Nations member states.

About five years ago, the working group made a breakthrough in language when it began referring to "indigenous peoples" rather than "indigenous populations."[90] As a result, many indigenous groups believed that the equal recognition of their right to self-determination, as possessed by all other peoples, necessarily followed. However, these new developments in language indicate that this is not the case. The propensities of lawyers to use double-speak and for the United Nations to establish double standards was forgotten.[91]

Part of the problem appears to be the willingness of the chair to listen to people who do not represent any indigenous group or, at least, a well-defined indigenous group, together with a lack of consensus among well-defined indigenous groups. Some speakers who do not represent any indigenous group, and who may be participating for some sort of intellectual gratification or professional ambition, are allowed to propose alternative language for the draft declaration as if it was entirely an academic exercise. Other people who participate assert that they represent a given indigenous group with very little in the way of verification.[92] The lack of consensus can be attributed to the worldwide geographic distribution of indigenous peoples, which makes it financially impossible for many of them to get together before the working group's session to try and reach an agreement. A number of indigenous representatives also appear to be exclusively concerned with their own problems and aspirations while being insensitive to the problems and aspirations of other indigenous groups.

The other acknowledged major weakness of the draft declaration is the lack of any provision that deals with treaties. This can be attributed to the unprecedented delay in finishing the *Study of the Problem of Discrimination against Indigenous Populations* (thirteen years), in conjunction with the further delay (until 1989) before the sub-commission confirmed the appointment of Miguel Alfonso Martinez as the special rapporteur on the *Study on Treaties, Agreements and Other Constructive Arrangements between States and Indigenous Populations*.

Since his appointment, the special rapporteur has been subjected to a series of obstacles. The sub-commission has made a number of outrageous time demands that appear to be calculated at destroying or compromising the integrity of the study. Just before his appointment became final, the sub-commission greatly expanded the special rapporteur's mandate to include "other constructive arrangements."[93] He was then directed to submit an outline to the sub-commission less than eight weeks after his appointment. His request for a single consultant was denied except on the basis of a four-month contract.[94] His critically important research trips to Washington, D.C., and Seville (where most of the documents are located, but not properly indexed) were limited to five days.

His study was also hindered by member states of the United Nations. The special rapporteur missed five hearings in the United States on indigenous treaties because of the delay by the United States in granting him a visa.[95] Moreover, to obtain information from United Nations member states, he mailed out a questionnaire. As of July 30, 1991, he had only received a handful of responses.[96]

Despite these difficulties, one very constructive preliminary suggestion was made by Drafting Group Two, headed by Danilo Türk. The following language was suggested: "The duty of States to honour and to implement treaties and other agreements concluded with indigenous peoples according to their original intent, pursuant to the principle of *pacta sunt servanda*."[97] This principle—that agreements must be observed—is a fundamental principle on which all international law is based. The reform of the rule of international law that allows members of the Family of Nations to unilaterally abrogate treaties with indigenous peoples is one of the most unjust and discriminatory in existence.[98] A provision such as the one proposed by Mr. Türk must be included in the draft declaration.

More generally, the issue of why the 1969 Vienna Convention on the Law of Treaties is not applied to treaties with indigenous peoples ipso facto should be addressed. When special rules are applied to treaties with the indigenous peoples of the Western Hemisphere, the only apparent distinction is race. Finally, the rule of international law that the negotiation of a bilateral treaty provides a country with recognition as a member of the Family of Nations is also not applied to indigenous peoples and should be included in the declaration.[99]

It is anticipated that the draft declaration will not go to the General Assembly before 1993. One of two basic scenarios will occur. Either the working group will submit a declaration that continues the institutionalized double standards that exist, or they will submit one that recognizes the rights of indigenous people as being equal to those of all other peoples. By all indications, the former possibility is much more likely than the latter. The delay in not having the draft declaration ready to present to the General Assembly for the cinquecentennial in 1992 appears calculated to deprive indigenous peoples of the impact of such an anniversary.[100] It also symbolizes the casual disregard, if not hostility, that the United Nations continues to exhibit toward indigenous peoples.

ORGANIZATION OF AMERICAN STATES

The Organization of American States (OAS) is a regional agency within the United Nations system.[101] The OAS grew out of a hemispheric concern for collective security. The origins of the OAS can be traced to Simon Bolivar, who expressed a desire by the newly independent Latin American countries to guard against possible Spanish attempts at reconquest.[102] This was followed in 1823 by the development of the United States' Monroe Doctrine, which set forth the following three principles: (1) The American continents would not be subject to future colonization by European powers, (2) there would be nonintervention by the Europeans in the Americas, and (3) there would be nonintervention by the United States in European affairs.[103] Around 1904, the Monroe Doctrine developed the (Theodore) Roosevelt Corollary under which the United States claimed the right to exercise an international police power to intervene anywhere in the Western Hemisphere.[104] This was changed in 1933 by Franklin Roosevelt's "Good Neighbor" policy, which repudiated the right of the United States to unilaterally intervene in the affairs of American states.[105]

These developments, along with a series of regional conferences, led to the signing of the Charter of the Organization of American States in 1948.[106] The OAS Charter came into force in 1951 and has since been ratified by "all the American Republics."[107] As a result of this genesis, the OAS developed special rules for the recognition of new governments that were based on the Jeffersonian concept of the consent of the governed and the right of revolution.[108] The OAS is also supposedly based on the principles of the sovereign equality of states, respect for human rights, and nonrecognition of rights claimed by conquest.[109]

However, the OAS totally ignored the rights of the indigenous peoples and nations of the Western Hemisphere. After becoming independent, the new American states continued the same policies of colonization, assimilation, and extermination of the native populations.[110] They continued to not recognize Indian nations as equal and to recognize discovery and conquest as constituting a valid title to Indian land. The only difference was that the indigenous peoples were being colonized overland by Christian, "civilized" successor states rather than being colonized overseas by European, Christian, "civilized" states. From the indigenous peoples' perspective, this is a distinction without a difference.[111]

The Charter of the OAS differs from the League of Nations Covenant and the United Nations Charter in one very significant way. It contains no reference to the international trust. The League of Nations Covenant recognized the sacred trust of civilization in the Mandates system and Native Inhabitants clause. The United Nations Charter recognized the sacred trust of civilization in the Trusteeship system and the Non-Self-Governing Territories provision. The OAS Charter omits any such reference. This is no minor omission, and it was obviously intentional. The American member states of the OAS do not recognize any international trust responsibility for the indigenous peoples of the Western Hemisphere, despite the evolution of the international trust from the writings of Victoria about the relationship between the Indians and the Spanish.

The two other basic documents of the OAS, the American Declaration of the Rights and Duties of Man and the American Convention on Human Rights, contain similar glaring omissions.[112] The American Declaration of the Rights and Duties of Man was patterned after the Universal Declaration of Human Rights. One would think that the substantive provisions of each should be very close to identical, but they are not.

Article 2 of the Universal Declaration of Human Rights provides for the recognition of all people as equal before the law and States that "no distinction shall be made on the basis of the political, jurisdictional or international status of the country or territory to which a person belongs, whether it be independent, trust, non-self-governing or under any limitation of sovereignty." Article 2 of the American Declaration of the Rights and Duties of Man provides for the recognition of all people as equal before the law but does not recognize the existence of territory that is under a "trust, non-self-governing or under any limitation of sovereignty." Apparently, this was intended to classify all the territory within the Western Hemisphere as being divided up between independent American states, and not recognizing the status of any indigenous territory as under a trust, non-self-governing, or "under any limitation of sovereignty," despite the fact that this is the case.

The American Convention on Human Rights was patterned after the two international covenants on human rights. Article 1 of each international human rights covenant contains the right of all peoples to self-determination. The American Convention on Human Rights contains no such provision. Nonetheless, the right of all peoples to self-determination "is widely regarded as an absolute prerequisite for the enjoyment of all individual human rights, be they civil or political or economic, social, and cultural rights."[113]

The two fundamental aspects of self-determination are economic and political. The economic aspect recognizes the right of all peoples to control their natural resources. The political aspect recognizes the right of all peoples to determine their political status. This right is generally exercised by a plebiscite, which gives the people the choice between the "establishment of a sovereign and independent State, the free association or integration with an independent State, or the emergence into any other political status freely determined by the people."[114] It would appear that the American Convention on Human Rights intends to institutionalize the status quo without recognizing the right of all peoples—especially indigenous peoples—to self-determination.

With the exclusion of the recognition of the indigenous peoples of the Western Hemisphere from any of these instruments, the OAS passed the International Convention Relative to Inter-American Indian Conferences and the Inter-American Indian Institute.[115] Beginning in 1953, the Inter-American Indian Institute (IAII) and Inter-American Indian Conferences were set up on a permanent basis. The IAII is one of six specialized agencies within the OAS. The other specialized agencies deal with agriculture, health, geography and history, children, and women.[116] Seventeen American states are members, including Argentina, Bolivia, Brazil, Chile, Colombia, Costa Rica, Ecuador, El Salvador, Guatemala, Honduras, Mexico, Nicaragua, Panama, Paraguay, Peru, the United States, and Venezuela.

The convention establishes three main organizations to achieve its purposes: (1) an Inter-American Indian Conference, (2) an Inter-American Indian Institute, and (3) National Indian Institutes. A total of ten Inter-American Indian Conferences have been held, in Patzcuaro, Mexico, in 1940; Cuzco, Peru, in 1949; La Paz in 1954; Guatemala City, Guatemala, in 1959; Quito, Ecuador, in 1964; Patzcuaro in 1968; Brasilia, Brazil, in 1972; Mérida, Mexico, in 1980; Santa Fe, New Mexico, in 1985; and Argentina in 1990. The agenda for each conference is cleared in advance by the OAS Council. The topic at the 1964 conference at Quito was Socio-Economic Development of the Indian Community, with seven meetings on the following subjects: socioeconomic development, personnel training, education and linguistics, health and social security, problems of the jungle populations, Indian folk arts and crafts, and the role of Indian women in development plans.[117] Indigenous participation at these conferences has been either nonexistent or grudgingly accepted on an unequal, censored basis.[118]

The IAII acts as a permanent standing committee of the Inter-American Indian Conferences. The institute's duties also include record keeping, publications, training experts "devoted to the problems of the Indian," and distributing reports on

> [s]cientific investigations in regard to the Indian problems[,] . . . legislation[,] . . . [m]aterial of all kinds utilizable by the Government as a basis for development of policies looking to economic and social improvement of living standards among Indian communities [, and] . . . [r]ecommendations made by the Indians.[119]

The official languages of the IAII are limited to those that are nonindigenous to the Western Hemisphere: English, Spanish, Portuguese, and French.[120] The IAII "maintains a library of items relevant to its functions, and displays very interesting exhibits of Indian crafts both at headquarters and in its permanent exhibit room in the Museum of Anthropology in Mexico City."[121] Of the seventeen members, only Mexico has established a National Indian Institute; it has several branches throughout the country.[122]

Criticism has been leveled at the Inter-American System on the grounds that

> it is an alien institution; even the IAII has not in the past invited Indian participation on an equal footing. More importantly, the Inter-American system is widely viewed as a combined force of governments already hostile or at least insensitive to Indian reality; moreover, the system is seen as a creation and tool of US imperialism, both historically and at present.[123]

The Inter-American System is based on some novel and contradictory assumptions. Foremost would be the lack of international trust responsibilities for the indigenous peoples. Although numerous domestic trust relationships are recognized by the legal systems of the American Republics, they do not recognize *any* international trust responsibilities. However, it is well established that the domestic trust relationships suffer from the same infirmities as those suffered by peoples before being brought under the international trust, namely, nonconsensual government, territorial aggrandizement, constant policy vacillation, and lack of accountability.[124] As mentioned above, the League of Nations and United Nations trust systems were based on the model of the relationship between Spanish-speaking peoples and the indigenous peoples of the Western Hemisphere. This is the most fundamental, although not the only, contradiction within the Inter-American System.

With the rejection of the usual international solution to the problem of indigenous peoples, the OAS plans to solve the "Indian Problem" on "the basis of mutual respect for the inherent rights of each [American Republic] to exercise absolute liberty in solving the 'Indian Problem' in America, by means of periodical meetings."[125] This planned solution would be laughable if it were not so serious a violation of Indian rights. Essentially, the OAS institutionalized the "Indian Problem" by not recognizing its normal international trust responsibilities, and then set out to solve the problems of Indian groups by destroying them via assimilation policies. This final solution to the "Indian Problem" has had few parallels in modern history.

The real problems that the indigenous peoples of the Western Hemisphere face are not addressed by the Inter-American System. The United Nations system has solved such problems through the application of international trust principles and the recognition of the human right of all peoples to political self-determination and self-determination over natural resources. Although the United States rejected assimilation policies in favor of the self-determination policy in 1975, the OAS has yet to change its policy. Special legal doctrines have been applied to the indigenous peoples of the Western Hemisphere for five hundred years, and there is no indication that the Inter-American System is doing anything to change the status quo.

NOTES

1. D. Sanders, Another Step: The UN Seminar on Relations between Indigenous Peoples and States, 4 C.N.L.R. 37 (1989).
2. W. Reisman and B. Weston, Toward World Order and Human Dignity 222 (1976).
3. Charter of the United Nations, Chapter XI, Declaration Regarding Non-Self-Governing Territories; *see* Appendix 2.
4. C. E. Toussaint, The Trusteeship System of the United Nations 248 (1956).
5. E. Sady, The United States and Dependent Peoples 77 (1956).
6. *Id.* at 77–80.
7. *Id.* at 80.
8. *Id.* at 77.
9. *Id.* at 78.
10. *Id.* at 81; *see also* S. Ahmad, The United Nations and the Colonies 273–82 (1974); G. Bennett, The Developing Law of Aboriginal Rights, International Commission of Jurists, The Review, no. 22, 42 (June 1979).
11. The "Belgian Thesis" may be found in the following sources: Text of Replies to the Ad Hoc Committee on Factors (May 8, 1952), U.N. Doc. A./AC.67/2, at 3–31; *see also* F. Van Langenhove, Le Probleme de la Protection des Populations Aborigines aux Nations Unies 89 Hague Racueil, 325 (1956); J. L. Kunz, Chapter XI of the United Nations Charter in Action, 48 Am. J. Int'l. L. 103, n. 34 (1954).
12. Belgian Government Information Center, The Sacred Mission of Civilization: To Which Peoples Should the Benefits Be Extended? The Belgian Thesis 59–64 (1953).
13. *Id.* at 7–8.
14. *Id.* at 8, 11, 27–28, 49–50, 56–57. Footnotes in that text:

> (1) See General Assembly resolution 275 (III), adopted on 11 May 1949, on the social problems of the aboriginal populations and other underdeveloped social groups of the American continent. (2) See the law of the Indies promulgated by the King of Spain at the beginning of the sixteenth century, under the humanitarian influence of Las Casas; article 111 of the 1946 Constitution of Ecuador; article 46 of the Constitution of India; article 72 of the 1947 Constitution of Venezuela; articles 5, 6 and 216 of the 1946 Constitution of Brazil. (3) See e.g. article 6 of the Berlin Act of 1885; the Convention of Saint-Germain of 1919; article 23 (b) of the League of Nations; the Recruiting of Indigenous Workers Convention 1936; the Final Act of the First Inter-American Congress on Indian Life, held at Patcuaro in 1940.

According to S. Hasan Ahmad:

> Mr. Langenhove of Belgium added that Article 23 of the covenant "reappeared, couched in almost identical terms in Chapter XI of the Charter." It was elementary humanitarian duty to restore to the millions of indigenous peoples the safeguards of which they had been deprived and to which they were entitled under the Charter. The continuance of the state of affairs, he lamented, would represent a deplorable retrogression in international law. GA (VIII), O.R., Pln. mtg. 459th, 27 Nov. 1953, pp. 309–10.

S. Hasan Ahmad, *supra* note 10, at 277 n. 61. *Cf.* C. Eagleton, Covenant of the League of Nations and Charter of the United Nations, Points of Difference (1946).

15. C. Eagleton, *supra* note 14, at 22.

16. *Id.* at 20.

17. *Id.* at 10; *see also* R. Barsh, Indigenous North America and Contemporary International Law, 62 Ore. L. Rev. 73, 84 (1983). During the San Francisco Conference, the terms "dependent territories," "dependent peoples," and "Non-Self-Governing Territories" were viewed as being synonymous and all-inclusive: S. Hasan Ahmad, *supra* note 14, at 172.

18. S. Hasan Ahmad, *supra* note 14, at 38. "American Indians suffered every 'colonialist' abuse from the European colonists in America that those colonists complained of in their Declaration of Independence, and more": F. Jennings, Empire of Fortune 478 (1988). Conversely, according to President Theodore Roosevelt, "Every argument that can be made for the Filipinos could be made for the Apaches": M. P. Rogin, Fathers and Children: Andrew Jackson and the Subjugation of the American Indian 313 (1975).

> It is indeed difficult for the British to understand why countries which have expanded across oceans, bringing under their protection backwards peoples and leading them towards civilization, prosperity, and self-government should be classed as brutal imperialists, while on the other hand nations which have expanded across continents, engulfing and sometimes almost exterminating backward peoples in the process, are subjected to no such stigma. In their own case, the Americans believe this expansion to be the fulfillment of a "manifest destiny." It is difficult also to understand why the governing classes of Latin America should be so emotionally hostile to "colonialism" when they themselves have so many dependent peoples under their control. It is not generally recognized that all the successful revolts in the New World against European rule were the work of immigrants and not of the indigenous races. . . . In colonial times the Amerindians were governed and employed by men from Spain and Portugal: today they are still governed and employed by the descendants of the former officials and settlers, and their dependent status has in no way changed.

Sir Alan Burns, In Defence of Colonies 18–19 (1957).

19. F. Van Langenhove, The Idea of the Sacred Trust of Civilization with Regard to the Less Developed Peoples 11–12 (1951), cited in Y. El–Ayouty, The United Nations and Decolonization: The Role of Afro-Asia 53 (1971).

> There is further confusion of thought in America regarding British colonialism. At the time of the American Revolution few people seriously considered that the aboriginal Red Indians (or the African slaves) had any political rights, or that the Red Indians had any inherent right to the lands which the white colonists coveted. . . . There is, in fact, little difference between the expansion of the United States across the continent of America and the British expansion overseas, except perhaps that fewer of the aboriginal inhabitants were killed in the present British colonies than perished in the American wars against the Indians.

Sir Alan Burns, *supra* note 18, at 128–29.

20. Belgian Government Information Center, *supra* note 12, at 38–39; *see also* C. Attlee, As It Happened 180 (1954); H. D. Hall, Mandates, Dependencies, and Trusteeship 43 (1948).

> [T]he fallacy that whereas expansion by a country over *land*, and the incorporation of large areas of territory inhabited by other races and peoples is apparently perfectly praiseworthy, the extension of one's jurisdiction over *sea* is stigmatised in certain quarters as "Colonial

imperialism," "oppression of subject races," and so forth. There is another aspect of this fallacy which implies that in some way jurisdiction or sovereignty is diluted when exercised across salt water. The truth is that any virile and enterprising nation is apt to overflow its original borders. It spreads its culture, its religion, its commerce and finally its jurisdiction.

Britain, a small island, expanded her influence over sea. The United States of America, for example, starting from the thirteen original States expanded her influence westward over land. . . . Russia has expanded enormously over land, eastwards.

Speech of Sir Hilton Poynton in the Fourth Committee of the General Assembly of the United Nations, on 3rd October, 1947; published in *Information on Non-Self-Governing Territories*, Colonial No. 228, at 36 (1948), cited in Sir Alan Burns, *supra* note 18, at 17.

21. Belgian Government Information Center, *supra* note 12, at 16, 49.

22. G. Bennett, Aboriginal Rights in International Law 13 (1978); *see also* J. A. Houston, Latin America in the United Nations 162–221 (1956).

23. G. A. Res. 1514, 15 U.N. GAOR, Supp. (No. 16) 188, U.N. Doc. N/323 Add. 1–6 (1960). According to the "geographically separate" requirement,

International law is thus asked to perceive a distinction between the historical subjugation of an alien population living in a different part of the globe and the historical subjugation of a population living on a piece of land abutting that of its oppressors. The former can apparently never be legitimated by the mere passage of time, whereas the latter is eventually transformed into a protected status quo.

L. Buchheit, Secession and the Legitimacy of Self-Determination 18 (1978).

24. G. Bennett, The Developing Law of Aboriginal Rights, *supra* note 10, at 42.

25. G. Bennett, Aboriginal Rights, *supra* note 22, at 13. The Belgians noted:

The third group is composed of completely savage tribes who not only live in isolation in territories inaccessible to civilized people but who offer armed resistance to any attempt on the part of civilized peoples to enter into contact with them. It is obviously these tribes which preserve their customs, institutions and languages in their purest state. The action of the Indian Protection Service with regard to this group varies according to the circumstances and the possibilities. Can it reasonably be said that the territories "inaccessible to civilized people" in which the peoples of this third group live are territories whose populations have a full measure of self-government? Regarding the geographic factor introduced by the Committee of Factors that they are separated by a stretch of land, sea or other natural obstacles, does or doesn't this criterion apply to the peoples designated in this Report of the International Labor Office?

Belgian Government Information Center, *supra* note 12, at 20. At least two American Indian nations are islands: the Squaxin Nation in the Puget Sound and the Metlakahtla Indians of the Annette Islands in Alaska: J. Ryan, Indian Nations Compared to Other Nations, 3 Am. Ind. J., no. 8, at nn. 134, 138 (1977). The land of the Hopi Indians consists of an enclave within the enclave of the Navajo Indians, and the Six Nations Indians own land in both Canada and the United States.

26. For a list of these non-self-governing territories, *see* E. Sady, *supra* note 5, at 80.

27. ILO, Studies and Reports, New Series no. 35 (1953).

28. *Id.*; *see also* G. Bennett, Aboriginal Rights, *supra* note 22, at 69.

29. International Labour Office Convention 107 and Recommendation 104 of 1957, reprinted in G. Bennett, Aboriginal Rights, *supra* note 22, at 70–85.

30. ILO Convention 107, preamble.

31. A. Eide, United Nations Action on the Rights of Indigenous Populations, in The Rights of Indigenous Peoples in International Law: Selected Essays on Self-Determination 27 (R. Thompson ed. 1987).

32. ILO Convention 107, art. 2(1).

33. G. Bennett, Aboriginal Rights, *supra* note 22, at 16–17.

34. U.N. Doc. E/CN.4/Sub. 2/1982/33, Annex at 13.

35. U.N. Doc. E/CN.4/Sub. 2/476/Add. 5, Annex at 13.

36. See P. Aspelin, Culture and Conquest, The Multinational Corporate Challenge to Native Resource Control: Hydroelectric and Other Development Projects in South America, 15 Akwesasne Notes, no. 3, at 8 (Early Summer 1983).

37. ILO Convention 107, arts. 2(2) and 3(3).

38. *Id.* art. 3(2).

39. *Id.* arts. 2(3), 3(3).

40. J. Folk-Williams, The American Indian—An Overview of the Issues, 15 Akwesasne Notes, No. 2, at 10 (Spring 1983).

41. U.N. Charter, art. 73.

42. ILO Convention 107, art. 6.

43. *Cf.* Charter of the United Nations, *supra* note 3.

44. International Labour Office Convention 169 of 1989, reprinted in R. Barsh, An Advocate's Guide to the Convention on Indigenous and Tribal Peoples, 15 Okla. City U.L. Rev. 209 (1990).

45. Resolution of the Indigenous Peoples Preparatory Meeting—Geneva Relating to the International Labour Organization's Convention Concerning Indigenous and Tribal Peoples in Independent Countries, 1989. The resolution:

> 1. Calls upon Indigenous Peoples all over the world to seize every opportunity to condemn the ILO and the revision process.
> 2. Calls upon states not to ratify the revised Convention.
> 3. Calls upon Indigenous Peoples to monitor the ILO and governments in the implementation of the Convention.
> 4. Calls upon support groups of Indigenous Peoples to urge states not to ratify the Convention and to publish lists of governments who ratify the revised Convention.
> 5. Calls upon members of the Working Group and the Sub-Commission on Prevention of Discrimination and the Protection of Minorities to condemn the racist revision.
> 6. Calls upon the Working Group to monitor the implementation of the revised Convention.
> 7. Calls upon governments and human rights experts involved in the process of drafting the Declaration on Rights of Indigenous Peoples not to repeat the mistake of the ILO.
> 8. Calls upon the Working Group, the Sub-Commission and governments to disregard the terms of the revised Convention in the process of achieving a meaningful development on the Declaration on the Rights of Indigenous Peoples.

A. Lawrey, Contemporary Efforts to Guarantee Indigenous Rights under International Law, 23 Vand. J. Transnat'l. L. 703, 719 n. 80 (1990).

46. R. Barsh, An Advocate's Guide, *supra* note 44, at 219.

47. General Assembly Res 1803(XVII), Permanent Sovereignty over Natural Wealth and Resources:

The General Assembly . . .

Bearing in mind its resolution 1314 (XVIII) of 12 December 1958, by which it established the Commission on Permanent Sovereignty over Natural Wealth and Resources and instructed it to conduct a full survey of the status of permanent sovereignty over natural wealth and resources as a basic constituent of the right of self-determination . . .

Noting that the creation and strengthening of the inalienable sovereignty of States over their natural wealth and resources reinforces their economic independence . . .

Declares that:

1. The right of peoples and nations to permanent sovereignty over their natural wealth and resources must be exercised in the interest of their national development and of the well-being of the people of the state concerned.

2. The exploration, development and disposition of such resources, as well as the import of the foreign capital required for these purposes, should be in conformity with the rules and conditions which the peoples and nations freely consider to be necessary or desirable with regard to the authorization, restriction or prohibition of such activities. . . .

4. Nationalization, expropriation or requisitioning shall be based on grounds or reasons of public utility, security or the national interest which are recognized as overriding purely individual or private interests, both domestic and foreign. In such cases the owner shall be paid appropriate compensation. . . .

5. The free and beneficial exercise of the sovereignty of peoples and nations over their natural resources must be furthered by the mutual respect of States based on their sovereign equality. . . .

7. Violation of the rights of peoples and nations to sovereignty over their natural wealth and resources is contrary to the spirit and principles of the Charter of the United Nations and hinders the development of international co-operation and the maintenance of peace.

48.

Another factor prevalent throughout the history of United States and Indian relations has been economic greed. Indians have possessed land and other resources that non-Indians have wanted. Non-Indians usually have prevailed. Often racism, expressed as white cultural superiority (whites would use the resource more appropriately), has been the justification for taking Indian land.

Indian Tribes: A Continuing Quest for Survival, A Report of the United States Commission on Civil Rights, at v (June 1981).

49. General 14 Dec. 1960. U.N. GAOR, XV, Supp. 16 (A/4684), Res. no. 1514 (XV), at 66–67.

50. R. Barsh and J. Henderson, The Road 48 (1980); *see also* text accompanying Chapter 6, notes 57–61.

51. ILO Convention 169, art. 13.

52. M. E. Galey, Indigenous Peoples, International Consciousness Raising and the Development of International Law, 8 H.R.J. 21, 23 (1975).

53. UN Sub-Commission on Prevention of Discrimination and Protection of Minorities, Study of the Problem of Discrimination against Indigenous Populations, U.N. Doc. E/CN.4/Sub.2/1986/7 & Adds. 1–4, at 25 (Jose R. Martinez Cobo, Special Rapporteur) (1986). The final volume, which contains the conclusions and recommendations of the study, is available as a UN publication: 5 UN Indigenous Study, U.N. Sales No. E.86.XIV.3. The original documents can be found at: U.N. Docs. E/CN.4/Sub.2/476/Adds. 1–6 (1981), E/CN.4/Sub.2/1982/2/Adds. 1–7 (1982), and E/CN.4/Sub.2/1983/21/Adds. 1–7 (1983), cited in H. Hannum, New Developments in Indigenous Rights, 28 Va. J. Int'l. L. 649, 658 n. 36 (1988). For further

literature, *see* B. Roy and G. Alfredsson, Indigenous Rights: The Literature Explosion, 13 Transnational Perspectives 19 (1987).

54. Y.El-Ayouty, *supra* note 19, at 229; S. O'Brien, Federal Indian Policies and the International Protection of Human Rights, in American Indian Policy in the Twentieth Century 38 (V. Deloria, Jr., ed. 1985).

55. H. Hannum, *supra* note 53, at 659–60; S. O'Brien, *supra* note 54, at 40–41.

56. S. O'Brien, *supra* note 54, at 39–40.

57. R. Barsh, Current Developments: Indigenous Peoples: An Emerging Object of International Law, 80 Am. J. Int'l. L. 369, 371 (1986).

58. See Appendix 3.

59. Declaration of the World Conference to Combat Racism and Racial Discrimination, reprinted in 1 UN Indigenous Study, *supra* note 53, at 31; cited in Hannum, *supra* note 53, at 659.

60. R. Barsh, Current Developments, *supra* note 57, at 372.

61. Sub-Commission on Prevention of Discrimination and Protection of Minorities Resolution 1984/35A, 4th preambular para. (Aug. 30); cited in R. Barsh, Current Developments, *supra* note 57, at 371.

62. U.N. Doc. E/CN.4/Sub.2/1984/SR.32, para. 48, cited in 5 UN Indigenous Study, *supra* note 53, at 2.

63. *Id.* at 4–5. The special rapporteur specially noted the absence of African countries and suggested that a study be undertaken just on those nations.

64. Cited in Erica-Irene Daes, Native People's Rights, 27 C. de D. 123, 131 (1986); *see also* Study of the Problem of Discrimination Against Indigenous Populations, ch. V, U.N. Doc. E/CN.4/Sub.2/1982/Add.6, at 3.

65. 5 UN Indigenous Study, *supra* note 53, at 16.

66. *Id.* at 20.

67. *Id.* at 4.

68. Economic and Social Council Resolution 1982/34 of 7 May 1982.

69. D. Sanders, The UN Working Group on Indigenous Populations, 11 H.R.Q. 406, 408 (1989).

70. D. Betz, Persistent Peoples and International Organizations: Expanding Linkage in a Time of Rapid Global Change, in Sovereignty Symposium III: The Dialogue Continues, sec. 10, at 11 (1990).

71. "All contributions, greatly needed and most welcome, should be addressed to: Voluntary Fund for Indigenous Populations, c/o the Centre for Human Rights, Palais des Nations, 1211 Geneva 10, Switzerland": World Campaign for Human Rights, Human Rights, The Rights of Indigenous Peoples, Fact Sheet No. 9, at 9–10.

72. IWGIA [International Workgroup for Indigenous Affairs] Yearbook 1990, at 167 (A. Gray & J. Dahl eds. 1991).

73. *Id.* at 13. The author attended the 1991 session of the working group, and a number of his observations are contained in this section.

74. At the 1991 session of the working group, The World Council of Churches informally agreed to allow their credentials to be used for this purpose.

75. Sub-Comm'n Res. 1985/22 (Aug. 29), cited in R. Barsh, Current Developments, *supra* note 57, at 373.

76. *Id.* at 383.

77. IWGIA Yearbook 1990, *supra* note 72, at 168–69; R. Brody, M. Convery, D. Weisbrodt, The 42nd Session of the Sub-Commission on Prevention of Discrimination and Protection of Minorities, 13 H.R.Q. 260, 285 (1991).

78. Report of the Working Group on Indigenous Populations on Its Eighth Session, U.N. Doc. E/CN.4/Sub.2/1990/42, at 4.

79. A. Eide, *supra* note 31, at 11, 29.

80. See Appendix 4 for the complete text of the 1991 version of the Draft Universal Declaration on the Rights of Indigenous Peoples.

81.

> Nothing in the foregoing paragraphs shall be construed as authorising or encouraging any action which would dismember or impair, totally or in part, the territorial integrity or political unity of sovereign and independent States conducting themselves in compliance with the principle of equal rights and self-determination of peoples as described above and thus possessed of a government representing the whole people belonging to the territory without distinction as to race, creed or colour.

General Assembly Resolution 2625 (xxv). *Cf.* C. Quaye, Liberation Struggles in International Law 52 (1991).

82. R. A. Williams, Jr., Encounters on the Frontiers of International Human Rights Law: Redefining the Terms of Indigenous Peoples' Survival in the World, 1990 Duke L. J. 660, 690.

83. Report of the Working Group on Indigenous Populations on Its Eighth Session, U.N. Doc. E/CN.4/Sub.2/1990/42, at 49.

84. *Id.* at 42. Emphasis added.

85. Erica-Irene Daes, *supra* note 64, at 123.

86. *Id.* at 127.

87. U.N. Doc. E/CN.4/Sub.2/1990/42, at 38; G. Morris, In Support of the Right of Self-Determination for Indigenous Peoples under International Law, 29 Ger. Y.B. Int'l. L. 277 (1986).

88. Erica-Irene Daes, *supra* note 64, at 128. Emphasis added.

89. U.N. Doc. E/CN.4/Sub.2/1990/42, at 37. Emphasis added.

90. See H. Hannum, New Developments, *supra* note 53, at 649 n. 1; *see also* G. Nettheim, "Peoples and Populations," in The Rights of Peoples chap. 7, at 107–26 (J. Crawford ed. 1988); G. P. Castile, Issues in the Analysis of Enduring Cultural Systems, in Persistent Peoples: Cultural Enclaves in Perspective (G. P. Castile & G. Kushner eds.) (1981).

91. T. Franck, Of Gnats and Camels: Is There a Double Standard at the United Nations? 78 Am. J. Int'l. L. 811, 831 (1984).

92. One example is President Yogesh Varhade of the Ambedkar Centre for Justice and Peace, Inc., of Toronto, Canada, whose card states, "Voice of 150 million natives of India (Untouchables and Tribes)."

93. U.N. Doc. E/CN.4/Sub.2/AC.4/1991/Misc.2, at 11.

94. *Id.* at 13.

95. *Id.* at 15.

96. *Id.* at 15.

97. U.N. Doc. E/CN.2/Sub.2/1990/42, at 50.

98. *Lone Wolf v. Hitchcock*, 187 U.S. 553 (1903); see Chapter 6, note 100 *infra*.

99. G. Brewsaugh, Federal Indian Policy: A Violation of International Treaty Law, 4 W.S.U.L. Rev. 229, 255 (1976–77). "In the case of bilateral treaties the presumption of recognition appears to be cogent to the point of being conclusive": H. Lauterpacht, Recognition in International Law 375 (1947).

100.

> The attitudes of UN member governments towards minorities and indigenous peoples as reflected in their cultural policies, have delayed the preparation of international instruments, have made difficult the defining of indigenous peoples and have prevented the development of an international non-governmental organization of indigenous peoples with access to the UN law-making process.

M. E. Galey, Indigenous Peoples, International Consciousness Raising and the Development of International Law on Human Rights, 8 H.R.J. 21, 24 (1975).

101. UN Charter, art. 52(1).

102. H. P. de Vries & J. Rodriguez-Novas, The Law of the Americas: An Introduction to the Legal Systems of the American Republics 3 (1965).

103. J. B. Moore, 6 A Digest of International Law, 401 (1906); A. Thomas and A. Thomas, Jr., The Organization of American States and the Monroe-Doctrine—Legal Implications, 30 La. L. Rev. 54 (1969–70).

104. J. Cabranes, Human Rights and Non-Intervention in the Inter-American System, 65 Mich. L. Rev. 1147, 1153 (1967).

105. *Id.* at 1155.

106. O. S. Stoetzer, The Organization of American States: An Introduction 116–44 (1965).

107. H. P. de Vries & J. Rodriguez-Novas, *supra* note 102, at 5.

108. *Id.* at 37–43.

109. M. Ball, The OAS in Transition 43–47 (1969); C. Fennick, The Organization of American States: The Inter-American Regional System 180 n. 35 (1963); *see also* OAS Charter, ch. II, art. 5(e).

110. R. Karen, Neighbors in a New World: The Organization of American States 51 (1906).

111.

> Mostly, the new Latin American States continued to be governed, politically and economically, by a small dominating class of Spanish or Portuguese ancestry—closely linked culturally to the civilization and religion of Catholic Latin Europe, and generally separated by an enormous social and economic gulf from their own native peasant populations—largely of Indian stock.

W. Friedmann, An Introduction to World Politics 305 (1965).

112. American Declaration of the Rights and Duties of Man, adopted by the Ninth International Conference of American States, Bogota, Columbia, 1948, repr. in 43 Am. J. Int'l. L., supp. 133 (1949); American Convention on Human Rights, signed at the Inter-American Specialized Conference on Human Rights, San Jose, Costa Rica, November 22, 1969, in Handbook of Existing Rules Pertaining to Human Rights in the Inter-American System (Organization of American States, updated to July 1983).

113. M. Tardu, Human Rights in the International Petition System (1979), p. 2, vi, Special Committee on the Situation with Regard to the Implementation of the

Declaration on the Granting of Independence to Colonial Countries and Peoples 15 (April 1980).

114. Declaration on Principles of International Law Concerning Friendly Relations and Co-Operation among States in Accordance with the Charter of the United Nations, G.A. Res. 2625, 25 U.N. GAOR, Supp. (no. 28) 121, 123, 124, U.N. Doc. A/8028 (1971).

115. Reprinted in A. J. Peaslee, 2 International Governmental Organizations Constitutional Documents 854 (1974). This Convention was based on the International Convention of Patzcuaro of 1940: O. C. Stoetzer, The Organization of American States 70–71 (1965).

116. R. Lawson, International Regional Organizations 319 (1964).

117. OAS, Secretary General, Annual Report, 1964–65, at 142 (1965).

118. R. Barsh, The IX Inter-American Indian Congress, 80 Am. J. Int'l. L. 682 (1986).

119. International Convention Relative to Inter-American Indian Conferences and the Inter-American Indian Institute, art. IV., in A. J. Peaslee, *supra* note 115, at 856.

120. *Id.* at art. XI, 861.

121. M. Ball, The OAS in Transition 353 (1969; footnotes omitted).

122. R. Dunbar Ortiz, Indians of the Americas: Human Rights and Self-Determination 46 (1984).

123. *Id.* at 47.

124. J. L. Andress & J. E. Falkowski, Self-Determination: Indians and the United Nations—The Anomalous Status of America's "Domestic Dependent Nations," 8 Am. Ind. L.Rev. 97, 107 (1980).

125. See A. J. Peaslee, *supra* note 115, preamble.

5

International Courts and Indigenous Peoples

The International Court of Justice and other international tribunals have essentially failed to recognize any of the rights of the indigenous peoples of the Western Hemisphere. This is hardly surprising, since the jurisdiction of the International Court of Justice is limited to disputes between member states and the indigenous nations of the Western Hemisphere are not recognized as member states. Further, the International Court of Justice applies general principles of law recognized by "civilized nations," and the indigenous nations of the Western Hemisphere are still considered to be "uncivilized nations."[1] Thus, the parties that the court recognizes and the law that it applies predetermine the results that it reaches.

The rights of the indigenous peoples of the Western Hemisphere have never been the central issue before any international tribunal. Their status and rights have only been addressed as peripheral to the rights of members of the Family of Nations. In one of these decisions, the main issue was whether land occupied by indigenous peoples is considered to be *terra nullius* (vacant land). Although this legal fiction may seem to make some sense in the context of ancient legal precedent, the continued viability of such a colonial doctrine in the twentieth century is by no means obvious.[2]

CAYUGA INDIANS (GREAT BRITAIN) V. UNITED STATES

The first international tribunal to address the rights of the indigenous peoples of the Western Hemisphere was the *Cayuga Indians (Great Britain) v. United States* case in 1926.[3] Although this case is often cited for the proposition that Indian nations are "not a legal unit of international law," this is a grossly oversimplified and convenient overstatement of the holding of the case. Additionally, to view this case in its proper perspective, it is necessary to understand the limitations on the tribunal's jurisdiction.

This case was decided by the American and British Arbitral Tribunal. The tribunal was the third commission instituted to settle claims between Great Britain and the United States. The jurisdiction of the first commission was limited to claims between the two nations which arose after the signing of the Treaty of Ghent in 1814. The jurisdiction of the second commission was limited to claims between the two nations arising out of acts committed during the "American War of Secession." The jurisdiction of the third commission was created to adjudicate pecuniary claims between the two nations that were unsettled under the previous arrangements.[4]

The facts before the third commission were as follows: In 1789 the state of New York entered into a treaty with the Cayuga Indians who remained at Cayuga Lake, even though a majority of the Cayugas lived at Buffalo Creek (in western New York) and Grand River (in Canada). In this treaty, the Cayuga Lake Cayugas ceded to New York State their remaining land, except for a reservation at Cayuga Lake, for a yearly annuity of $500. The remaining Cayugas were dissatisfied with this treaty because they had not been properly represented. In 1790 and 1795, the Buffalo Creek and Grand River Cayugas confirmed the prior treaty and sold the land reserved at Cayuga Lake for a yearly annuity of $1,800, which was to be paid to the "Cayuga Nation."[5] From 1795 to 1810, the annuity was paid to Cayugas living in Canada. Afterwards, as a result of the War of 1812, the annuity was paid to Cayugas living in the United States. Before this third tribunal, Great Britain brought a claim "on behalf of the Cayuga Indians in Canada against the United States by virtue of certain treaties between the State of New York and the Cayuga Nation in 1789, 1790 and 1795, and the Treaty of 1814 between the United States and Great Britain known as the Treaty of Ghent."[6] Great Britain invoked "article IX of the Treaty of Ghent, by which the United States agreed to restore to the Indians with whom that Government had been at war 'all the possessions, rights, and privileges which they may have enjoyed or been entitled to' in 1811 before the war."[7] Britain claimed that the Cayugas, or Britain on their behalf, were entitled to the whole amount of the annuity from 1810 to the present, or, in the alternative, a proportion of the annuity for the future.[8]

The tribunal held in favor of Great Britain and based liability on equitable considerations and Article IX of the Treaty of Ghent. To get to the equitable considerations, the tribunal had to find that the Canadian Cayugas were "not a legal unit of international law"[9] and that Great Britain was the Canadian Cayugas' "quasi guardian" or stood "in loco parentis"; otherwise, the court would not have had jurisdiction to make an award.[10] The tribunal found that the Cayugas were a "legal unit of New York law" and that New York was competent to decide "what constituted the [Cayuga] 'Nation' ";[11] however, it stated:

It does not follow, however, that Great Britain may not maintain a claim on behalf of the Cayuga Indians in Canada. These Indians are British Nationals. They have been settled in Canada, under the protection of Great Britain.... There was no definite political constitution of the Cayuga Nation, and it is impossible to say with legal precision just what would constitute a migration of the nation as a legal and political entity. When the Cayugas divided, some going to Canada and some remaining in New York, and when that cleavage became permanent in consequence of the War of 1812, Great Britain might, if it seemed desirable, treat the Canadian Cayugas as a unit of British law or might deal with them individually as British nationals.... If, therefore, the Canadian Cayugas have a just claim, according to "the principles of international law and of equity," Great Britain is entitled to maintain it.... [W]e "ought not to permit words such as 'sovereign states,' 'treaties,' and the like to conceal the real facts." The substance of the matter was that New York agreed to pay the then Cayuga Indians and their posterity, and on the division of the tribe the annuity ought to have been apportioned as, indeed, was done when the New York Cayugas afterward divided.... Nor can we examine the evidence and come to any other conclusion than that as a matter of right and justice such an apportionment should have been and ought to be made.... The claim of the Canadian Cayugas, who are in fact the greater part of that people, is founded in the elementary principle of justice that requires us to look at the substance and not stick in the bark of the legal form.[12]

After clearing these legal hurdles, the court next addressed the issue of whether the United States could be held liable for a treaty made by the state of New York and whether the claim was barred by laches. The tribunal found that the treaty was clearly a contract of the state of New York to pay money and that, generally, the United States could not be held liable for New York's failure to pay.[13] However, the tribunal found that the United States had become liable when it had assumed responsibility under Article IX of the Treaty of Ghent, after New York failed to recognize the claim of the Canadian Cayugas, and after the matter was brought to the attention of the United States in 1849.[14]

The United States then put forth the defense of the doctrine of laches, or equitable estoppel, due to Great Britain's delay in filing the claim. Even though the tribunal found laches on the part of Great Britain, the Canadian Cayugas could not equitably be barred by laches since they were Indians, who were treated like "persons under disability."[15]

The tribunal next fashioned an award in accordance with its factual findings and within its limited power to only award money damages. The court awarded Great Britain, as the Canadian Cayugas' "quasi-guardian," the sum of one hundred thousand dollars. This money represented a just share of the annuity payments from 1849 until 1926, and "a capital sum which at 5% interest will yield half of the amount of the annuity for the future."[16]

There are two additional points that should be addressed. First, the authority for the tribunal's use of the language that the Cayugas were "not a legal unit of international law" is debatable. The tribunal merely cited Hyde, who cited *Cherokee Nation v. Georgia.*[17] *Cherokee Nation v. Georgia*, however, held that the Cherokee Indians were a state within the meaning of international law, although they were not a "foreign state" within the meaning of Article III of the United States Constitution.[18] If the tribunal merely meant that the Cayugas were not recognized as a member of the Family of Nations, that was a given. The tribunal only had jurisdiction to decide pecuniary claims between Great Britain and the United States. If it had found the Cayugas to be a "legal unit of international law," it would not have had jurisdiction to hear the claim or render a decision in favor of the equities of the case.

Second, the tribunal stated that there "was no definite political constitution of the Cayuga Nation."[19] This statement is erroneous and demonstrates a widespread biased and racist view of Indian governmental organization. The Cayuga Nation was a member of the Six Nations Confederacy, which most definitely *did* have a "definite political organization."[20] Regardless, and despite some of the unfortunate use of language and reasoning by the tribunal, the result that it reached does seem to be a fair, equitable, and appropriate resolution of the monetary claim before it.

ISLAND OF PALMAS CASE

The next case that involved an examination of the rights of indigenous peoples by an international tribunal was the *Island of Palmas* case.[21] The rights of the indigenous people were almost irrelevant to the decision, since it was based on the premise that either the United States or the Netherlands was sovereign and that the indigenous people were not.

This case was brought by the United States and the Netherlands in the Permanent Court of Arbitration at the Hague "to determine whether the Island of Palmas (or Miangas) in its entirety forms a part of territory belonging to the United States of America or of Netherlands territory."[22] The United States claimed territorial sovereignty over this inhabited island (halfway between the Philippine Islands and the Netherlands East Indies) as a successor to the rights of Spain over the Philippines based on the doctrine of discovery and the principle of geographical contiguity (a variety of the Hinterlands doctrine).[23] The Netherlands claimed territorial sovereignty based on colonization by the East India Company as evidenced by "conventions entered into with native princes."[24]

The sole arbitrator, Max Huber,[25] decided against the United States because the Spanish discovery (although within the limits of the Bull Inter Caetera of Pope Alexander VI) was not followed by effective occupation[26] and because the title claimed by contiguity had "no foundation in international law."[27] The arbitrator decided in favor of the Netherlands because the "conventions" with the native rulers, along with other evidence, established a "continuous and peaceful display of State authority (so-called prescription)."[28]

The rights of the indigenous peoples were relevant to the court only "in so far as the rights of the Parties to the dispute may be derived from them."[29] In response to the evidence presented to the tribunal by the parties, the court made the following statement:

> It is admitted by both sides that international law underwent profound modifications between the end of the Middle-Ages and the end of the 19th century, as regards the rights of discovery and acquisition of uninhabited regions or regions inhabited by savages or semi-civilized peoples. Both Parties are also agreed that a juridical fact must be appreciated in the light of the law contemporary with it, and not of the law in force at the time when a dispute in regard to it arises or falls to be settled.... International law in the 19th century, having regard to the fact that most parts of the globe were under the sovereignty of States members of the community of nations, and that territories without a master had become relatively few, took account of a tendency already existing and especially developed since the middle of the 18th century, and laid down the principle that occupation, to constitute a claim to territorial sovereignty, must be effective.... However, according to the view that has prevailed at any rate since the 19th century, an inchoate title of discovery must be completed within a reasonable period by the effective occupation of the region claimed to be discovered. This principle must be applied in the present case, for the reasons given above in regard to the rules determining which of successive legal systems is to be applied (the so-called intertemporal law).[30]

In this passage, the tribunal found that international law only recognized the sovereign rights of "States members of the community of nations." Indigenous peoples—referred to as "savages or semi-civilized peoples"—could have no sovereign rights, and land that they occupied was regarded as "territories without a master."

The decision also addressed the legal effect of "so-called political contracts between native rulers" and the Dutch East India Company:

> As regards *contracts between a State* or a Company such as the Dutch East India Company and *native princes or chiefs of peoples* not recognized as members of the community of nations, they are not, in the international law sense, treaties or conventions capable of creating rights and obligations such as may, in international

law, arise out of treaties. But, on the other hand, contracts of this nature are not wholly void of indirect effects on situations governed by international law; if they do not constitute titles in international law, they are none the less facts of which that law must in certain circumstances take account. From the time of the discoveries until recent times, colonial territory has very often been acquired, especially in the east Indies, by means of contracts with the native authorities, which contracts leave the existing organisation more or less intact as regards the native population, whilst granting to the colonizing Power, besides economic advantages such as monopolies or navigation and commercial privileges, also the exclusive direction of relations with other Powers, and the right to exercise public authority in regard to their own nationals and to foreigners. The form of the legal relations created by such contracts is most generally that of suzerain and vassal, or of the so-called colonial protectorate.

In substance, it is not an agreement between equals; it is rather a form of internal organization of a colonial territory, on the basis of autonomy for the natives. . . . And thus suzerainty over the native State becomes the basis of territorial sovereignty as towards other members of the community of nations.[31]

Thus, the arbitrator determined that international law did not recognize indigenous peoples as members of the international community and that "treaties" with indigenous peoples were not equal to treaties between members of the community of nations. Rather, the arbitrator found that such treaties created the feudal relationship known as a suzerain.

According to this concept, the native people do not own their land. Rather, they become a tenant holder of a fief of—in this case—the East India Company, which is the immediate vassal to Her Majesty the Queen of the Netherlands, who owns the ultimate title to the land. It is unlikely that the native rulers had any such understanding or that the language of the "treaty" (none of which was ever cited by the arbitrator) was readily susceptible to such an interpretation.

LEGAL STATUS OF EASTERN GREENLAND

In 1933 the Permanent Court of International Justice rendered the next decision that ignored the human rights of indigenous peoples. In the case of the *Legal Status of Eastern Greenland*, which was contested between Denmark and Norway, the issue before the court was which of these two Christian-European states had sovereignty over eastern Greenland.[32] It was once again assumed that only "white races" could have sovereignty over land and that the indigenous people (Eskimos or Inuit) could not.[33]

Norway claimed that eastern Greenland was *terra nullius*—territory belonging to no one—because it had not been effectively occupied by any other member of the Family of Nations. Therefore, that nation's Proclamation of July 10, 1931—that it had proceeded to occupy certain territory in eastern Greenland—gave it the right to colonize the area.[34] Denmark claimed sovereignty over eastern Greenland on the basis of colonies in the western part of Greenland, the recognition of its sovereignty by other members of the Family of Nations, and its activities in eastern Greenland. Its claim was based on—"to use the phrase employed in the Palmas Island decision of the Permanent Court of Arbitration, April 4th, 1928—a title 'founded on the peaceful and continuous display of State authority over the island.' "[35]

The court decided in favor of Denmark. It found Norway's proclamation unlawful and invalid because it constituted "a violation of the existing legal situation."[36] Denmark had satisfied the two elements of a claim based on continued display of authority: "the intention and will to act as sovereign, and some actual exercise or display of such authority."[37] Denmark established its intention to occupy the whole island in a number of bilateral treaties with members of the Family of Nations.[38]

The court also ruled that Denmark had sufficiently acted on its assertion of sovereign rights. In this regard, the court observed

> that in many cases the tribunal has been satisfied with very little in the way of the actual exercise of sovereign rights, provided that the other State could not make out a superior claim. This is particularly true in the case of claims to sovereignty over areas in thinly populated or unsettled countries.[39]

These activities consisted largely of hunting and fishing, on a very limited scale, over a vast extent of territory.[40] Paradoxically, the indigenous people were involved in the same activities on a much more extensive, continuous, and long-term basis. Nonetheless, these activities, and the rights that should attach to them, were totally ignored by the court. The court's reasoning appears to be that such activities by "the white races" give sovereign rights over territory, yet the same activities by indigenous people do not. This assumption appears to be a logical extension—or a more honest illustration—of the reasoning used by Vattel, who was not cited.[41]

WESTERN SAHARA CASE

The next case dealing with the rights of indigenous people is the *Western Sahara* case.[42] This case is different from the previous cases for a number of reasons. First, it dealt with people who are not from the Western Hemisphere. Second, the case was decided following a number of important developments in international law, including the entry into force of the United Nations Charter and the passage of UN General Assembly Resolution 1514(XV). Third, the politics surrounding the decision appear more important than the legal issues decided by the court.

There was a series of unique events that led Morocco to request that the General Assembly refer this matter to the International Court of Justice for an advisory opinion. The Western Sahara consists of about 100,000 square miles of mostly desert, which is sparsely inhabited by a small number of people (estimates range from about 30,000 to 100,000) who are mostly nomadic Arab-Berbers. These nomadic people have close racial, linguistic, religious, and cultural ties with neighboring people in Morocco and Mauritania, and therefore "it is extremely difficult to determine who among them is a Saharan indigenous to the Territory."[43] Beginning in 1884, a Spanish colonial protectorate was established over this area, and it was administered as a "province" of Spain.[44] Spain initially colonized the territory as a fishing and stopping-off point between the Canary Islands and the mainland.

After becoming independent in 1956, Morocco claimed the Western Sahara as an integral part of its precolonial territory, based on "immemorial possession . . . [and] the public display of sovereignty [which was] uninterrupted and uncontested for centuries."[45] It cited the *Eastern Greenland* case "to establish Morocco's claim to a title based 'upon continued display of authority' . . . on the same principles as those applied by the Permanent Court in upholding Denmark's claim to possession of the whole of Greenland."[46] After becoming independent in 1960, Mauritania also claimed the Western Sahara as an integral part of its precolonial territory.[47]

As a result of the passage of General Assembly Resolution 1514, the Fourth Committee on Decolonization and the General Assembly began to address the question of the Western Sahara. The General Assembly

> called upon Spain to determine at the earliest possible date together with the inhabitants of the territory, and in consultation with Morocco and Mauritania and any other interested party, the procedures for the holding of a referendum under United Nations auspices to enable the indigenous population to exercise freely its right to self-determination.[48]

Morocco pushed for a referendum based on the assumption that it would result in the Western Sahara "reintegrating" with Morocco. Although initially reluctant, Spain agreed to the holding of a United Nations–supervised referendum.

Around 1965, the situation was complicated with the discovery in the Western Sahara of 1.7 billion tons of high-grade phosphate (which is used in the manufacture of fertilizer) and growing suspicions that the territory contained other valuable natural resources.[49] Spain's position was predicated on the assumption that there were no valuable resources in the area. Morocco, a large exporter of phosphates, was very concerned about how this would effect its economy and the outcome of the referendum. It was also concerned about creating another Kuwait—a small population of very rich people with very poor neighbors.

In 1973, Spain gave the local government of the Western Sahara assurances that it would freely determine the latter's future status and guarantee its territorial integrity. In 1974 Spain passed a statute that provided for the holding of a United Nations–supervised referendum during the first half of 1975. In response to these developments, Morocco attempted in vain to get Spain to consent to a joint submission of the dispute to the International Court of Justice as a contentious case. Morocco then lobbied the General Assembly to request an advisory opinion from the International Court of Justice, which would obviate the need to obtain Spain's consent. Morocco, becoming fearful of losing a referendum, was obviously seeking to obtain a decision that would strengthen its claim for reintegration of the Western Sahara.

On December 13, 1974, the General Assembly, after extensive revision and discussion, adopted Resolution 3292 which authorized the advisory opinion on the following two questions:

> I. Was Western Sahara (Rio de Oro and Sakiet El Hamra) at the time of colonization by Spain a territory belonging to no one (*terra nullius*)?
>
> If the answer to the first question is in the negative,
>
> II. What were the legal ties between this territory and the Kingdom of Morocco and the Mauritanian entity?[50]

The resolution was adopted by a vote of eighty-seven to zero with forty-three abstentions. The unprecedented number of abstentions was attributed to a desire not to delay the referendum and to reservations about the merits of Moroccan claims.[51]

The first substantive question put to the court was whether the Western Sahara, at the time of Spanish colonization in 1884, was a territory belonging to no one. Curiously, none of the interested parties (except Algeria) argued this position. The court split fourteen to two and found that the Western Sahara was not a *terra nullius* and that "agreements with local rulers, whether or not considered as an actual 'cession' of the territory, were regarded as derivative roots of title, and not original titles obtained by occupation of *terrae nullius*."[52] This statement is rather unsatisfactory because it sidesteps any discussion of "those late nineteenth-century theorists [who denied] any force of international legal personality inherent in non-European style State entities."[53]

The separate opinion of Vice-President Ammoun took a rather more direct approach. Judge Ammoun concluded:

> [T]he concept of *Terra nullius*, employed at all periods, to the brink of the twentieth century, to justify conquest and colonization, stands condemned. It is well known that in the sixteenth century Francisco de Vittoria protested against the application to the American Indians, in order to deprive them of their lands, of the concept of *res nullius*.[54]

In a more forthright manner, this view acknowledges the existence of the doctrine of *terra nullius*, but denies it any present-day application because of its discriminatory nature and the development of intertemporal law.

The second substantive question put to the court was whether there were "legal ties" between the Western Sahara, on the one hand, and the kingdom of Morocco and the Mauritanian entity, on the other. On this point, Spain took the position that a United Nations–supervised referendum should be held, while Morocco and Mauritania argued that since the Western Sahara was a part of their territory at the time of Spanish colonization in 1884, it should be recognized as part of their territory now. The court found as follows:

162. The materials and information presented to the Court show the existence, at the time of Spanish colonization, of legal ties of allegiance between the sultan of Morocco and some of the tribes living in the territory of Western Sahara. They equally show the existence of rights, including some rights relating to the land, which constituted legal ties between the Mauritanian entity, as understood by the Court, and the territory of Western Sahara. On the other hand, the Court's conclusion is that the materials and information presented to it do not establish any tie of territorial sovereignty between the territory of Western Sahara and the Kingdom of Morocco or the Mauritanian entity. Thus the Court has not found legal ties of such a nature as might affect the application of resolution 1514 (XV) in the decolonization of Western Sahara, and, in particular, of the principle of self-determination through the free and genuine expression of the will of the peoples of the Territory.[55]

The court's choice of language in this operative paragraph is rather unfortunate. It was apparently struggling with the words "legal ties" in Resolution 3292—which had no previous definition in international law—in an attempt to reach a near-unanimous decision. The court's solution of finding "legal ties" but not "legal ties of such a nature as might affect the application of resolution 1514," as subsequent events have shown, was an extremely poor choice of language.

Paragraphs 54 through 58 place the decision into the context of the development of intertemporal law regarding self-determination. These paragraphs cite the Namibia opinion, General Assembly Resolution 1514, and General Assembly Resolution 2625 as authority for the primacy of the principle of self-determination. Thus, the court concluded that Morocco and Mauritania's "claim to what has been called automatic retrocession is not applicable to the Western Sahara."[56] The court made this comment to rationalize the apparent inconsistency between the General Assembly's treatment of Ifni, which it allowed to be retroceded to Morocco, and the Western Sahara.[57]

The separate opinion of Judge de Castro amplified the aspect of the court's opinion concerning self-determination and the development of international law. He took the position that essentially it did not matter whether there were legal ties in 1884 because intertemporal law made those ties subject to new facts and new law. At the time of the colonization by Spain,

> the territory had a status which was governed by the law in force at that time. But that status had not crystallized and was not fixed *ad aeternum*. . . .
>
> After the entry into force of the United Nations Charter, the territory of Western Sahara became a "non-self-governing territory," and the administering Power therefore has a duty to recognize the principle that the interests of the inhabitants of the territory are paramount, and to develop self-government (Art. 73 of the Charter).
>
> The advisory opinion of the Court is confined to the statement that, whatever the existing legal ties with the territory may have been at the time of colonization by Spain, *legally* those ties remain subject to intertemporal law and that, as a consequence, they cannot stand in the way of the application of the principle of self-determination.[58]

Despite the court's opinion that the people of the Western Sahara were entitled to self-determination and a report from a United Nations Visiting Mission "that there was an overwhelming consensus among Saharans within the Territory in favour of independence," the United Nations–supervised referendum has not yet been held.[59] Morocco intentionally misinterpreted the first sentence of paragraph 162 of the opinion as a recognition of Moroccan sovereignty over the Western Sahara. The king of Morocco organized an invasion—which became known as the "Green March"—of 350,000 unarmed civilians into the Western Sahara to gain recognition of Morocco's "right to national unity and territorial integrity."[60]

This unarmed invasion was followed by an armed invasion, which resulted in a "secret" trilateral agreement between Morocco, Mauritania, and Spain. The agreement recognized the territorial division of the Western Sahara between Morocco (the northern two-thirds) and Mauritania (the southern third), along with the establishment of an interim Moroccan and Mauritanian regime. In return for Spanish withdrawal, Spain retained a 35 percent interest in the Saharan phosphate industry and fishing rights off the Saharan and Moroccan coasts.

The indigenous response in the Western Sahara to this agreement and the invasion of their country was the organization of groups of freedom fighters (the largest group is known as Polisario) to carry out armed resistance to the occupation. They were successful in expelling Mauritania from the southern third of their territory, but remain hopelessly stalemated with the vastly superior military forces of Morocco.[61] The UN response to these developments to date has been ineffective, although hopes for a future United Nations–supervised referendum remain. There also has been little outrage expressed by the vast majority of the international community against the overland colonization of this territory by Morocco.[62]

NOTES

1. "[T]he Statute of the International Court of Justice still mentions, as a source of law, principles recognized by civilized nations, a terminology in conflict with the equality of all nations and originating at a time when colonial peoples were openly considered as non-civilized": M. Mushkat, An African Approach to Some Basic Problems of International Law, 7 Indian J. Int'l. L. 354 (1967), cited in The Rights of Indigenous Peoples in International Law: Selected Essays on Self-Determination 8 (R. Thompson ed. 1987).

2.

> The elaborate "European" legal fictions upon which post-Westphalia, "classical" International Law was based are perhaps best expressed in the specially concurring opinion of Vice-President Ammoun of the World Court in the *Western Sahara* Advisory Opinion rendered by the Court in 1975. . . . In Roman antiquity, as Judge Ammoun notes, any territory that was not Roman was legally considered by the Romans as *terra nullius* and therefore subject to legal appropriation by them; and in the later epoch of the great European maritime expansion and exploration in the 16th and 17th centuries and the resultant discovery of "new" lands overseas, any territory not belonging to a Christian sovereign was deemed, by the International Law of the time, to be *terra nullius* and therefore capable of yielding full legal title to the fact of European discovery and assertion of sovereignty over it. By the 19th century, as Judge Ammoun further noted, the key International Law phrasing had shifted from "Christian" to "civilized" state, but the legal result remained the same: the European state authority was legally entitled to treat non-European, autochthonous peoples as legal non-persons and the lands they inhabited as *terra nullius* and therefore ripe for the successful assertion of European territorial sovereignty over them. The ethno-culturally limited and particularistic, Eurocentrist character of the "classical" International law rules as to acquisition of territorial sovereignty through discovery and occupation and conquest, are patent. [footnotes omitted]

E. McWhinney, The International Court of Justice and the Western Tradition of International Law 5–8 (1987). *See also* G. Orwell, Not Counting the Niggers, in An Age Like This 1920–1940, The Collected Essays, Journalism and Letters of George Orwell 394 (S. Orwell & I. Angus ed. 1968); J. McDonell, Occupation and Res Nullius, 1 J. Soc. Comp. Leg. 276 (ser. II, 1899); Legal Consequences for States of the Continued Presence of South Africa in Namibia (South West Africa) Notwithstanding Security Council Resolution 276 (1971), Order No. 1 of 26 January 1971, I.C.J. Reports 1971, 3, 86 (1971).

3. 6 R. Int'l Arb. Awards 173 (1926).

4. *Id.* at 5.

5. *Id.* at 175–76.

6. *Id.* at 175.

7. *Id.* at 176.

8. *Id.* at 176.

9. *Id.* at 176.

10. *Id.* at 177. *In loco parentis* means "in the place of a parent," or that the Canadian Cayugas were the children of their parent Great Britain.

11. *Id.* at 184: "Legally the New York Cayugas' organization was now the nation for the strict legal purposes of the covenant in the Treaty of 1795."
12. *Id.* at 177–79. Citations omitted.
13. *Id.* at 187–88.
14. *Id.* at 188–89.
15. *Id.* at 189.
16. *Id.* at 189.
17. *Id.* at 176–77.
18. *See* Chapter 6, text and notes 66–67 *infra.*
19. *Id.* at 177.
20. *See* the White Roots of Peace, The Great Law of Peace of the Longhouse People (1973); *see also* The Great Law of Peace and the Constitution of the United States of America, 19 Akwesasne Notes, no. 4, at 5 (Summer 1987); Bruce E. Johansen, Forgotten Founders: Benjamin Franklin, The Iroquois and the Rationale for the American Revolution (1982), cited in D. Johnson, The Quest of the Six Nations Confederacy for Self-Determination, 44 U. Toronto Fac. L. Rev. 1, 7 n. 34 (1986); The History and Culture of Iroquois Diplomacy: An Interdisciplinary Guide to the Treaties of the Six Nations and Their League (F. Jennings ed. 1985); P. A. Wallace, The White Roots of Peace (1946); R. Burlingame & A. Stevens, Victory without Peace 61–62 (1944): The League of Nations was patterned in part after the Six Nations Confederacy.
21. (*U.S. v. Neth.*), 2 R.I.A.A. 831 (1928).
22. *Id.* at 832.
23. *Id.* at 837.
24. *Id.* at 837–38; it appears that the Netherlands overlooked a good argument that Spain did not have any rights because they were sold to Portugal in 1529. *See* European Treaties Bearing on the History of the United States and Its Dependencies to 1648, at 169 (F. G. Davenport & C. P. Paullin eds. 1967).
25. *Id.* at 834.
26. *Id.* at 848.
27. *Id.* at 869.
28. *Id.* at 868.
29. *Id.* at 837.
30. *Id.* at 845–46; *see also* T. O. Elias, The Doctrine of Intertemporal Law, 74 Am. J. Int'l. L. 285 (1980).
31. *Id.* at 858.
32. (*Den. v. Nor.*), 1933 P.C.I.J., Ser. A/B, No. 53.
33. *Id.* at 37–39.
34. *Id.* at 23.
35. *Id.* at 45.
36. *Id.* at 75.
37. *Id.* at 46.
38. *Id.* at 56–62.
39. *Id.* at 46.
40. *Id.* at 62; *see also* N. Doubleday, Aboriginal Subsistance Whaling: The Right of Inuit to Hunt Whales and Implications for International Environmental Law, 17 Den. J. Int'l. & P. 373 (1989).

41. *See also* Chapter 2, text and notes 44–46 *supra*, and Chapter 7, notes 15–26 *infra*.

42. Western Sahara, Order of 3 January 1975, I.C.J. Reports 1975, at 3 (1975).

43. Report of the United Nations Visiting Mission to Spanish Sahara, 1975, in The Report of the Special Committee on the Situation with Regard to the Implementation of the Declaration on the Granting of Independence to Colonial Countries and Peoples, U.N. Doc. A/10023/Add.5, Annex, at 28 (1975), cited in T. Franck, The Stealing of the Sahara, 70 Am. J. Int'l. L. 694, 697 n. 18 (1976).

44. Western Sahara, Order of 3 January 1975, I.C.J. Reports 1975, at 3, 25 (1975).

45. *Id.* at 42; Morocco also claimed parts of Algeria, Mali, Senegal, Ceuta, Melitta, Ifni, and Mauritania: Morocco, A Country Study (Harold D. Nelson ed. 1985).

46. Western Sahara, Order of 3 January 1975, I.C.J. Reports 1975, at 42–43 (1975).

47. *Id.* at 47.

48. G.A. Resolution 2229 (XXI), cited in M. Shaw, The Western Sahara Case, 49 Br. Y.B. Int'l. L. 119, 122 (1978).

49. A. Byman, The March on the Spanish Sahara: A Test of International Law, 6 Den. J. Int'l. L. & P. 95, 96 (1976–77); *see also* E. Riedel, Confrontation in Western Sahara in the Light of the Advisory Opinion of the International Court of Justice of 16 October 1975: A Critical Appraisal, 19 Ger. Y.B. Int'l. L. 405 (1976).

50. Western Sahara, Order of 3 January 1975, I.C.J. Reports 1975, at 13–14 (1975).

51. M. Shaw, The Western Sahara Case, 49 Br. Y.B. Int'l. L. 119, 124 n. 3 (1978).

52. Western Sahara, Order of 3 January 1975, I.C.J. Reports 1975, at 39 (1975).

53. M. Shaw, *supra* note 51, at 133.

54. Western Sahara, Order of 22 May 1975, I.C.J. Reports 1975, at 6, 86–87 (1975).

55. *Id.* at 68.

56. Western Sahara, Order of 3 January 1975, I.C.J. Reports 1975, at 3, 120 (1975) (separate opinion of Judge Dillard).

57. *Id.* at 34; *see also* M. Shaw, *supra* note 51, at 122.

58. *Id.* at 169–71; *cf.* M. Khadduri, Iraq's Claim to the Sovereignty of Kuwayt, 23 N.Y.U.J. Int'l. L. & Pol. 5 (1990); *see also* M. Bos, A Methodology of International Law (1984), ch. 10, at 286.

59. Report of the United Nations Visiting Mission to Spanish Sahara, *supra* note 43, at 708.

60. Letter dated 18 October 1975 from the Permanent Representative of Morocco to the United Nations, addressed to the President of the Security Council. U.N. Doc. S/11852 (1975), cited in T. Franck, The Stealing of the Sahara, 70 Am. J. Int'l. L. 694, 712 n. 111 (1976).

61. 2 Encyclopedia of Public International Law 293 (1981).

62. The Sahrawi Arab Democratic Republic (SADR), proclaimed in 1976, is recognized by seventy-four mainly Third World countries. IWGIA Yearbook 1990, at 149 (1991).

6

Special Legal Doctrines Used by the United States to Restrict the Right of Indian Peoples to Own Land and Be Self-Governing

CASE LAW

Except for the provisions mentioned earlier, the rights of indigenous peoples were ignored by the international legal system. Instead, their rights were determined by the domestic law of the overland European colonizers. A survey of the case law and policy of the United States will, therefore, be instructive for a number of reasons. First, the following cases illustrate the restrictions placed on the collective right of Indians to own land more fully than does the U.S. response to the questionnaire sent to the special rapporteur on the Study of the Problem of Discrimination against Indigenous Populations.[1] These cases, especially the cases developing the domestic trust, are also relevant to the civil and political rights of Indians, in particular their right to self-government.[2] Second, because the case law of the United States is the most highly developed body of law on indigenous peoples,[3] these cases are followed in other countries, including Australia,[4] Canada,[5] and New Zealand.[6] Therefore, they reflect state practice or customary international law.

Third, the United States has rejected assimilation policies in favor of a policy called self-determination. This has created a dilemma because prior case law is founded on assumptions leading to assimilation and not to self-determination. This case law must be reexamined before its relevance to the current self-determination policy can be fully understood, since "the judicial process is by nature evolutionary, building on what has gone before."[7] This also parallels the dilemma the United Nations faces in considering the rejection of the assimilation policy of the ILO and the emerging agenda of the Working Group on Indigenous Populations.

The first case addressing the nature of the right of Indians to own land was *Fletcher v. Peck*.[8] It was also the first case involving an interpretation of the contract clause of the federal Constitution, and it arose out of one of the largest land frauds perpetrated during the early years of the American Republic.[9] Additionally, it set the precedent of deciding Indian rights in cases to which they are not a party.

The facts of the case are as follows: In 1795 the Georgia legislature passed legislation enabling the state of Georgia to sell the right to buy Indian land to speculating land companies.[10] In 1796 a new legislature repealed the 1795 enabling legislation.[11] A "feigned" diversity suit was brought for the recovery of money paid, because of a breach of warranty of title over land conveyed to Fletcher by Peck.[12] In his deed to Fletcher, Peck covenanted

> that the state of Georgia aforesaid was, at the time of the passing of the act of the legislature thereof, (entitled as aforesaid,) legally seised in fee of the soil thereof, subject only to the extinguishment of part of the Indian title thereon. And that the legislature of the said state at the time of passing the act of sale aforesaid; had good right to sell and dispose of the same in manner pointed out by the said act. . . . And further, that the title to the premises so conveyed by the State of Georgia, and finally vested in the said Peck, has been in no way constitutionally or legally impaired by virtue of any subsequent act of any subsequent legislature of the said state of Georgia.[13]

The U.S. Supreme Court's decision, written by Chief Justice John Marshall, found for Peck because Georgia's first grant was a legal contract and its repeal violated the contract clause.[14]

The nature of Indian title arose tangentially, because Fletcher argued that Peck breached the covenant in the deed that the state of Georgia had a right to sell fee title to the land that was in the possession of the Indians.[15] Peck argued that the covenant was not breached because the state could sell its right to buy the land subject to Indian title.[16] Peck cited Vattel's *Law of Nations* to support his argument:

> What is the Indian title? It is mere occupancy for the purpose of hunting. It is not like our tenures; they have no idea of a title to the soil itself. It is overrun by them, rather than inhabited. It is not a true and legal possession.[17]

Chief Justice Marshall found that the state of Georgia had the right to sell the Indian land. Therefore, the covenant was not breached.[18] Not only did Georgia have a right to sell Indian land, but Marshall—who was forced to use this language because of the words used in the covenant—described

Georgia's title as "seisin in fee" subject to Indian title.[19] Marshall even noted that the use of this language implied that a grantee could maintain an action of ejectment against the Indians.[20]

Justice Johnson's dissent strongly disagreed with Marshall's use of language in the majority opinion:

Can, then, one nation be said to be seised of a fee-simple in lands, the right of soil of which is in another nation? It is awkward to apply the technical idea of fee-simple to the interests of a nation, but I must consider an absolute right of soil as an estate to them and their heirs. A fee-simple estate may be held in reversion, but our law will not admit the idea of its being limited after a fee-simple. In fact, if the Indian nations be the absolute proprietors of their soil, no other nation can be said to have the same interest in it. What, then, practically, is the interest of the states in the soil of the Indians within their boundaries? Unaffected by particular treaties, it is nothing more than what was assumed at the first settlement of the country, to wit, a right of conquest or of purchase, exclusively of all competitors within certain defined limits.[21]

Subsequent case law demonstrates that the misuse of words with precise legal meanings has resulted not only in a great deal of confusion, but also in a loss of Indian rights.[22] There have been two interpretations given to Marshall's language. One interpretation describes Indian title "as sacred as the fee-simple of the whites."[23] However, another, more recent interpretation describes "aboriginal title" as "not a property right but a 'mere possessory right' subject to the whim of the sovereign."[24]

The nature of Indian title next came before the Supreme Court in *Johnson v. McIntosh.*[25] Once again, Indians were not a party to the controversy, so the issues were framed without any consideration of their interests.[26] The plaintiffs claimed land under grants made to them, via a private individual, by the Illinois and Piankeshaw Indian nations in 1773 and 1775.[27] The defendant claimed the same land under grants made to him by the U.S. government, which bought the land from the same Indians in 1795.[28]

The issue in the case was whether the courts of the United States were bound to recognize the plaintiffs' title.[29] The plaintiffs argued that since both parties claimed from the same source, it would be "unnecessary, and merely speculative, to discuss the question respecting the sort of title or ownership, which may be thought to belong to savage tribes, in the lands on which they live."[30] Therefore, the only issue was whether individuals could buy land from the Indians or whether that was the exclusive prerogative of the United States.[31]

The plaintiffs also argued that individuals had the right to purchase Indian lands since they were not prohibited from doing so when the purchases were made in 1773 and 1775.[32] Further, the plaintiffs argued that a statute passed by Virginia in 1779 asserting that the state had "the exclusive right of pre-emption from the Indians" was not competent to take away vested rights.[33] The fact that Indians held their land in common "did not affect the strength of their title by occupancy."[34]

The defendant argued that the Indians had no right to sell their land to a private individual because "the civilized powers of Europe and of this continent . . . have uniformly disregarded their supposed right to the territory included within the jurisdictional limits of those powers."[35] The foundation of title was the doctrine of discovery by which the United States acquired sovereignty and dominion and that "overlooks all proprietary rights in the natives."[36] Accordingly, Indians "remain in a state of nature, and have never been admitted into the general society of nations."[37] "The Statutes of Virginia, and of all the other colonies, and of the United States, treat them as an inferior race of people, without the privileges of citizens and under the perpetual protection and pupilage of the government."[38]

According to the defendant, Indian title was "a mere right of usufruct and habitation, without power of alienation."[39] Since the Indians owned their land collectively, they

> could have acquired no proprietary interest in the vast tracts of territory which they wandered over; and their right to the lands on which they hunted could not be considered as superior to that which is acquired to the sea by fishing in it. The use in the one case, as well the other, is not exclusive. According to every theory of property, the Indians had no individual rights to land; nor had they any collectively, or in their national capacity; for the lands occupied by each tribe were not used by them in such a manner as to prevent their being appropriated by a people of cultivators. All the proprietary rights of civilized nations on this continent are founded upon this principle.[40]

Chief Justice Marshall, writing for the majority, found for the defendant, and built further on the unfortunate choice of language that he had used in *Fletcher*.[41] *Fletcher* found that whites held fee title subject to Indian title.[42] *Johnson* found Indian title to be a mere "right of occupancy."[43] Marshall justified this diminution of the right of Indians to own land to a mere possessory interest based on the doctrine of discovery. The doctrine of discovery was "confined to countries 'then unknown to all Christian people.' . . . Thus [it] assert[s] a right to take possession notwithstanding the occupancy of the natives, who were heathens."[44]

As far as Chief Justice Marshall was concerned, the "character and religion" of the Indians "afforded an apology for considering them as a people over whom the superior genius of Europe might claim an ascendancy."[45] In exchange for unlimited independence, Christian-European states "made ample compensation to the inhabitants of the new [world] by bestowing on them civilization and Christianity."[46] In other words, according to U.S. Supreme Court Chief Justice John Marshall, Indians could not own land because they were uncivilized heathens. Thus, "discovery gave an exclusive right to extinguish the Indian title of occupancy, either by purchase or conquest; and gave also a right to such a degree of sovereignty as the circumstances of the people would allow them to exercise."[47] Supreme Court Justice Story, in his *Commentaries*, recognized that *Johnson* was in conflict with the laws of nature,[48] but he rationalized Marshall's reasoning as follows:

> European nations . . . claimed an absolute dominion over the whole territories afterwards occupied by them, not in virtue of any conquest of or cession by, the Indian natives, but as a right acquired by discovery. Some of them, indeed, obtained a sort of confirmatory grant from the papal authority. But as between themselves they treated the dominion and title of territory as resulting from priority of discovery; and that European power which had first discovered the country and set up marks of possession was deemed to have gained the right, though it had not yet formed a regular colony there. We have also seen that the title of the Indians was not treated as a right of propriety and dominion, but as a mere right of occupancy. As infidels, heathens, and savages, they were not allowed to possess the prerogatives belonging to absolute, sovereign, and independent nations. The territory over which they wandered and which they used for their temporary and fugitive purposes, was, in respect to Christians, deemed as if it were inhabited only by brute animals.[49]

Chief Justice Marshall also was aware that his decision was "opposed to natural right, and to the usages of civilized nations."[50] It was opposed to natural right because the decision hinged on distinctions that failed to recognize the inherent equality of all human beings.[51] Marshall had already developed some expertise in finessing racial issues by couching them in less than totally candid language. Through the use of neutral principles of property law, Marshall had upheld chattel slavery.[52] The decision was opposed to the usages of civilized nations because Marshall confined the usages of civilized nations to Christian-European nations, with special legal doctrines applying to "wandering hordes" of Indians.[53]

An alternative analysis that was not opposed to natural law or the usages of civilized nations was only briefly considered by Marshall. International law recognized that when Indian nations ceded land to the United States by treaty, a plaintiff's interest in the land was governed by the land tenure system of the new sovereign.[54] Rights acquired before the cession were lost unless reserved by the treaty or guaranteed by the new sovereign.[55] In the plaintiff's case, since neither was done, the only recourse would be against the Indian nation that originally sold him the land. When the plaintiff bought the land from the Indians he incorporated himself with them and his rights were governed exclusively by the law of these Indians.[56] The situation would be the same today if an American citizen were to purchase land in Canada.

A great deal of confusion has been caused by the following language used in *Johnson*:

That law which regulated, and ought to regulate in general, the relations between the conqueror and conquered, was incapable of application to a people under such circumstances. The resort of some new and different rule, better adapted to the actual state of things, was unavoidable. Every rule which can be suggested will be found to be attended with great difficulty.

However extravagant the pretension of converting the discovery of an inhabited country into conquest may appear; if the principle has been asserted in the first instance, and afterwards sustained; if a country has been acquired and held under it; if the property of the great mass of the community originates in it, it becomes the law of the land, and cannot be questioned.[57]

In this passage, Marshall recognized that the doctrine of conquest did not apply to the Indians.[58] Rather, Marshall was converting the doctrine of discovery into the doctrine of conquest "by judicial fiat."[59] Only by pretending that Indian nations were conquered nations could Marshall justify his decision. The Supreme Court recognized that it was making no distinction between vacant land and land occupied by Indians.[60]

Thus, in this passage, Marshall invented a self-conscious legal fiction—the "myth of conquest"—to overlook the territorial integrity and political independence of Indian nations.[61] It should also be noted that language in this passage is totally unnecessary to the holding of the decision (*obiter dicta*), since the land at issue had been sold by the Indians. *Johnson*, with very few exceptions, "has been the basis of all subsequent determinations of Indian rights."[62]

The next important case, which not only reaffirmed the nature of Indian title as defined in *Johnson* but also established the domestic U.S. version of the sacred trust of civilization, was *Cherokee Nation v. Georgia*.[63] The rules developed in *Johnson* and *Cherokee Nation* are fundamental to understanding the unique legal doctrines that the U.S. courts apply only to Indians.

The facts of *Cherokee Nation v. Georgia* are as follows: The Cherokee Nation of Indians was having a dispute with the state of Georgia. The Cherokee Nation of Indians sought original jurisdiction before the Supreme Court of the United States under Article III of the U.S. Constitution.[64] Article III gives the Supreme Court original jurisdiction to hear disputes between states of the Union and "foreign States."[65] The Supreme Court held that the Cherokee nation was a foreign state within the meaning of international law:

Is the Cherokee nation a foreign state, in the sense in which that term is used in the constitution? The counsel for the plaintiffs have maintained the affirmative of this proposition with great earnestness and ability. So much of the argument as was intended to prove the character of the Cherokees as a state, as a distinct political society, separated from others, capable of managing its own affairs and governing itself, has, in the opinion of a majority of the judges, been completely successful. They have been uniformly treated as a state, from the settlement of our country. The numerous treaties made with them by the United States, recognize them as a people capable of maintaining the relations of peace and war, of being responsible in their political character for any violation of their engagements, or for any aggression committed on the citizens of the United States, by any individual of their community. Laws have been enacted in the spirit of these treaties. The acts of our government plainly recognize the Cherokee nation as a state, and the courts are bound by those acts.[66]

However, the Supreme Court ruled that "an Indian tribe or nation within the United States" was not a foreign state within the meaning of Article III.[67]

There were three major reasons given by the Supreme Court to support inventing this distinction.[68] First, the Supreme Court seized on the language used in the commerce clause of the Constitution to distinguish an Indian nation from a foreign nation. The Commerce clause gives Congress the power to "regulate commerce with foreign Nations, and among the several States, and with the Indian Tribes."[69] In the majority opinion, Marshall wrote: "We perceive plainly that the constitution, in this article, does not comprehend Indian tribes in the general term 'foreign nations'; not, we presume, because a tribe may not be a nation, but because it is not foreign to the United States."[70]

Second, and the point for which the case is most often cited, Marshall created the domestic trust relationship by interpreting the protection language of the Treaty of Holstein as making the Cherokee nation—and by analogy, all other Indian nations—"domestic dependent nations."[71] Marshall viewed Indians as being "in a state of pupilage; their relations to the United States resembles that of a ward to his guardian."[72] Although Marshall cited no authority for this analogy, he apparently derived this language from the writings of Victoria[73] and Burke.[74] These are the same sources from which the international trust developed.[75] However, the objectives of the domestic and international trusts are diametrically opposed. The ultimate objective of the international trust is the development of self-government, while the ultimate objective of the domestic trust is the destruction of self-government.[76]

Third, and a point that is often overlooked, is the fact that the guardianship notion was founded on the rule established in *Johnson* that did not recognize the right of Indians to own land. Based on this rule, Indian enclaves were placed "a grade below" the enclaves of Europe.[77] Marshall wrote that "the Indian territory is admitted to compose a part of the United States . . . [and] the Indians . . . occupy a territory to which we assert a title independent of their will."[78] Thus, Indian nations were not foreign nations because Marshall did not consider their land to be foreign. Rather, the Supreme Court regarded the land of this vanishing race as a "certain future acquisition."[79] This is how Marshall found an "aggregate of aliens composing a state" not to be a foreign state.[80]

Cherokee Nation's companion case, and the leading case to reject the *Johnson–Cherokee Nation* doctrine on the nature of the rights of Indians to own land and be self-governing, is *Worcester v. Georgia.*[81] Although *Worcester* is no longer "good law," it does provide a point of contrast against which the development of all subsequent domestic Indian law ought to be viewed. *Worcester* incorporates much of the dissenting opinion of *Cherokee Nation*, which found the Cherokees to be a foreign nation within the meaning of both international law and Article III.[82]

Worcester was a test case challenging the constitutionality of laws passed by the state of Georgia that extended their jurisdiction over the Cherokees.[83] Reverend Worcester had been residing on Cherokee territory and preaching the Christian gospel, with the permission of the Cherokees but in violation of a Georgia law that "forbade the residence of whites in Cherokee country without an oath of allegiance to the state and a license to remain."[84] Reverend Worcester was sentenced by a Georgia trial court to serve four years in jail, and he lost an appeal of this decision before the Georgia Supreme Court.[85]

The case was then appealed to the U.S. Supreme Court. Reverend Worcester argued that the laws passed by Georgia were unconstitutional as they were repugnant to the treaties between the Cherokee Nation and the federal government.[86] The U.S. Supreme Court held that the Georgia laws were void and that all "intercourse" with the Indians was to be carried on exclusively by the federal government.[87]

However, in reaching this decision, Chief Justice Marshall took a radically different view of the nature of Indian title. Marshall set the stage for his rejection of the theories of Vattel when he wrote:

> America, separated from Europe by a wide ocean, was inhabited by a distinct people, divided into separate nations, independent of each other and of the rest of the world, having institutions of their own, and governing themselves by their own laws. It is difficult to comprehend the proposition, that the inhabitants of either quarter of the globe could have rightful original claims of dominion over the inhabitants of the other, or over the lands they occupied; or that the discovery of either by the other should give the discoverer rights in the country discovered, which annulled the pre-existing rights of its ancient possessors.
>
> After lying concealed for a series of ages, the enterprise of Europe, guided by nautical science, conducted some of her adventurous sons into this western world. They found it in the possession of a people who had made small progress in agriculture or manufactures, and whose general employment was war, hunting, and fishing.
>
> Did these adventurers, by sailing along the coast, and occasionally landing on it, acquire for the several governments to whom they belonged, or by whom they were commissioned, a rightful property in the soil, from the Atlantic to the Pacific;

> or rightful dominion over the numerous people who occupied it? Or has nature, or the great Creator of all things, conferred these rights over hunters and fishermen, on agriculturists and manufacturers?[88]

In rejection of the principles set forth in *Johnson* and *Cherokee Nation*, the rights of both Indians and whites to own land were recognized as being equal with one exception. This exception was the belief that discovery gave the discovering European nation the exclusive right to purchase Indian land should the Indians choose to sell it.[89] Although discovery gave the discovering European nation the exclusive right to purchase, it did not "found that right on a denial of the possessor to sell."[90] Discovery "asserted a title against Europeans only, and [was] considered as blank paper so far as the rights of the natives were concerned."[91]

Further, the existence of the Cherokee Indians as a nation and their right to self-government and territorial integrity were explicitly recognized by treaty:

> This treaty, thus explicitly recognizing the national character of the Cherokees, and their right of self government; thus guarantying their lands; assuming the duty of protection, and of course pledging the faith of the United States for that protection has been frequently renewed, and is now in full force. . . . From the commencement of our government, congress has passed acts to regulate trade and intercourse with the Indians. . . . All of these acts, and especially that of 1802, which is still in force, manifestly consider the several Indian nations as distinct political communities, having territorial boundaries, within which their authority is exclusive, and having a right to all the lands within those boundaries, which is not only acknowledged, but guarantied by the United States. . . .
>
> The treaties and laws of the United States contemplated the Indian territory as completely separated from that of the states; and provide that all intercourse with them shall be carried on exclusively by the government of the union . . . the articles so often repeated in Indian treaties; extending to them, first, the protection of Great Britain, and afterwards that of the United States. These articles are associated with others, recognizing their title to self government. The very fact of repeated treaties with them recognizes it; and the settled doctrine of the law of nations is, that a weaker power does not surrender its independence—its right to self government, by associating with a stronger, and taking its protection. A weak state in order to provide for its safety, may place itself under the protection of one more powerful, without stripping itself of the right of government, and ceasing to be a state. Examples of this kind are not wanting in Europe. "Tributary and feudatory states," says Vattel, "do not thereby cease to be sovereign and independent states, so long as self government and sovereign and independent authority are left in the administration of the state."[92]

Thus, not only was the state of Georgia preempted from exercising any jurisdiction within Cherokee territory, but the Indians' authority within their own territorial boundaries was also exclusive.[93] The only legitimate power of either the federal or state governments over Indians was based on consent as expressed in treaties.[94] No other rule would recognize the inherent right of all peoples to self-government. The situation would be the same today if New York State passed the same law asserting jurisdiction over Canada.

In recognizing the human rights and treaty rights of the Cherokee Nation of Indians, the seventy-seven-year-old Marshall knew that he would have a confrontation with President Andrew Jackson, who was an old Indian fighter and an advocate of the removal of Indians. Jackson is reported to have said, "John Marshall has made his decision, now let him enforce it."[95] Since Marshall had no power to enforce the decision, Reverend Worcester continued to languish in the Georgia jail.

Before *Worcester*, Marshall knew that he would go down in history as the inventor of a body of law that applied special legal doctrines to Indians that were different from the laws applied to whites. *Worcester* has been viewed by some as Marshall's attempt to right the wrongs that he had perpetrated on Indian peoples in his prior decisions.[96] After *Worcester*, the institution of the U.S. Supreme Court was shaken to its roots by being so rudely confronted with the reality of the limits of its powers. As a result of this decision, neither Marshall nor the Supreme Court ever again confronted the other branches of government with a decision that applied the same rules to Indians and whites alike. To understand American Indian law, it is important to understand the two opposing views of the nature of Indian rights, mentioned above. Unfortunately, contemporary cases have rejected the *Worcester* view of Indian title in favor of the *Johnson–Cherokee Nation* view. Contemporary analysis rejects *Worcester* as being based on "platonic [*sic*] notions of Indian sovereignty"[97] and allows both the states and the federal government to assert jurisdiction over Indian land without Indian consent.

Federal interference is based on a perversion of the guardianship notion first mentioned in *Cherokee Nation*. The trust ought to be limited to a duty of protection in the best interests of the Indians and an obligation to encourage their self-government.[98] Instead, the domestic trust presumes that Indians are incompetent to govern their own affairs, and the federal government in its self-appointed role as guardian has asserted plenary power to steal Indian land and destroy Indian self-government.[99] In the leading case of *Lone Wolf v. Hitchcock*, the Supreme Court upheld the federal government's power to unilaterally abrogate treaties with Indians and take their land,[100] although such abrogations violate the most fundamental principles of international and trust law.[101] Furthermore, the Supreme Court, which established the domestic trust relationship, has refused to provide remedies for breaches of trust duties.[102] One leading authority found that "the net result is the creation of a new power, a power to regulate Indians."[103]

Not only has the federal government failed to protect Indians from itself, it has also failed to protect them from state governments. In early cases, the U.S. Supreme Court protected Indians from state governments because the Indians "owe no allegiance to the States, and receive from them no protection. Because of the local ill feeling, the people of the States where they are found are often their deadliest enemies."[104] More recently, in addition to expressly delegating authority over Indians to state governments,[105] the federal government has also recognized certain "inherent" limitations on the authority of Indians over their land vis-à-vis state governments.[106] The federal courts have also reversed the presumption in *Worcester* that state governments have no jurisdiction over Indians in favor of "creating a presumption of state jurisdiction."[107]

Under current analysis, state jurisdiction is not preempted by the federal government unless the Indians can show that tribal self-government would be impaired by it. In *Williams v. Lee*, the Supreme Court reversed earlier cases that protected Indians from state governments when it found that "absent governing Acts of Congress, the question has always been whether the state action infringed on the right of reservation Indians to make their own laws and be ruled by them."[108] This standard invites litigation, and it has been an enormous financial drain on the Indians, who are the poorest segment of the population. Federal courts have also upheld state jurisdiction in numerous other cases despite the fact that treaties are often involved and that "[i]mplicit in these treaty terms . . . was the understanding that the internal affairs of the Indians remained exclusively within the jurisdiction of whatever tribal government existed."[109]

All these assertions of power over Indians are based on the doctrines of discovery and wardship which apply only to Indians. These doctrines are derived from the nature of the right of Indians to own land as defined in *Johnson*. Using these doctrines, any interference with Indian self-government can be easily rationalized. If the Indians' land does not really belong to them,[110] or if they can be treated as a race of incompetents,[111] then their consent does not need to be obtained. Rather than follow any of the limitations that should have been placed on these doctrines, the U.S. Supreme Court has been further expanding on the *Johnson* view of Indian title and Indian rights.

The best example is *Tee-Hit-Ton Indians v. United States*.[112] In 1955, the Tee-Hit-Ton Indians of Alaska sued the United States for taking timber from land "claimed, occupied, and used" by the Tee-Hit-Ton Indians "from time immemorial."[113] The federal government—demonstrating the inherent conflict of interest it faces as the Indians' "guardian"—argued that

> the Tee-Hit-Tons' property interest, if any, is merely that of the right to use the land at the Government's will; [and] that Congress has never recognized any legal

interest of petitioner in the land and therefore without such recognition, no compensation is due the petitioner for a taking by the United States.[114]

The U.S. Supreme Court decided the case on "the rule derived from *Johnson v. McIntosh* that the taking by the United States of unrecognized Indian title is not compensable under the Fifth Amendment."[115] The Supreme Court described the "nature of aboriginal interest in land" as "original Indian title or *permission from the whites to occupy*."[116] Thus, such Indian land can be taken without due process or just compensation.[117]

The Supreme Court also gave its traditional allusion to the "myth of conquest":

Every American schoolboy knows that the savage tribes of this continent were deprived of their ancestral ranges by force and that, even when the Indians ceded millions of acres by treaty in return for blankets, food and trinkets, it was not a sale but the conquerors' will that deprived them of their land.[118]

Once again, the doctrine of conquest was totally inapplicable to the Tee-Hit-Tons, or any other Indians in Alaska, because there were never any hostilities between whites and Indians in the entire state.[119]

In addition to what "every American schoolboy" knows about the savage tribes of this continent, the Supreme Court cited Wheaton as an authority.[120] Wheaton's position is enlightening:

The Spaniards and Portuguese took the lead among the nations of Europe, in the splendid maritime discoveries in the East and the West, during the fifteenth and sixteenth centuries. According to the European ideas of that age, the heathen nations of the other quarters of the globe were the lawful spoil and prey of their civilized conquerors, and as between the Christian powers themselves, the Sovereign Pontiff was the supreme arbiter of conflicting claims. Hence the famous bull, issued by Pope Alexander VI, in 1493, by which he granted to the united crowns of Castile and Arragon all lands discovered, and to be discovered, beyond a line drawn from pole to pole, one hundred leagues west from the Azores, or Western Islands, under which Spain has since claimed to exclude all other European nations from the possession and use, not only of the lands but of the seas in the New World west of that line.... On the other hand, Great Britain, France, and Holland, disregarded the pretended authority of the Papal See, and pushed their discoveries, conquests, and settlements, both in the East and West Indies; until conflicting with the paramount claims of Spain and Portugal, they produced bloody and destructive wars between the different maritime powers of Europe. But there was one thing in which they all agreed, that of almost entirely disregarding the right of the native inhabitants of these regions. Thus the bull of Pope Alexander VI reserved from the grant to Spain all lands which had been previously occupied by any Christian nation.... It thus became a maxim of policy and law, that the right of the native Indians was subordinate to that of the first Christian discoverer, whose paramount claim excluded that of every other civilized nation, and gradually extinguished that of the natives.[121]

Not only did Wheaton ignore Pope Paul III's bull, he also gave the grants of the English monarchs equal dignity with the bull of Pope Alexander VI. This was a rather creative way of not recognizing the right of Alaskan Indians to own land. The Russians "discovered" Alaska and sold the right of preemption to the United States.[122] Therefore, what the Spanish or English governments did was of questionable relevance to Alaska.

However, in *Tee-Hit-Ton*, the Supreme Court even went beyond the expansive interpretation that Marshall gave to Vattel's theories in *Johnson*. The description of Indian title as "permission from the whites to occupy" implies that Indians are "tenants at will": If the whites revoked their "permission," the Indians would be trespassing on their own land![123]

The real reason for the Supreme Court's decision was buried in a footnote. Somehow the government got into evidence the fact that if the Supreme Court gave just compensation for the taking of unrecognized Indian title, estimated pending claims would be worth $9 billion.[124] This compares to the $800 million paid for all the land purchased from the Indians in the United States.[125] Really, this was a purely economic decision.

The decision also has a macabre twist. The Supreme Court failed to cite or distinguish as authority a law review article written by Felix S. Cohen (who had died two years earlier) that would have reached the opposite result.[126] Clearly the judges were aware of the article written in 1947 because they plagiarized one of its key phrases—"every American schoolboy"—out of context. Cohen wrote:

> Every American schoolboy is taught to believe that the lands of the United States were acquired by purchase or treaty from Britain, Spain, France, Mexico, and Russia, and that for all the continental lands so purchased we paid about 50 million dollars out of the Federal Treasury. Most of us believe this story as unquestioningly as we believe in electricity or corporations. We have seen little maps of the United States in our history books and big maps in our geography books showing the vast area that Napoleon sold us in 1803 for 15 million dollars and the various other cessions that make up the story of our national expansion. As for the original Indian owners of the continent, the common impression is that we took the land from them by force and proceeded to lock them up in concentration camps called reservations.
>
> Notwithstanding this prevailing mythology, the historic fact is that practically all of the real estate acquired by the United States since 1776 was purchased not from Napoleon or any other emperor or czar but from its original Indian owners.[127]

Compare this language to the opinion of the Supreme Court that "every American schoolboy" knows the continent was taken from the Indians by conquest.[128] This followed the Supreme Court's tradition of creating mythology in Indian law cases rather than following historical fact.

The Supreme Court's position was based on what Cohen referred to as the "menagerie" theory of Indian title. According to this theory; "Indians are less than human and . . . their relations to their lands is not the human relation of ownership but rather something similar to the relation that animals bear to the areas in which they may be temporarily confined."[129] As to the origins of this theory, Cohen wrote:

> The sources of this "menagerie" theory are many and varied and sometimes elegantly pedigreed. There is the feudal doctrine, which has seldom been heard in this country for a century or so except in Indian cases, that ultimate dominion over land rests in the sovereign. . . . There are other subtler sources of the "menagerie" theory of Indian reservations which are seldom set forth in legal briefs but exert a deep influence on public administration. One of the most insidious of these is the doctrine that the only good Indian is a dead Indian, when it follows, by frontier logic, that the only good Indian title is one that has been extinguished, through transfer to a white man or a white man's government. And finally there is the more respectable metaphysical doctrine that since government is the source of all rights there are no rights against the Government, from which it may be deduced that Indians who have been deprived of their possessions by governmental action are without redress. All these doctrines, it may be hoped, have been finally consigned to the dust bins of history by the course of decisions of the Supreme Court that culminates in the *Alcea* case.[130]

However, the Supreme Court does not find the body of law treating Indians as less than human to be invidious racial discrimination. In the leading case of *Morton v. Mancari*, the Court upheld an Indian hiring preference statute.[131] Although a higher standard of review is applied to other racial classifications (the strict scrutiny test), a lower standard of review is applied to an "Indian" classification ("reasonably and directly related to a legitimate, nonracially based goal").[132] The Court was concerned that if it applied the same standard of review to an "Indian" classification, "an entire Title of the United States Code (25 U.S.C.)" would be declared unconstitutional.[133]

The Court reasoned, in a footnote, that the term "Indian" was not a racial classification because it only dealt with federally recognized Indians.[134] In other words, a subclassification of a racial group does not constitute a racial classification. Additionally, it is the federal government that determines whether someone is a member of the subclassification. Moreover, on its face, the statute applies to all members of the racial group "Indians" and is not limited to "federally recognized Indians."[135] The same reasoning could have been used to uphold black slavery as nonracial on the grounds that some black people were not slaves.

This review establishes the fact that the U.S. Supreme Court that laid the foundation for domestic Indian law was a racist institution.[136] Not only did it uphold chattel slavery, but it also relied on the racist line of writers of international law as authority for its denial of the rights of Indians to own land and be self-governing. The Supreme Court still follows the same line of cases although it omits some of the most offensive language. In 1883, the Supreme Court found that the whites were "superiors of a different race."[137] When the current chief justice of the Supreme Court, William Rehnquist, cited this language as authority in 1978, he omitted the offensive language "superiors of" and wrote, "a different race."[138]

FEDERAL INDIAN POLICY

Federal Indian policy, although often couched in language that claims to help or protect Indians, has often been used as a pretext for taking or controlling Indian land.[139] The ultimate objective of the domestic trust has been the coerced assimilation of Indians into mainstream American society at the expense of Indian land ownership and self-government. One author has noted, "We sometimes fail to realize that the formulation of all Indian policies in American history; even the most just, has been based on certain attitudes that could best be described as racial."[140]

After the Revolutionary War, the United States continued to follow many of the precedents set by the British government in dealing with the Indians. The first policy statement made by Congress was the Northwest Ordinance of 1787, which read:

> The utmost good faith shall always be observed towards the Indians, their lands and property shall never be taken from them without their consent; and in their property rights and liberty, they never shall be invaded or disturbed, unless in just and lawful wars authorized by Congress; but laws founded in justice and humanity shall from time to time be made, for preventing wrongs being done to them, and for preserving peace and friendship with them.[141]

This policy was built on the themes first set forth by Victoria and Pope Paul III recognizing the human rights of indigenous peoples.[142] However, this policy has rarely been carried out in practice.

In these early years, the federal government's major concerns were with the regulation of trade and land cessions with the Indians.[143] A federal monopoly was established in both areas. In 1790, the first Nonintercourse Act was passed. In addition to regulating trade with Indians, this act forbid the conveyance of Indian lands without the consent of the federal government.[144] The legal status of the Indians was described as follows:

> From the earliest times the Indians, though treated as subject to the sovereignty first of the foreign colonizing powers, then of the colonies or States, and finally, of the United States, have been considered not as citizens or subjects, that is, as members of the various bodies politic within whose midst they have lived, but, from the constitutional viewpoint, as aliens, and their tribes as foreign nations to be dealt with as such, namely, by treaties and agreements rather than by statutes.[145]

Despite the First Amendment's express prohibition against the establishment of religion, this did not apply to the Indians. Congress began appropriating funds to missionaries to Christianize and civilize the Indians.[146] The government would often authorize a large number of missionaries from different Protestant denominations to convert the Indians on a single reservation.

Within fifty years of becoming the first state in the Western Hemisphere to be recognized as a member of the Family of Nations, in 1823 the United States developed the Monroe Doctrine. This policy was based on the " 'doctrine of two spheres' which assumed that the nations of the 'New World' and those of the 'Old World' were essentially different in political and economic terms."[147] This rule of American international law recognized existing European colonies and the independence of former European colonies. It also continued the nonrecognition of indigenous nations and established the legitimacy of the overland colonization of indigenous nations free from international reproach.

In the development of Indian policy, one author noted five basic alternatives:

> Alternative 1: destroy the status quo: violate, or render inoperative, treaty guarantees; destroy tribal integrity; kill or remove Indians, or wait for them to die off.
>
> Alternative 2: maintain the status quo: support existing treaty guarantees, tribal integrity, and the right of tribes to hold land in common; protect the individual Indian against white aggression.
>
> Alternative 3: change the status quo by voluntary agreement of tribes, leading gradually to individual allotment of lands and adoption of "civilized" ways.
>
> Alternative 4: change the status quo by involuntary means by destroying tribal autonomy, and forcing Indians rapidly into individual allotment of lands, subjection to the white man's law, and mandatory citizenship.
>
> Alternative 5: any of the above alternatives, but with the addition of benefits to white farmers greedy for Indian land, to white miners eager to exploit Indian mineral wealth, and to railroad companies anxious for Indian land and rights-of-way.[148]

The federal government adopted a combination of the first, fourth, and fifth alternatives.

In the 1830s the federal government initiated the Removal policy.[149] Under this policy, land-hungry whites took the Indians' eastern lands in exchange for land west of the Mississippi River. This area was known as the Great American Desert, and it "was then considered to be uninhabitable by white people."[150] The justification for this policy was that "only if the Indians were removed beyond contact with whites could the slow process of education, civilization and Christianization take place."[151] This exchange of land was a way to "avoid dealing with the more difficult and more basic political conflicts of interest inherent in allowing a 'sovereign nation' to exist within a state without being incorporated into the federal system."[152]

The already educated, civilized, and Christianized Cherokees were among those eastern Indians removed to the western lands. This episode in Cherokee history is known as the "Trail of Tears" because about one-fifth of the Cherokees died when they were removed by the United States in the middle of winter.[153] New treaties were made with the Cherokee Nation of Indians, and they were promised

> a permanent home, . . . which shall, under the most solemn guarantee of the United States, be, and remain, theirs forever—a home that shall never, in all future time, be embarrassed by having extended around it the lines, or placed over it the jurisdiction of a Territory or State, nor be pressed upon by the extension, in any way, of any of the limits of any existing Territory or State.[154]

In 1871, in a rider attached to an appropriation bill, Congress passed a law providing:

> No Indian nation or tribe within the territory of the United States shall be acknowledged or recognized as an independent nation, tribe, or power with whom the United States may contract by treaty; but no obligation of any treaty lawfully made and ratified with any such Indian nation or tribe prior to March 3, 1871 shall be hereby invalidated or impaired.[155]

"By this section, the policy of the government, maintained for nearly 100 years of entering into treaties with the various tribes of Indians within the geographical limits of the United States as with a foreign nation was changed."[156] Although existing treaty rights were not intended to be impaired and Indians were still supposed to be dealt with on the basis of consent, Congress began passing legislation affecting Indians without the Indians' consent.[157]

The U.S. Supreme Court upheld such legislation based on a perversion of the trust concept. Indians were regarded as incompetent wards, and the federal government was presumed to be acting in their best interest.[158] In fact, the leading case upheld the sale of Indian lands to non-Indians by the federal government without Indian consent.[159] This is how consent is dispensed with in a country where all just government is supposed to be based on the consent of the governed.[160] Although the 1871 act appears on its face to be racially discriminatory and a violation of the separation of powers clause, it has not been declared unconstitutional.[161]

In 1887 the General Allotment policy was initiated even though previous experiments with allotments had disastrous effects on Indians.[162] The Allotment Act was supposed to make the entire race of Indian people into farmers in twenty-five years by allotting each Indian an individually owned parcel of land out of the communally held Indian lands, most of which were guaranteed to them by treaty. During the twenty-five-year trust period, the federal government was to hold trust title to the Indian land. After the twenty-five-year period was over, the Indian allottee, if declared competent, would be given fee title to the land. This would make the Indian an American citizen, without his or her consent, and the jurisdiction of the Indian nation over that plot of land would come to an end.[163]

After the allotments were made to Indians, the "surplus" Indian land was sold to non-Indians.[164] This was the real reason for the policy, and was well known at the time. During the debates on this legislation, a small minority of congressmen spoke out against the legislation in the following terms:

> The main purpose of this bill is not to help the Indian, or solve the Indian problem, or provide a method for getting out of our Indian troubles so much as it is to provide a method for getting at the valuable Indian lands and opening them up to white settlement. The main object of the bill is in the last sections of it, not in the first. The sting of this animal is in its tail. . . . The provisions for the apparent benefit of the Indian are but the pretext to get at his lands and occupy them. With that accomplished, we have securely paved the way for the extermination of the Indian races upon this part of the continent.[165]

Even the sponsor of the bill, Senator Henry L. Dawes (R-Mass.), acknowledged that the act was a "violation of treaties" and a "flagrant disregard of inalienable rights."[166]

Under the Allotment Act, almost two-thirds of the remaining Indian land passed into the hands of the whites.[167] The numbers are staggering. For various reasons, 20 million acres of Indian land were spared from the Allotment Act. The remaining 118 million acres of land held by Indians in 1887 had been reduced to 28 million acres by 1934. Additionally, most of the land taken by the whites was the best farming land, and most of the land remaining with the Indians is desert or semidesert. This transparent land theft scheme has been called an "orgy of plunder and exploitation unparalleled in American history."[168]

When this policy was finally repudiated by the federal government and the trust period was extended, the Indians' "right of occupancy" was subject to the further restriction that the federal government held trust title to their land. "Equally important with the outright loss of land is the effect of the allotment system in making such lands as remain in Indian ownership unusable."[169] After the original Indian allottee died, the allotted land was divided up among that person's heirs, resulting in small parcels of land that were not economically feasible units. In this way, the federal government obtained control over the leasing and management of much of the remaining Indian land.[170] This policy is responsible for the poverty in which many Indian peoples live today.

With respect to the Cherokees, the United States unilaterally allotted their lands in 1906. The Cherokee Indians were declared to be citizens, and they were forced to incorporate within the state of Oklahoma, in violation of the promises made to them when they were forcibly removed from their traditional lands in the eastern part of the United States.[171]

"From the first settlement of the American colonies the Indians were treated as alien peoples outside of the control of domestic laws."[172] In 1924, without Indian consent, Congress unilaterally declared all Indians born in the United States to be U.S. citizens.[173] Although this was done under the pretext of giving Indians rights—especially the right to vote—in effect, it took away the Indians' right to be citizens of their own indigenous nations without interference from the United States.[174] It reduces Indians from what ought to be a people with the right to control their remaining land to a small, insignificant minority in a majority rule system. One example is the Navajo Indians, who have a 25,000-square-mile reservation and a population of 200,000. Although this reservation is larger than forty UN member states, the Navajo are not allowed any representation in the U.S. Senate, and their potential congressional voting strength is split between four states of the Union.[175]

In 1934, after the allotment policy was acknowledged to be a failure, Congress passed the Indian Reorganization Act.[176] The Indian Reorganization Act stopped allotments, but only if the Indians would accept a constitution written by the federal government. The Indian Reorganization Act constitutions, among other things, imposed a separation of church and state on the Indians' traditional theocratic governments.[177] The legitimacy of these governments is often called into question in view of the known Indian tradition of not attending meetings or participating in elections with which they did not agree. Such governments were often voted in by a nontraditionalist, Christian minority, and the United States no longer recognizes the authority of the traditional Indian governments with whom they previously had negotiated treaties.[178]

The ultimate solution to the "Indian Problem" was the Termination policy, initiated in the 1950s.[179] The goal of the Termination policy was the complete integration of Indians "into the mass of the population as full, tax-paying citizens."[180] Under this policy, the federal government withdrew recognition of all special Indian rights (treaty, executive order, statutory, and aboriginal). Indian land was divided into individual parcels, and this land again soon passed into the hands of the white population. Over one hundred Indian groups were terminated. Although the Termination policy has been rejected as "morally and legally unacceptable," only one terminated Indian group has been reinstated.[181]

The final reversal of federal Indian policy to date occurred in 1970 with the initiation of the Self-Determination policy.[182] The name of this policy is very misleading. It has almost nothing to do with the meaning of self-determination under international law. This domestic policy only gives Indians very limited control over some of their educational programs.

As this review of domestic Indian policy has shown, it can be changed at any time. Only a constitutional amendment requiring Indian consent would be adequate to really protect the right of Indians to self-government.[183] It is also clear that the United States still regards Indian rights to be only temporary.[184]

NOTES

1. The response of the U.S. Government was so misleading and incomplete that an American Indian rebuttal was made. United States' Response to the Study of the Problem of Discrimination of Indigenous Populations, 7 American Indian Law Newsletter, no. 11, special issue (1974).

2. *Id.* at 75.

3. G. Bennett, Aboriginal Title in the Common Law: A Stony Path Through Feudal Doctrine, 27 Buf. L. Rev. 617 (1978).

4. *Millirrpum v. Nabalco Pty. Ltd.* (1971) 17 F.L.R. 141; *see also* P. Biskup, Not Slaves, Not Citizens: The Aboriginal Problem in Western Australia 1898–1954 (1973); S. Haas, An Outward Sign of an Inward Struggle: The Fight for Human Rights of the Australian Aborigine, 5 Fla. Int'l. L.J. 81 (Fall 1989).

5. L. Green, Trusteeship and Canada's Indians, 3 Dalhousie L.J. 104 (1976); *see also* Native Rights in Canada (P. A. Cumming & N. H. Mickenberg eds. 1972); M. Asch, Home and Native Land: Aboriginal Rights and the Canadian Constitution (1984); B. H. Wildsmith, Aboriginal Peoples and Section 25 of the Canadian Charter of Rights and Freedoms (1988); B. Slattery, Ancestral Lands: Alien Laws: Judicial Perspectives on Aboriginal Title (1983); Pathways to Self-Determination: Canadian Indians and the Canadian Constitution (L. Little Bear, M. Boldt & J. A. Long eds. 1984).

6. N. Smith, Maori Land Law (1960); *see also* R. Falk, The Role of Domestic Courts in the International Legal Order (1964); I. H. Kawharu, Waitangi, Maori and Pakeha Perspectives on the Treaty of Waitangi 98–99 (1989).

7. R. Ericson & D. R. Snow, The Indian Battle for Self-Determination, 58 Ca. L. Rev. 445, 486 (1970).

8. 10 U.S. (6 Cranch.) 87 (1812).

9. C. Haines, The Role of the Supreme Court in American Government and Politics 1789–1835, at 309 (1960).

10. 10 U.S. (6 Cranch.) 87, 88 (1812).

11. *Id.* at 89.

12. C. Haines, *supra* note 9, at 314; *see also* J. Norgren, Protection of What Rights They Have: Original Principles of Federal Indian Law, 64 N.D.L. Rev. 73, 83 (1988); G. T. Dunne, Justice Joseph Story and the Rise of the Supreme Court 70–76 (1970).

13. 10 U.S. (6 Cranch.) 87, 88 (1812).

14. *Id.* at 139.

15. *Id.* at 124.

16. *Id.* at 121.

17. *Id.*
18. *Id.* at 142.
19. *Id.* at 142–43; *see also* R. L. Barsh and J. Y. Henderson, The Road: Indian Tribes and Political Liberty 38 (1980).
20. *Id.* at 142.

Ejectment is an action to restore possession of property to the person entitled to it. Not only must the plaintiff establish a right to possession in himself, but he must also show that the defendant is in wrongful possession. If the defendant has only trespassed on the land, the action is for trespass (i.e. damages).

Black's Law Dictionary 464 (1979).
21. Black's Law Dictionary, *supra* note 20, at 147.
22. H. Berman, The Concept of Aboriginal Rights in the Early Legal History of the United States, 27 Buf. L. Rev. 637, 638 (1978); *see also* Veeder, Greed and Bigotry: Hallmark of American Indian Law, 3 Am. Ind. J., no. 12, at 2, 8 (1977).
23. *Mitchell v. United States*, 34 U.S. (9 Pet.) 711, 746 (1835).
24. N. J. Newton, At the Whim of the Sovereign: Aboriginal Title Reconsidered, 31 Hast. L.J. 1215 (1980).
25. 21 U.S. (8 Wheat.) 543 (1823).
26. N. J. Newton, *supra* note 24, at 1221–22.
27. 21 U.S. (8 Wheat.) 543, 553–55 (1823).
28. *Id.* at 572.
29. *Id.*
30. *Id.* at 562–63.
31. *Id.* at 563.
32. *Id.* at 563.
33. *Id.* at 565 n.a.
34. *Id.* at 563.
35. *Id.* at 567.
36. *Id.*
37. *Id.*
38. *Id.* at 569.
39. *Id.*
40. *Id.* at 569–70.
41. *Id.* at 592.
42. *Fletcher v. Peck*, *supra* note 8, at 142–43.
43. *Johnson v. McIntosh*, *supra* note 25, at 574, 591.
44. *Id.* at 576–77.
45. *Id.* at 573.
46. *Id.* at 573.
47. *Id.* at 587.
48. J. Story, 1 Commentaries on the Constitution of the United States 4 (1858).
49. *Id.* at 106 (footnotes omitted). *Cf.* J. Story, A Discourse Pronounced at the Request of the Essex Historical Society 71 (1928): "If, abstractly considered, mere discovery could confer any title, the natives already possessed it by such prior discovery." *See also* D. Getches, D. Rosenfelt & C. Wilkinson, Cases and Materials on Federal Indian Law 297 (1979); Sir James McIntosh, Progress of Ethical Philosophy 49–50 (Philadelphia ed. 1832). "A state is also distinguishable from an

unsettled horde of wandering savages not yet formed into civil society": J. B. Moore, A Digest of International Law 15 (1906).

50. 21 U.S. 543, 591 (1823).

51. H. Berman, *supra* note 22, at 651.

52. D. M. Roper, In Quest of Judicial Objectivity: The Marshall Court and the Legitimation of Slavery, 21 Stan. L. Rev. 532 (1969).

53. *Cherokee Nation v. Georgia*, 30 U.S. (5 Pet.) 1, 27 (1831).

54. R. Barsh and J. Henderson, *supra* note 19, at 45–46.

55. *Id.* at 46.

56. *Id.*

57. 21 U.S. 543, 591 (1823).

58. See also H. Berman, *supra* note 22, at 691; F. S. Cohen, Handbook of Federal Indian Law 282 n. 20 (1942).

59. H. Berman, *supra* note 22, at 648.

60. 21 U.S. 453, 596 (1823).

61. H. Berman, *supra* note 22, at 647; *see also* R. Barsh and J. Henderson, *supra* note 19, at 48, 143 n. 24, 278; F. Jennings, The Invasion of America: Indians, Colonialism, and the Cant of Conquest 15–16, 32 (1975); R. A. Williams, Jr., The American Indian in Western Legal Thought: The Discourses of Conquest 315, 330–33 n. 14 (1990); *cf.* J. Y. Henderson, Unraveling the Riddle of Aboriginal Title, 5 Am. Ind. L. Rev. 75, 92 (1977).

62. Indian Tribes, A Report of the United States Commission of Civil Rights 16–17 (June 1981).

63. 30 U.S. (5 Pet.) 1 (1831).

64. *Id.* at 15.

65. U.S. Const. art. 3, sect. 2.

66. 30 U.S. 1, 15 (1831).

67. *Id.* at 19.

68. See N. J. Newton, *supra* note 24, at 1224.

69. U.S. Const. art. 1, sect. 8.

70. 30 U.S. 1, at 18 (1831).

71. *Id.* at 17; *see also* F. S. Cohen, *supra* note 58, at 46–48.

72. *Id.*; *see also* R. L. Barsh & J. Y. Henderson, *supra* note 19, at 55.

73. J. B. Scott, The Spanish Origin of International Law 78 (1934); *see also* J. Norgren, Protection of What Rights They Have: Original Principles of Federal Indian Law 64 N. D. L. Rev. 73, 77 nn. 12–17 (1988); R. A. Williams, Jr., The Medieval and Renaissance Origins of the Status of the American Indian in Western Legal Thought, 57 So. Cal. L. Rev. 1, 68 (1983); Rethinking the Trust Doctrine in Federal Indian Law, 98 Harv. L. Rev. 422, 424 (1984); H. Krieger, Principles of the Indian Law and the Act of June 18, 1934, in 3 Geo. Wash. L. Rev. 279, 288 (1935); F. S. Cohen, The Spanish Origin of Indian Rights in the Law of the United States, 31 Geo. L. Rev. 1, 17 (1942).

74. C. Toussaint, Trusteeship System of the United Nations (1956); *see also* Rethinking the Trust Doctrine in Federal Indian Law, 98 Harv. L. Rev. 422, 425 (1984); A. Beverridge, The Life of John Marshall 10–12 (1919); Who Was Who in America, Historical Volume 1607–1896, at 404 (rev. ed. 1967).

75. *Id.*; *see also* Y. El-Ayouty, The United Nations and Decolonization (1971); E. Sady, The United Nations and Dependent Peoples (1956).

76. The domestic trust relationship in the Western Hemisphere has deviated from the trust relationship first envisaged by Victoria. It now appears to be modeled after the regime of tutelage derived from Roman law (ST/HR/SER.A/11, at 6). Under Roman law, "children were things for their father, and he was in legal possession of them": S. W. Dyde, Hegel's Philosophy of Right 50 (1890). The treatment of Indians as incompetent wards is one of the aspects of the domestic trust that Indians are trying to have changed: *see* U.N. Doc. E/CN.4/Sub. 2/NGO/98, reprinted in 13 Akwesasne Notes, no. 4, at 21–22 (Autumn 1981); Felix S. Cohen, writing in 1942, found this wardship language to be susceptible to over a thousand different meanings: F. S. Cohen, *supra* note 58, at 170 n. 289.

77. 30 U.S. 1, 26 (1831).

78. *Id.* at 17.

79. *Id.* at 25.

80. *Id.* at 15.

81. 31 U.S. (6 Pet.) 515 (1832).

82. *Cherokee Nation v. Georgia*, 30 U.S. (5 Pet.) 1, 49 (1831).

83. J. Burke, The Cherokee Cases: A Study in Law, Politics, and Morality, 21 Stan. L. Rev. 500, 510 (1969); *see also* U. B. Phillips, Georgia and State Rights 66–68 (1968).

84. F. S. Cohen, *supra* note 58, at 55.

85. 31 U.S. (6 Pet.) 515, 536 (1832).

86. *Id.* at 538.

87. *Id.* at 560.

88. *Id.* at 542–43.

89. *Id.* at 559.

90. *Id.* at 544.

91. *Id.* at 546.

92. *Id.* at 556–61.

93. *Id.* at 556.

94. *Id.* at 557.

95. J. P. Kinney, A Continent Lost—A Civilization Won 71 (1975); *see also* A. M. Josephy, Red Power: The American Indians Fight for Freedom 32 (1971); *cf.* R. N. Satz, American Indian Policy in the Jacksonian Era 60 n. 31 (1975); S. P. McSloy, American Indians and the Constitution: An Argument for Nationhood, 14 Am. Ind. L. Rev. 139 (1989).

96. R. L. Barsh & J. Y. Henderson, *supra* note 19, at 60–61.

97. *McClanahan v. Arizona State Tax Commission*, 411 U.S. 164; *see also* W. Walters, Review Essay: Preemption, Tribal Sovereignty, and *Worcester v. Georgia*, 62 Ore. L. Rev. 127 (1983).

98. *See* Appendix 2; *see also* Rethinking the Trust Doctrine in Federal Indian Law, 98 Harv. L. Rev. 422, 429, 439 (1984).

99. Indian Tribes, *supra* note 62, at 27–28, *see also* N. Carter, Race and Power Politics as Aspects of Federal Guardianship over American Indians: Land Related Cases 1887–1924, 4 Am. Ind. L. Rev. 197 (1976).

100. *Lone Wolf v. Hitchcock*, 187 U.S. 553 (1903).

Treaties with Indians were viewed as ruses, and violated with complete unscrupulousness. . . . United States policy . . . drifted in the middle of the nineteenth century to a policy of the destruction of all Indian organisation. . . . It became—and was actually called officially—a policy of liquidation applied to Indian properties and Indian life.

J. Collier, America's Colonial Record 31 (1947), cited in Sir Alan Burns, In Defence of Colonies: British Colonial Territories in International Affairs 30 n. 4 (1957). *Cf.* J. Crawford, The Creation of States in International Law 182 (1979).

101. All treaty law is based on the principle of *pacta sunt servanda*, or the belief that it is binding on the parties to it and must be performed by them in good faith: Vienna Convention on the Law of Treaties, art. 26 (1969).

102. *United States v. Mitchell*, 445 U.S. 535 (1980); *cf. Tito v. Waddell*, 2 W.L.R. 496 (1977).

103. W. G. Rice, Jr., The Position of the American Indian in the Law of the United States, 16 J. Comp. Leg., ser. III, at 78, 81 (1934), cited in F. S. Cohen, *supra* note 58, at 89; *see also* M. Savage, Native Americans and the Constitution: The Original Understanding, 16 Am. Ind. L. Rev. 57 (1991).

104. *United States v. Kagama*, 118 U.S. 375, 384 (1886).

105. 18 U.S.C. sect. 1162 *et seq.*

106. *United States v. McBratney*, 104 U.S. 621 (1881); *Oliphant v. Suquamish Indian Tribe*, 435 U.S. 191 (1978); Indigenous Law and the State (B. W. Morse & G. R. Woodman eds. 1988).

107. D. Getches, D. Rosenfelt & C. Wilkinson, *supra* note 49, at 299.

108. *Williams v. Lee*, 358 U.S. 217 (1959); *see also* C. F. Wilkinson, American Indians, Time, and the Law (1987).

109. *Id.* at 221–22.

110. "The True basis of guardianship, as revealed by the cases between 1887 and 1924, was nothing more than raw power applied to a subjugated people who were considered to be racially inferior": N. Carter, *supra* note 99, at 225.

111. Indian Tribes, *supra* note 99, at 33–35; R. L. Barsh & J. Y. Henderson, *supra* note 19, at 185–86.

112. 348 U.S. 272 (1955); *see also* R. T. Coulter, The Denial of Legal Remedies to Indian Nations under U.S. Law, 13 Am. Ind. J. 5, 7 (1987).

113. *Id.* at 277.

114. *Id.*; *see also* E. S. Cahn, Our Brother's Keeper: The Indian in White America 156–62 (1969); American Indian Policy Review Commission Final Report, submitted to Congress 129 (May 17, 1977) (re conflict of interest).

115. *Id.* at 289.

116. *Id.* at 279. Emphasis added.

117. R. T. Coulter, *supra* note 112, at 5, 7.

118. 348 U.S. 272, 89–90 (1955).

119. N. J. Newton, *supra* note 24, at 1242–44; *see also* K. Kickingbird & K. Ducheneaux, One Hundred Million Acres 34 (1973); J. Youngblood Henderson, Unraveling the Riddle of Aboriginal Title, 5 Am. Ind. L. Rev. 75, 115–16 (1977) (noting that conquest generally extinguishes external sovereignty only and not rights to private property); The Aggressions of Civilization: Federal Indian Policy since the 1880's, at 194–95 (S. Cadwalader & V. DeLoria, Jr., eds. 1984).

120. F. S. Cohen, Original Indian Title, 32 Minn. L. Rev. 28, 34–35 (1948); *see also* N. J. Newton, *supra* note 24, at 1215 n. 1.

121. H. Wheaton, Elements of International Law (W. B. Lawrence ed. 1866).

122. 348 U.S. 272, 275; *see also* J. C. Wise & V. DeLoria, Jr., The Red Man in the New World Drama: A Politico-Legal Study with a Pageantry of American Indian History 35–44 (1971).

123. A. K. Weinberg, Manifest Destiny 34, 97 (1935).

124. *Tee-Hit-Ton Indians v. United States, supra* note 112 at 283 n. 17.

125. F. S. Cohen, *supra* note 120, at 28, 46.

126. *Id.*

127. *Id.* at 34–35; Cohen cites Jefferson as his authority:

> That the lands of this country were taken from them by conquest, is not so general a truth as is supposed. I find in our historians and records, repeated proofs of purchase, which cover a considerable part of the lower country; and many more would doubtless be found on further search. The upper country, we know, has been acquired altogether by purchases made in the most unexceptional form.

T. Jefferson, Notes on the State of Virginia, 1781–1785, repr. in P. Padover, The Complete Jefferson 632 (1943).

128. See *supra* text accompanying note 118.

129. F. S. Cohen, *supra* note 58, at 288.

130. F. S. Cohen, *supra* note 120, at 58; *Referring to Alcea Band of Tillamooks v. United States* 341 U.S. 48, 71 S. Ct. 552, 95 L. Ed. 738 (1951).

131. 417 U.S. 535 (1974).

132. *Id.* at 554.

133. *Id.* at 552.

134. *Id.* at 553 n. 24.

135. Section 12 of the Indian Reorganization Act, 25 U.S.C., section 472, provides:

> The Secretary of the Interior is directed to establish standards of health, age, character, experience, knowledge, and ability for Indians who may be appointed, without regard to civil-service laws to the various positions maintained, now or hereafter, by the Indian office, in the administration of functions or services affecting any Indian tribe. Such qualified Indians shall hereafter have the preference to appointment to vacancies in any such positions.

136. United States Supreme Court cases indicate a "virulently racist attitude": Rethinking the Trust Doctrine, *supra* note 98, at 426. "Slaves and Indians were those unfortunate men essentially outside of America's civil society, but ruled by it": R. K. Faulkner, The Jurisprudence of John Marshall 58 (1968). "Their position demanded the strictest interpretation of the legal definition of Indians as 'wards of the nation,' and of the racialist characterization of the Indians as permanent inferiors": R. Slotkin, The Fatal Environment: The Myth of the Frontier in the Age of Industrialization 1800–1890, at 320–21 (1985). *See also* I. Harvey, Constitutional Law: Congressional Plenary Power over Indian Affairs—A Doctrine Rooted in Prejudice, 10 Am. Ind. L. Rev. 117 (1982); J. Burke, The Cherokee Cases: A Study in Law, Politics, and Morality, 21 Stan. L. Rev. 500 (1969); R. F. Weston, Racism in U.S. Imperialism (1972); W. Washburn, The Moral and Legal Justification for Dispossessing the Indians (1959).

137. *Ex parte Crow Dog*, 109 U.S. 556, 557 (1883); *see also* S. L. Harring, Crow Dog's Case: A Chapter in the History of Tribal Sovereignty, 14 Am. Ind. L. Rev. 191 (1989).

138. *Oliphant v. Suquamish Indian Tribe* 435 U.S. 191, 211 (1978); *see also*

R. A. Williams, Jr., The Algebra of Federal Indian Law: The Hard Trail of Decolonizing and Americanizing the White Man's Indian Jurisprudence, 1986 Wis. L. Rev. 219, 266–74 (1986).

139. Indian Tribes, *supra* note 99, at 16–17; *see also* F. Prucha, The Indians in American Society from the Revolutionary War to the Present 2–4 (1984); F. Prucha, Indian Policy in the United States: Historical Essays (1981).

140. R. A. Trennert, Alternatives to Extinction 1 (1975); *see also* M. B. Hooker, Legal Pluralism: An Introduction to Colonial and Neo-Colonial Laws 312–31 (1957).

141. Northwest Ordinance, July 13, 1787, ch. 8, 1 Stat. 50, art. III.

142. F. S. Cohen, *supra* note 73, at 12; *see also* J. Norgren, Protection of What Rights They Have: Original Principles of Federal Indian Law, 64 N. Dak. L. Rev. 73, 80–81 (1988).

143. F. Prucha, American Policy in the Formative Years: Indian Trade and Intercourse Acts, 1790–1834 (1962); J. M. Sosin, The Revolutionary Frontier 1763–1783, at 82 (1967).

144. 25 U.S.C. section 177.

145. W. Willoughby, The Constitutional Law of the United States 294–95 (1910).

146. Indian Tribes, *supra* note 99, at 19; L. Priest, Uncle Sam's Stepchildren 28 (1942); R. H. Keller, American Protestantism and United States Indian Policy 149 (1983); R. Berkhofer, Jr., The White Man's Indian 149–51 (1978); R. Berkhofer, Jr., Salvation and the Savage: An Analysis of Protestant Missions and American Indian Response 1787–1862 (1972); R. Pierce Beaver, Church, State, and the American Indians: Two and a Half Centuries of Partnership in Missions between Protestant Churches and Government (1966).

147. 7 Encyclopedia of Public International Law, Monroe Doctrine 339 (1984); *see also* M. Kryzanek, U.S.–Latin American Relations (1990); A. Thomas & A. Thomas, Jr., The Organization of American States and the Monroe Doctrine—Legal Implications, 30 La. L. Rev. 541 (1969–70). The Monroe Doctrine was mentioned in Article 21 of the League of Nations Covenant: M. F. Lindley, The Acquisition and Government of Backward Territory in International Law, Being a Treatise on the Law and Practice Relating to Colonial Expansion 77–79 (1926). The Monroe Doctrine "implied or carried with it, an assumption of superiority, and of a right to exercise some kind of protectorate over the countries to whose territory that doctrine applies": E. Dickson, The Equality of States in International law 178 (1920, repr. 1977).

148. W. Washburn, The Assault on Indian Tribalism: The General Allotment Law (Dawes Act) of 1887, at 4–5 (1975).

149. R. Berkhofer, Salvation and the Savage (1967).

150. Indian Tribes, *supra* note 99, at 18.

151. F. Prucha, *supra* note 143, at 224.

152. R. Ericson & D. R. Snow, The Indian Battle for Self-Determination, 58 Ca. L. Rev. 445 (1970).

153. L. French, The Death of a Nation, 4 Am. Ind. J., no. 6, at 6 (1978); A. Debo, And Still the Waters Run: The Betrayal of the Five Civilized Tribes (1940).

154. F. S. Cohen, *supra* note 58, at 45–46.

155. 25 U.S.C. section 71.

156. *In re Heff*, 197 U.S. 488 (1905); *see also* R. T. Devlin, The Treaty Power

under the Constitution of the United States, Chapter XII Treaties with Indians 404–19 (1908).

157. F. S. Cohen, *supra* note 58, at 67; *United States v. Sante Fe Pac. R. Co.*, 314 U.S. 329 (C.C.A. 1940).

158. U.S. Congress, 1 American Indian Policy Review Commission, Final Report Submitted to Congress 3 (1977).

159. *Lone Wolf v. Hitchcock*, 187 U.S. 553 (1903).

160. C. Scott, Administrative Law: Self-Determination and the Consent Power: The Role of the Government in Indian Decisions, 5 Am. Ind. L. Rev. 195 (1977); U.S. Congress, *supra* note 158, at 59–60.

161. E. McGimpsey, Indian Tribal Sovereignty, in 2 Studies in American Indian Law 14–15 (Johnson ed. 1971); G. W. Rice, Indian Rights: 25 U.S.C. Section 71: The End of Indian Sovereignty or a Self-Limitation of Contractual Ability? 5 Am. Ind. L. Rev. 239, 246 (1977).

162. 25 U.S.C. section 331, *et seq.*; *see also* F. E. Leupp, The Indian and His Problem 61 (1910); H. Fritz, The Movement for Indian Assimilation 1860–1890 (1963); L. Priest, Uncle Sam's Stepchildren 177 (1942); P. Gates, Indian Allotments Preceding the Dawes Act (1971).

163. W. Willoughby, *supra* note 145, at 310.

164. 25 U.S.C. section 348 (1970).

165. W. Washburn, *supra* note 148, at 39 (dissenting opinion of Representatives R. Errett, C. Hooker, and T. Gunter).

166. *Id.* at 47.

167. F. S. Cohen, *supra* note 58, at 216.

168. A. Debo, *supra* note 153, at 91; *see also* W. Washburn, *supra* note 148; J. Kinney, A Continent Lost—A Civilization Won (1975).

> After the passage of the Dawes Act in 1887, the agricultural affairs of the Indians rapidly deteriorated. The allotment of individual landholdings was a travesty of justice, because the vast majority of Indian lands were located in the semiarid Great Plains and the arid West. There, allotments of 160 acres or fewer were totally inadequate to enable the Indians to become self-sufficient farmers.

R. Hurt, Indian Agriculture in America 231 (1987).

169. John Collier, Memorandum, Hearing on H.R. 7920 before the House Commission on Indian Affairs, 73d Cong., 2d Sess., 16–18 (1934), cited in D. Getches, D. Rosenfelt & C. Wilkinson, *supra* note 49, at 74; *see also* K. Kickingbird & K. Ducheneaux, *supra* note 119, at 14–31.

170. D. Getches, D. Rosenfelt & C. Wilkinson, *supra* note 49, at 72–77.

171. W. Willoughby, *supra* note 145, at 317–18; A. Debo, *supra* note 153.

172. W. Willoughby, *supra* note 145, at 296.

173. 8 U.S.C. section 1401(a)(2); *see also* F. S. Cohen, *supra* note 58, at 153.

174. F. S. Cohen, *supra* note 58, at 153–59; V. DeLoria, Jr., Behind the Trial of Broken Treaties, An Indian Declaration of Independence 166–68 (1974).

175. T. Wyckoff, The Navajo Nation Tomorrow—51st State, Commonwealth, or . . . ? 5 Am. Ind. L. Rev. 267 (1977); *see also* The Navajo Nation: An American Colony, A Report of the United States Commission on Civil Rights (September 1975).

176. Tribal Self-Government and the Indian Reorganization Act of 1934, 70 Mich. L. Rev. 955 (1972).

177. 25 U.S.C. section 476.

178. The Jury's Report: Report of the Fourth Russell Tribunal on the Rights of the Indians of the America's November 1980, 12 Akwesasne Notes, no. 5, at 31–35 (Winter 1980); *see also* Communication to the United Nations Commission on Human Rights and Sub-Commission On Prevention of Discrimination and Protection of Minorities, Violations of the Human Rights of the Mohawk People by the United States of America, The Right to Self-Determination, March 11, 1980; *Id.* Violations of the Human Rights of the Hopi People by the United States of America, The Right of Self-Determination and the Right to Own Land, March 11, 1980 (submitted by the Indian Law Resources Center).

179. C. F. Wilkinson, The Evolution of the Termination Policy, 5 Am. Ind. L. Rev. 139 (1977).

180. D. Getches, D. Rosenfelt & C. Wilkinson, *supra* note 49, at 86.

181. *Id.* at 107; *see also* J. F. Preloznik & S. A. Felsenthal, The Menominee Struggle to Maintain Their Tribal Assets and Protect Their Treaty Rights Following Termination, 51 N.D.L. Rev. 53 (1974); The American Indian Policy Review Commission has recommended that Congress adopt legislation permitting the restoration of all terminated tribes: *See* U.S. Congress, *supra* note 158, ch. 13.

182. 25 U.S.C. section 450 *et seq.*

183. E. McGimpsey, *supra* note 161, at 36; R. Barsh & J. Henderson, *supra* note 19, at 280. As a matter of American constitutional law, Indians not taxed are still excluded from some constitutional protections: U.S. Const., art. I, section 2. *See also* J. White, Taxing Those They Found Here (1972); U.S. Census Bureau, Report on Indians Taxed and Indians Not Taxed in the United States (except Alaska) at the Eleventh Census: 1890 (1894).

184. United States' Response to the Study of the Problem of Discrimination against Indigenous Populations, *supra* note 1, at 12.

7

Overview of Theories Justifying Colonization

The foregoing review of the treatment of indigenous peoples by both domestic and international law shows a constant tension between two basic positions. One position limits the application of general principles of international and natural law to Christian-European peoples, while having special rules that apply to other peoples.[1] The other basic position, while recognizing the existence of this historical limitation, attempts to expand the application of the principles of international law to all peoples regardless of religion, civilization, race, or any other distinction. Existing law is a compromise between these two positions.

At this point, it may be appropriate to explore the reasoning used to justify colonial expansion. Both France, with regard to its overseas territories, and the United States, with respect to the Indians, had policies of colonial expansion by means of assimilation. Both governments perverted the theory of natural law to justify colonial expansion while denying the natural right of the native peoples to self-determination.[2] However, both nations have now rejected assimilation policies because these have been recognized to be immoral.

France also rejected the "salt-water fallacy," noting that from a historical perspective, it was indefensible to assert that colonization only occurred over salt water and not overland.[3] It found that all colonial theories were basically justifications for the domination by one people over another.

Colonization was seen as the survival of the fittest in the struggle over the limited resources of the world.[4]

In response to the position that as a result of the equality of all races, no one race had the right to interfere with the activities of another, France asserted that

> no race had the right to refuse economic intercourse with others, nor did it have the right to leave its land undeveloped. . . . Rousseau's noble savage uncorrupted by civilization should not be allowed to prevail where such conditions exist. . . . Rather the law of natural selection must play its part unhindered.
>
>> The progressive extinction of inferior races by civilized ones, or, if one does not like these words, the destruction of the weak by the strong, is the very condition of progress.[5]

Another Frenchman, Charles Régismanset, was "desirous of removing all justifications from imperialism and of revealing it as he saw it: the result of naked force."[6] The history of colonial expansion was nothing more than "a series of acts in which the stronger party expropriated the land of the weaker."[7] Further, neither religious nor humanitarian pretexts were valid motivations "when the real goal is one of conquest. The foolishness of assimilation is clear: one race cannot assimilate another; it has only two choices: subjugation or annihilation."[8]

Another French writer, Jules Harmand,

> explained all colonial activity as the result of the natural instinct toward expansion. . . . [M]an, like all animals, seeks to expand in order to assure his self-preservation. . . . [T]his instinct toward preservation was nothing more than Nietzsche's will to power. . . . In primitive societies the will to power appears in all its simplicity and brutality, but in more advanced societies it is so well hidden by pretenses and elaborated motives that it is not initially seen. . . . Until mankind finds some sort of lasting equilibrium[,] . . . the expansion of nations can only be accomplished by means of continuous violence. Force alone will prevail.[9]

Harmand used Roman overland colonization as an example of the fallacy of attempting assimilation where the peoples involved were separated by a wide cultural gap: "Where important differences did exist the Romans never attempted a policy of assimilation but rather employed a system comparable to that of the modern protectorate."[10] This led the French to reject assimilation, because "all conquests are immoral. . . . To rob a people of its independence is an immoral act."[11]

American colonial expansion was justified on religious and utilitarian pretexts. The "white race" had a superior right to the land occupied by an "inferior race," "because [whites] used it according to the intentions of the CREATOR."[12] "America's incorporation of all adjacent lands was the virtually inevitable fulfillment of a moral mission delegated to the nation by Providence itself."[13] The Puritans were the first to use theology to justify their trespass. The biblical command to till the earth was used to justify the dispossession of the Indians, even though "the Scriptures . . . contain no statement whatever that the agriculturist has the right to expropriate those who do not till [the earth]."[14]

Vattel's theories lie at the foundation of the justifications used to dispossess Indians in American case law. A closer examination of these theories must be made in order to determine their validity. One of Vattel's assumptions was that Indians were hunters and whites were cultivators. This assumption is highly questionable since many Indian groups had a highly developed system of agriculture.[15]

However, even assuming the validity of Vattel's hunter/agriculturist distinction for the sake of argument, his theory was subject to further limitations. Vattel made the right of expropriation contingent on being " 'too closely pent up'; he declare[d] that those unable to cultivate their land have no right to expand."[16] There is no historical evidence that European colonizers were motivated by the lack of cultivatable land in Europe. Today, England has over ten times the population it had in 1700 and it is still self-sufficient in food. Thus, the application of Vattel's theories to English colonies in the sixteenth century appears to be patently fraudulent.[17] Moreover, if Vattel's theory of "international communism" is valid, could colonization by the Asians to less densely populated areas be justified today?

Vattel's theory was also subject to the limitation that the colonizers must confine themselves within just bounds.[18] Land could be expropriated from "backward peoples only when their lands are actually and immediately needed for world advantage, not merely for land hunger."[19] The European colonizers clearly expropriated far more territory than they had the capacity to cultivate.[20] Even today there are millions upon millions of acres of national forests, parks, and wilderness areas in the United States. White farmers are even paid not to grow crops.

Yet another limitation on Vattel's theory is that the hunters usurped only "more extensive territories than with a reasonable share of labour they would have occasion for."[21] Although Indians could be "confined within narrower limits," they could not be totally dispossessed because this would violate their "natural right to inhabit [the land], and to derive from it whatever is necessary for their subsistence, and suitable to their wants."[22] In numerous cases, Indians were completely dispossessed. Thus, the inconsistencies between the theory and practice of Vattel's "doctrine of beneficent territorial utilization" demonstrated that the pretended interest in the use of the soil was merely an interest in dispossession.[23]

In addition, the application of Vattel's theories by the U.S. Supreme Court takes on further racial overtones:

Gardens, orchards, and grain fields attested to [the Cherokees'] agricultural skill. Indians had no desire to abandon their own culture. The Cherokee who made a last stand against the English in 1760 were such expert farmers that William Wirt, their legal defender in the controversy over their later removal to the Far West in 1830, found whites fearful that Indian skills would prevent Georgia's occupation of Cherokee land. The Georgians insisted upon regarding the Cherokee as hunters and argued that these Indians "had no right to alter their condition to become husbandmen." This remarkable argument denies, of course, the right of the Cherokee to become farmers within the area of Georgian territory. Georgia's argument was carried forward until "it was made clear that, though the Georgian soil was destined to be tilled, it was destined to be tilled by the white man and not the Indian." Thus white racist rationale was twisted to justify taking lands occupied by the Cherokee, one of the great Indian people who had tilled the land for centuries.[24]

In *Cherokee Nation*, Chief Justice Marshall applied Vattel's theories to land actually cultivated by the Cherokees.[25] Thus, Indians continued to be treated as "wandering hordes" or a "race of hunters," despite their use of agriculture and their adoption of "civilized" ways.[26]

Felix S. Cohen, writing in 1951, expressed much the same sentiments:

[Before the Europeans came] to North America, this country was claimed by Indians who thought they owned it. Ever since the arrival of the first white immigrants, they have been devoting some of their finest legal talents to discovering defects in these Indian titles and, in that way, devising justifications for the removal of land, minerals, and timber from Indian ownership to white ownership, in the interest of progress. One of the most brilliant and ingenious justifications of this process is that which is given by Justice Jackson in his concurring opinion in [the] Northwest Shoshone case. He advances the theory that Indians were really communists, who did not understand or appreciate property rights. Ownership of land, he says, "meant no more to them than . . . sunlight and the west wind, and the feel of spring in the air. Acquisitiveness, which develops a law of real property, is an accomplishment only of the civilized." It follows, then, that the United States being civilized, is under no legal obligation to pay Indians when it takes away their homes, their timber, their fisheries, their water power, or anything else that might be needed for railroads, canneries, pulp companies, or other progressive organizations that appreciate property rights. In advancing this theory that civilized people have the right to relieve less civilized people of their possessions, Justice Jackson insists that the moral and the legal have nothing to do with each other.[27]

In more modern times, Vattel's theory has gone through another transformation. This transformation reveals the real utility of the theory:

It is thus a curiosity of the history of ideas that the same doctrine originated by the agriculturist to dispossess the huntsman was used ultimately by the industrialist to dispossess the agriculturist. But the jest is entirely on the darker races, the victims of the doctrine first as huntsmen and then as agriculturists.[28]

Hence, whatever rationale is used, the result is the same—the dispossession of indigenous peoples.

NOTES

1. *See supra* Chapter 1, note 2.
2. A. K. Weinberg, Manifest Destiny (1935).
3. R. Betts, Assimilation and Association in French Colonial Theory 102 (1961); *see also* R. Betts, Europe Overseas Phases of Imperialism 4 (1968).
4. R. Betts, Assimilation, *supra* note 3, at 94.
5. *Id.* at 95. Footnotes omitted.
6. *Id.* at 97.
7. *Id.* at 98.
8. *Id.* at 100.
9. *Id.* at 100–101.
10. *Id.* at 103.
11. *Id.*
12. A. K. Weinberg, *supra* note 2, at 73.
13. *Id.*
14. *Id.* at 76.
15. *Id.* at 85; *see also* C. Harvey, Agriculture of the American Indian: A Selected Bibliography (1979).
16. C. Harvey, *supra* note 15, at 78.
17. The Geographical Impact of Migration 69 (P. White & R. Woods eds. 1980).
18. *See* Chapter 2, text accompanying note 46 *supra.*
19. A. K. Weinberg, *supra* note 2, at 99.
20. *Id.* at 78–79.
21. *Id.* at 35.
22. *Id.*
23. *Id.* at 99.
24. W. Jacobs, Dispossessing the American Indian 148 (1972).
25. A. K. Weinberg, *supra* note 2, at 85.
26. *Cherokee Nation v. Georgia*, 30 U.S. (5 Pet.) 1, 21, 27 (1831).
27. F. S. Cohen, Judicial Ethics, in the Legal Conscience 162–3 (1960). First printed in 12 Ohio St. L.J. 3 (1951), cited in S. M. Feldman, Felix S. Cohen and His Jurisprudence: Reflections on Federal Indian Law 35 Buf. L. Rev. 479, 501 (1986), quoting *Northwestern Band of Shoshone Indians v. United States*, 324 U.S. 335, 358 (1945).
28. A. K. Weinberg, *supra* note 2, at 94; *see also* R. A. Williams, Jr., The Medieval and Renaissance Origins of the Status of the American Indian in Western Legal Thought, 57 So. Ca. L. Rev. 1, 5, and notes cited therein (1983).

8

Conclusion

Indian law can best be understood as a branch of international law. U.S. Supreme Court Chief Justice John Marshall said this in 1832,[1] and Felix S. Cohen said it in 1940.[2] This branch of international law has two further divisions. One, represented by positive law, treats Indians as an inferior race because of their perceived lack of "civilization" and because of their religion. The other division, which is based on human rights principles, calls for the reform of existing international law to apply the same rules to Indian nations that are applied to non-Indian nations.

The development of international law can be seen dramatically from the perspective of the impact that the discovery of the Western Hemisphere had on it. After the Americas were discovered by the Europeans, they were ruled by kings, queens, and popes, who claimed the authority to rule based on divine right. Through exposure to the democratic indigenous governments of the Western Hemisphere, writers on natural law created a revolution in thinking about the nature of government. Based on the writings of Victoria, Las Casas, Locke, Rousseau, Jefferson, and others, the notion developed that all peoples and all nations are created equal and that all just government is based on the consent of the governed.

Since that time, international law has evolved through the replacement of the old rules based on divine right by those based on principles of natural law. However, the transition is still not complete today. International law as it is still applied to indigenous peoples today is a remnant of those principles based on the natural slave theory of Aristotle justifying overland colonization and the use of force to preserve the status quo.

Originally, the Greeks discriminated against all non-Greeks whom they colonized, both overland and overseas. Based on this precedent, the emerging European Law of Nations replaced this with discrimination against all non-Catholic nations. The Protestant Reformation replaced this with discrimination against non-Christian nations. Originally, much of the European discrimination was directed against Arab and Jewish peoples. The discovery of the Western Hemisphere resulted in the extension of this discrimination to the indigenous nations and peoples of the Western Hemisphere. The European invaders—based on the expertise they developed during the Spanish Inquisition—carried out forced conversions on an unprecedented scale.[3] They also carried out the largest mass genocide in the history of the world against the indigenous peoples of the Western Hemisphere.[4]

The primary focus of international law has always been the regulation of disputes between members, while the secondary focus has always been the treatment of nonmembers. The nonmembers were viewed as an obstacle to the exploitation of the land and natural resources that were "discovered" by the members. Much of the rest of the development of international law can be seen as a refinement of these principles.

In the early stages of the development of international law, the treatment of the indigenous peoples was a matter exclusively within the domestic jurisdiction of the colonizing nation, and the rule that might makes right prevailed. Gradually, the treatment of indigenous peoples became a matter of international concern: first in theory, and then in practice. Victoria laid the theoretical foundation for the development of the international trust, but these principles were not implemented until much later, and only on a limited scale.

The first development in the international treatment of indigenous peoples did not occur until the abolition of slavery in the Congo Basin in 1885. All that has changed since that time is the progressive removal of both subject matter and geographic limitations placed on the treatment of indigenous peoples. Gradually, the defense of "matters essentially within the domestic jurisdiction" of United Nations member states has virtually disappeared.

With the founding of the League of Nations in 1919, the international protection of, and concern for, indigenous peoples was crystallized in the Mandate system and Native Inhabitants clause. Upon the signing of the United Nations Charter in 1945, these responsibilities were taken over under the Trusteeship system and Non-Self-Governing Territories provision. Although in theory they were intended to apply to the indigenous peoples of the Western Hemisphere, these peoples have been excluded through the application of a geographic limitation on what are supposed to be universally recognized human rights.

The next step that should be taken by the international legal system to remove the legacy of five hundred years of discrimination is the passage of a Universal Declaration on the Rights of Indigenous Nations and Peoples that recognizes the rights of indigenous peoples as equal to the rights of all other peoples. The first and most important right of all peoples is the right of self-determination, which necessarily involves the element of self-determination over natural resources. The definition of self-determination in international law has a long history. It is not something that needs to be invented by the United Nations Working Group on Indigenous Populations. Its origins can be traced to the U.S. Declaration of Independence and the French Declaration of the Rights of Man. It has been a cardinal principle of the United Nations since its inception and is enshrined in the Charter of the United Nations. Since the charter has gone into effect, further developments in the principle of self-determination have taken place:

> 6. The General Assembly first recognized "the right of peoples and nations to self-determination" as a fundamental human right in resolution 421 D (V) of 4 December 1950. . . .
>
> 7. The Assembly, in resolution 545 (VI) of 5 February 1952, decided "to include in the International Covenant or Covenants on Human Rights an article on the right of all peoples and nations to self-determination in reaffirmation of the principle enunciated in the Charter of the United Nations." It further decided that:
>
>> This article shall be drafted in the following terms: "All peoples shall have the right of self-determination," and shall stipulate that all States, including those having responsibility for the administration of Non-Self-Governing Territories, should promote the realization of that right, in conformity with the Purposes and Principles of the United Nations, and that States having responsibility for the administration of Non-Self-Governing Territories should promote the realization of that right in relation to the peoples of such Territories.
>
> 8. In resolution 637 A (VII) of 16 December 1952, the General Assembly, recognizing that "the right of peoples and nations to self-determination is a prerequisite to the full enjoyment of all fundamental human rights." . . .
>
> To States Members of the United Nations responsible for the administration of Non-Self-Governing and Trust Territories it recommended that they should "take practical steps, pending the realization of the right of self-determination and in preparation thereof, to ensure the direct participation of the *indigenous populations* in the legislative and executive organs of government of those Territories, and to prepare them for complete self-government or independence.[5]

In 1966, the precise definition of self-determination according to international law was set in concrete with the passage of the International Covenant on Economic, Social, and Cultural Rights and the International Covenant on Civil and Political Rights. The language of Part I, Article 1, of both covenants reads:

1. All peoples have the right of self-determination. By virtue of that right they freely determine their political status and freely pursue their economic, social and cultural development.
2. All peoples may, for their own ends, freely dispose of their natural wealth and resources without prejudice to any obligations arising out of international economic co-operation, based upon the principle of mutual benefit, and international law. In no case may a people be deprived of its own means of subsistence.
3. The States Parties to the present Covenant, including those having responsibilities for the administration of Non-Self-Governing and Trust Territories, shall promote the realization of the right of self-determination, and shall respect that right, in conformity with the provisions of the Charter of the United Nations.[6]

The language that should be contained in a Universal Declaration of the Rights of Indigenous Peoples should read:

1. All *indigenous* peoples have the right of self-determination. By virtue of that right they freely determine their political status and freely pursue their economic, social and cultural development.
2. All *indigenous* peoples may, for their own ends, freely dispose of their natural wealth and resources without prejudice to any obligations arising out of international economic co-operation, based upon the principle of mutual benefit, and international law. In no case may a people be deprived of its own subsistence.
3. The States Parties to the present Covenant, including those having responsibility for the administration of Non-Self-Governing and Trust Territories, shall promote the realization of the right of self-determination, and shall respect that right, in conformity with the provisions of the Charter of the United Nations. [emphasis added]

The drafting process of the Working Group on Indigenous Populations reminds one of George Orwell's *Animal Farm*[7]: One day, the words "All Animals are equal" are written on the side of the barn, but the next day the slogan reads, "Some Animals are more equal than others." The UN Working Group on Indigenous Populations' current version of the draft declaration should really be called the Universal Declaration of the Rights of United Nations Members States over the Backwards Races or the Cinquecentennial Declaration of Limitations on the Human Rights of Indigenous Peoples by the Members of the United Nations.[8]

Some people believe that the next step should be the passage of a binding Covenant on the Human Rights of Indigenous Peoples.[9] The problems with this are (1) passage will not occur for many years, (2) the covenant would not have an effective enforcement mechanism unless there was an optional protocol that was ratified by all United Nations member states with indigenous populations, and (3) indigenous peoples would be stuck in a human rights system that is, at best, ineffective.

The Human Rights Commission of the United Nations does very little to actually stop violations of human rights. The commission has been described as "as a 'conspiracy of governments' to deprive people of their rights."[10] The United Nations has already indicated that it intends to funnel indigenous peoples into the minority "protections" system,[11] which proved to be totally ineffective during the Holocaust of World War II.[12] In other words, if this is the only avenue pursued by indigenous peoples, it will be a very long time before any changes are actually implemented.

On the other hand, the Non-Self-Governing Territories provision of the UN Charter has been one of the most effective instruments for the realization of the rights of indigenous peoples. The origins of the sacred trust, being derived from the relationship between the indigenous peoples of the Western Hemisphere and the Spanish government, is a topic that ought to be addressed by the working group and the United Nations. Efforts should be made by indigenous groups to focus the attention of the working group on the removal of the narrowly defined, "geographically separate" limitation that has been placed on the Non-Self-Governing Territories provision. This indefensible geographic restriction on what are supposed to be universal rights has been the only reason given by the international legal system for the denial of human rights to indigenous peoples. This is one of the great omissions in all the working group's discussions.

This geographic restriction on the human rights of indigenous peoples cannot be justified on any theoretical level of human rights analysis. Those who reject the idea of the application to indigenous peoples of the human rights principles of the sacred trust of civilization that are contained in the Non-Self-Governing Territories provision are basically expressing their opinion that there is nothing wrong with overland colonization and assimilation. This restriction cannot be justified on any level other than the continuation of the historical exclusion of the last remaining so-called "backward race"—Indians—from the circle of the Family of Nations. This is the key to understanding how existing law is racially discriminatory against the indigenous peoples of the Western Hemisphere.

The international obligations that United Nations member states assumed under the Non-Self-Governing Territories provision came into full force and effect upon the acceptance of membership. Many indigenous peoples in the Western Hemisphere live in well-defined, geographically separate (under any reasonable interpretation of that language), non-self-governing territories. They are commonly referred to as "reservations" in the United States and Canada and as "parks" in other parts of South America. The United Nations has said that it wants to see an end to colonialism "in all of its manifestations," and yet it is blind to this manifestation of colonialism. The United Nations perpetuates the myth of salt water colonialism. Although it has been rather successful in ending overseas colonialism, it has done everything possible to continue the prerogatives of the "overland colonization" of its member states.

Indigenous groups have argued that they are "peoples" within the meaning of the Non-Self-Governing Territories provision. At the first session of the working group, one indigenous delegation said: "Those peoples we call indigenous are nothing more than colonized peoples who were missed by the great wave of global decolonization following the second world war[,] . . . particularly where independence was granted, not to the original inhabitants of a territory, but to an intrusive and alien group newly arrived."[13] The United Nations has confined the scope of the Non-Self-Governing Territories provision to about two hundred million people, and there are now another two hundred million people living in non-self-governing territories who want to be recognized. The time is long overdue for the United Nations to recognize that human rights cannot be subject to geographic limitations.[14]

Concepts such as "nation building" and "territorial integrity" are nothing more than shibboleths used by United Nations member states to disguise the use of force against indigenous peoples. It is the United Nations that has failed to recognize the territorial integrity or political independence of one single indigenous nation in the entire Western Hemisphere, and not the other way around.[15] Clearly, the United Nations members have not lived up to their international legal obligations under any reasonable interpretation of the international trust provisions that were derived from the writings of Victoria. In fact, the narrower interpretation of the Non-Self-Governing Territories provision by the United Nations—when compared to the Native Inhabitants clause of the League of Nations Covenant—is one of the rare instances where international law has devolved rather than evolved. This is an area that must be continually addressed by indigenous peoples until something is done to apply these provisions to all non-self-governing territories as originally intended.

What is needed now is the admission of at least one indigenous nation of the Western Hemisphere into the United Nations so that it can act as an essential spokesperson for the injustices that indigenous peoples have endured since the European invasion of their hemisphere began five hundred years ago. Someone needs to speak out against the genocide that continues to be committed against a number of indigenous peoples today.[16] This includes actual physical genocide,[17] causing serious bodily harm,[18] deliberately inflicting on the group conditions of life calculated to bring about its physical destruction,[19] preventing births within the group,[20] and forcibly transferring children of the group to another group.[21] After this step is taken, the right of all of the indigenous groups in the Western

Hemisphere to self-determination must be recognized before the historical discrimination against them by the international legal system can finally be removed.

One of the great ironies of history is the fact that many European colonizers to the United States came to this country for religious freedom. Many of them have found it, yet they still deny recognition to numerous indigenous governments that are theocratic on the grounds that they are "heathens." In fact, many United Nations member states have routinely and forcibly removed these "heathen" governments from power and replaced them with Christian-dominated tribal councils.[22] This nonrecognition of the theocratic indigenous governments of the Western Hemisphere is one of the most deeply ingrained discriminations that they have suffered. There is no separation between their religion and their governments. Failure to recognize their governments is the same as failure to recognize their religions, and this greatly restricts their ability to freely exercise their indigenous religions.

Recent world events may have some impact on the development of the rights of indigenous peoples. The double standard that is applied to the indigenous peoples of the Western Hemisphere can be seen from the *Western Sahara* case. The UN General Assembly and the International Court of Justice recognized the right of a very small number of nomadic people to self-determination because of the development of intertemporal law. However, the same international legal system still applies a 1493 Papal bull to deny the entire indigenous population of the Western Hemisphere their right to self-determination. The enormity of the inconsistency between the treatment of these two groups of peoples is something that must be addressed by the United Nations.[23] The doctrine of two spheres is alive and well in the Western Hemisphere.

The breakup of the overland colonial empire of the Soviet Union was long overdue, as is the breakup of the overland colonial empires of the American Republics. The recognition of the Navajo Indian nation as an independent state is about as big a threat to the United States as the recognition of Moldavia was to the Soviet Union.[24] All that is lost is the right of the overland colonizers to exploit the people and the land that was colonized.

The ILO Convention of 1989 also must be condemned. Article 6, which does not require indigenous consent, is not acceptable. This provision continues the discriminatory treatment of indigenous peoples by members of the United Nations. A provision that violates such a fundamental and self-evident human rights principle simply cannot be justified.

Article 15 of the new ILO Convention, which denies the right of indigenous peoples to own subsurface natural resources, is a continuation of the racist doctrines based on Aristotle's natural slave theory, which states that only "civilized" people own or use such resources. This provision is merely a continuation of the notion that in 1992, indigenous peoples are merely wandering hordes of savages. This provision also pulls the carpet out from under the right of indigenous peoples to own land. It reduces their right to own land to a right to own only land that has no subsurface natural resources, and it allows nonindigenous peoples to interfere with indigenous peoples' surface rights. The new ILO Convention does not specify the depth of indigenous peoples' right to surface resources. Are they entitled to the top inch, or foot, or meter of soil? Apparently, their rights do not include the bones of their ancestors.[25] The whole idea is absurd and demonstrates how far beyond their area of competence the ILO wandered.[26]

Numerous other provisions in the 1989 ILO Convention, including those dealing with forced removal and not requiring indigenous consent, also violate these peoples' human rights. These provisions are again an extension of the "menagerie theory" of international law to indigenous peoples. Any just system of international law would not only recognize the right of indigenous peoples to self-determination and subsurface natural resources, it would also recognize their right to restitution for five hundred years of genocide, ethnocide, and theft of land and natural resources.

A number of commemorations are being planned for 1992. The pope and the Spanish king are planning a number of celebrations during the cinquecentennial of Columbus's voyage. The pope apparently believes that the end justifies the means, the ignominious forced conversions and genocide of the past five hundred years have been forgotten, and the current genocide that is occurring against the indigenous peoples of the Western Hemisphere is too small—by comparison—for his comment. Apparently, the discriminatory effect that the papal bull Inter Caetera has had on the development of international and domestic legal systems is also beyond his concern.[27] The Spanish king will also join the pope in celebrating the past colonial enterprises of his country, without showing any remorse for the millions upon millions of human beings that were slaughtered by his people in the process.

Indigenous peoples plan to celebrate 1992 as symbolizing five hundred years of resistance. Although they were denied any formal recognition of the event by the United Nations, they have continued their plans outside that organization. From 1492 until 1992, the international legal system has discriminated against them. Indigenous nations have not been recognized as full members of the Family of Nations because of their race and religion. In view of the continued unwillingness of members of the international legal system to recognize their rights as being equal to those of all other peoples, perhaps the indigenous peoples should refer to their celebrations as the first five hundred years of resistance.

Columbus died thinking that he had discovered India, and the indigenous peoples of the Western Hemisphere are still referred to by the misnomer "Indians." English is supposed to be the most expressive language on the planet, yet no English word has evolved to accurately describe these people. Would the rights of the indigenous peoples of the Western Hemisphere be any different if we called them "Human Beings"? Not a single indigenous nation of the Western Hemisphere is recognized as an equal member of the United Nations, and not a single indigenous language of the Western Hemisphere is spoken as the official language of a United Nations member state. After five hundred years, even though the Indians in India are recognized as equal members of the United Nations, the indigenous peoples of the Western Hemisphere are still the invisible race.

If Victoria were alive today, he would be surprised and disappointed by the impact of his writings on the development of international law. The fact that his writings on the international trust formed the basis for the decolonization of Africa, Asia, and the Pacific Islands would be very surprising. However, he would be astonished to see that these international trust responsibilities have not been applied to the indigenous peoples of the Western Hemisphere—the very people about whom he was writing.

The foregoing review demonstrates how the international legal system has created one system of law that applies to "civilized" peoples and another system that applies to the so-called "backwards races" or, in modern patois, "indigenous populations." In 1493, the rights of the indigenous population of the entire Western Hemisphere were ignored. In 1919, under the League of Nations, the rights of indigenous peoples were recognized, but nothing was done about them. In 1945, under the UN Charter, the rights of indigenous peoples were once again recognized but they were then defined out of existence through the adoption of a geographic limitation. With the establishment of the UN Working Group on Indigenous Populations, the United Nations once again was given an opportunity to redress the historical wrongs that have been perpetrated on the indigenous peoples of the Western Hemisphere. Unfortunately, once again it looks like the United Nations is unwilling to universalize the application of existing human rights standards to include indigenous peoples. International law continues to discriminate in favor of Christians and against the "heathens" of the Western Hemisphere.

Any talk of the recognition of the human rights of the indigenous peoples of the Western Hemisphere must begin and end with self-determination, which is an absolute prerequisite for the enjoyment of all other human rights. "[Some] of the most destructive and genocidal conflicts have been waged precisely in the repression of claims for greater autonomy or for independence by large, distinctive, and regionally separate peoples."[28] The working group has been presented with ample evidence of that fact at each and every one of its annual meetings. The struggle for the rights of indigenous peoples can be seen as a continuation of the replacement of the old rules of international law based on divine right and the use of force with those based on human rights principles.

The remedy to the discrimination that indigenous peoples have suffered is simple. All that is needed is the application of the Non-Self-Governing Territories provision of the UN Charter. That objective appears to be difficult to reach because United Nations member states want to retain their control over Indians, their land, and their natural resources. The fact that this violates the rights of the indigenous peoples is of little concern, since these rights have been violated for so long. A new world order based on principles of human rights is not something that is perceived to be in the short-term self-interest of United Nations member states, even though it is their best long-term hope for the future.

In conclusion, the international legal system does not now, and has never, recognized the human rights of the indigenous peoples of the Western Hemisphere. All that is required to recognize their human rights is the application of the Non-Self-Governing Territories provision. Rather than recognize and implement the human rights of indigenous peoples, the United Nations is continuing to implement refinements in the separate body of law that applies to them and has failed to provide any effective means for enforcing their rights. The institutionalized legal discrimination that these peoples have encountered since the writing of the papal bull Inter Caetera in 1493 continues. The denial of the right of the indigenous peoples of the Western Hemisphere to self-determination is merely a continuation of the doctrine of two spheres.

NOTES

1. *Worcester v. Georgia*, 31 U.S. (6 Pet.) 515 (1832).
2.

> In the first place, we must recognize that our Indian law originated, and can still be most clearly grasped, as a branch of international law, and that in the field of international law the basic concepts were all hammered out by the Spanish theological jurists of the sixteenth and seventeenth centuries, most notably by the author of the lectures *De Indis*, Francisco de Vitoria.

F. S. Cohen, The Spanish Origin of Indian Rights in the Law of the United States, 31 Geo. L. Rev. 1, 17 (1942). *See also* M. Savelle, Empires to Nations 138–43 (1974).

3.

> Inasmuch as the conversion of the Indians to Christianity was stated to be the principle aim of the Spanish conquerors, they have dissimulated the fact that only with blood and fire have the Indians been brought to embrace the Faith and to swear obedience to the kings of Castile or by threats of being slain or taken into captivity. As if the Son of God who died for each one of them would have countenanced such a thing! . . . Christ Jesus would have made no such demands on these peaceable infidels who cultivate the soil of their native lands.

Bartolome de Las Casas, The Devastation of the Indies: A Brief Account 17–18 (H. Briffault trans. 1974).

4. *Id.* at 12–13. Las Casas's estimates, which were based on firsthand experiences, were summarized as follows:

> Las Casas' opponents did not hesitate to make him responsible . . . for the irrationality of the genocide. There is no trusting his figures it was and still is said; they betray a medieval relationship to arithmetic. South and Central America never held 12, 15 or 20 million inhabitants during the time of the conquest; as in the reports of the crusaders the word "million" simply means many people. Such an approach has something repulsive about it from the outset. It would like to prove Las Casas a liar but let the murders [*sic*] go scot-free because they only killed 8, 5 or 3 million Indians instead of 20 million. That is the way the *National Zeitung* protects the German fascists, claiming that not 6 million Jews were killed but at most 5.
>
> Aside from the moral insanity manifested by such sophistry, it is also factually wrong. Two American scholars who have investigated the demographic conditions in old Mexico in recent years reached the conclusion that in the 30 years between Cortez's landing and the writing of the *Brief Account* the population of Central Mexico dwindled from 25 to roughly 6 million victims in Mexico alone; Las Casas names only 4.

M. van Nieuwstadt, A Dossier on the Extermination of the Indies in Present-Day Brazil, 143–76 (1974); *see also* B. de Las Casas, The Tears of the Indians: Being an Historical and True Account of the Cruel Massacres and Slaughters of Above Twenty Millions of Innocent People; Committed by the Spanish in the Islands of Hispaniola, Cuba, Jamaica, etc. As Also, in the Continent of Mexico, Peru, and Other Places of the West Indies, To the Total Destruction of Those Countries (J. Phillips trans., 1656); *see also* Chapter 1, note 33 *supra*, and notes 16–21 infra.

5. United Nations, United Nations Action in the Field of Human Rights 16–17 (1985) ST/HR/2/Rev. 2. Emphasis added.

6. International Covenant on Civil and Political Rights, Adopted and Opened for Signature, Ratification and Accession by General Assembly Resolution 2200 A (XXI) of 16 December 1966.

7. Flaws in the UN drafting process have been noted in the following two articles: T. Meron, The Meaning and Reach of the International Convention on the Elimination of All Forms of Racial Discrimination, 79 Am. J. Int'l. L. 283 (1985); and T. Meron, Reform of Lawmaking in the United Nations: The Human Rights Instance, 79 Am. J. Int'l. L. 664 (1985).

8. "The conventions do not recognize the independent political rights of Indigenous Peoples, but rather seek to merely impose obligations on existing nation-states in their relations with Indigenous Peoples": M. Jackson, Self-Determination—Two Views from the Front, On the Record, July 26, 1991, at 3.

9. R. Barsh, Current Developments, Indigenous Peoples: An Emerging Object of International Law, 80 Am. J. Int'l. L. 369, 378 (1986). "No new international legislation should be necessary; all that is required is the consistent application of existing norms to indigenous situations. Some indigenous groups strongly oppose the formulation of new and separate standards in fact, believing that this would constitute racial discrimination": *Cf.* R. Barsh, Indigenous Peoples and the Right to Self-Determination in International Law, in International Law and Aboriginal Human Rights 69 (B. Hocking ed. 1988).

10. D. Sidorsky, Essays on Human Rights: Contemporary Issues and Jewish Perspectives 30 (1979).

11. *Lovelace Case*, Report of the Human Rights Committee, GAOR 36th. Sess., Supp. 40(A/36/40), Annex XVII, 166–75, cited in The Rights of Peoples (J. Crawford ed. 1988), ch. 9, at 141, 152–54; *see also* O. Prounis, The Human Rights Committee: Toward Resolving the Paradox of Human Rights Law, 17 Colum. H.R.L. Rev. 103 (1985–86).

12. During a joint UN/OAS meeting, Secretary of State Henry Kissinger commented on the need for an effective international human rights system and the inadequacy of minority protections while failing to mention anything about the problems of indigenous peoples:

> The obscene and atrocious acts systematically employed to devalue, debase, and destroy human life during World War II vividly and ineradicable impressed the responsible peoples of the world with the enormity of the challenge to human rights. It was precisely to end such abuses and to provide moral authority in international affairs that a new system was forged after the war—globally in the United Nations and regionally in a strengthened inter-American system.

Secretary Kissinger's Statement at the U.N. Economic Commission for Latin America, Santiago, Chile, June 1976, Sixth General Assembly of the Organization of American States.

13. R. Barsh, Current Developments, *supra* note 9, at 375–76.

14. J. Donnelly, Universal Human Rights in Theory and Practice 152–54 (1989).

15. This point was clearly made to the working group by Howard Berman in 1991.

16. Genocide Convention, 9 December 1948:

> In the present Convention, genocide means any of the following acts committed with intent to destroy in whole or in part, a national, ethnical, racial, or religious group as such:
>
> (a) Killing members of the group;
>
> (b) Causing serious bodily or mental harm to members of the group;
>
> (c) Deliberately inflicting on the group conditions of life calculated to bring about its physical destruction in whole or in part;
>
> (d) Imposing measures intended to prevent births within the group;
>
> (e) Forcibly transferring children of the group to another group.
>
> See also Resolution 260-C (III) Application with respect to dependent territories, of the Convention on the Prevention and Punishment of the Crime of Genocide.
>
> The General Assembly recommends that Parties to the Convention on the Prevention and Punishment of the Crime of Genocide which administer dependent territories should take such measures as are necessary and feasible to enable the provisions of the Convention to be extended to those territories as soon as possible.

17. R. Strickland, Genocide at Law: An Historical and Contemporary View of the Native American Experience, 34 U. Kan. L. Rev. 713, 714 (1986) (estimates twenty-five million); Genocide in Paraguay (R. Arens ed. 1976). The Indian Law Resources Center in Washington, D.C., has been doing extensive work in this area.

18. R. Davis & M. Zannis, The Genocide Machine in Canada: The Pacification of the North 112 (1973); L. Kuper, Genocide: Its Political Use in the Twentieth Century (1981).

19. Resource Exploitation: The Cutting Edge of Genocide, 10 Akwesasne Notes, no. 2, at 9 (Late Spring 1978); Genocide in North America: The Violation of the Land and Human Rights of Native Peoples, Report to the UN Commission on Human Rights by the International Indian Treaty Council, International NGO Conference on Indigenous Peoples and the Land, 15–18 September 1981, Geneva, cited in 7 Human Rights Internet Reporter, no. 2, at 260 (1981); Zah Vows to Battle for Due Payment, 31 Navajo Times, no. 34, Aug. 22, 1991: Stewart Udall is attempting to obtain compensation for about two thousand Navajos from the federal government which failed to warn them of health dangers of working in uranium mines, after the federal courts denied relief because the uranium mining industry during that time was immune from suit; F. Abele, Confronting "Harsh and Inescapable Facts," in Sovereignty and Security in the Arctic 175–93 (E. J. Dojman ed. 1989); C. Cline, Pursuing Native American Rights in International Law Venues: A *Jus Cogens* Strategy after *Lyng v. Northwest Indian Cemetery Protection Association*, 42 Hast. L. J. 591, 627 (1991); D. Cycon, When Worlds Collide: Law, Development and Indigenous People, 25 New Eng. L. Rev. 761 (1990–91); "If examined in perspective, the disappearance of tribal cultures over much of the world in the past 150 years can be seen as the direct result of government exploitation of tribal resources for the benefit of industrial civilization": J. Bodley, Alternatives to Ethnocide: Human Zoos, Living Museums, and Real People, in Western Expansion and Indigenous Peoples: The Heritage of Las Casas 31, 36 (E. Sevilla-Casas ed. 1977). *See also* Resource Development and Indigenous Peoples: A Comparative Bibliography (J. Narby & S. Davis comps. 1983); *cf.* R. N. Farmer, Benevolent Aggression: The Necessary Impact of the Advanced Nations on Indigenous Peoples (1972).

20. Killing Our Future Sterilization and Experiments, 9 Akwesasne Notes, no. 1, at 4 (Early Spring 1977): Sterilization of Indian women was "generally not in compliance" with government regulations requiring informed consent, nor was misinformation or duress; *see also* Cook, Masterson & Trahant, Fraud in Indian Country, A Billion Dollar Betrayal, Arizona Republic, Oct. 4–11, 1987; and IHS Physicians Faulty or Frayed: Shortage Looms, Arizona Republic, Oct. 7, 1987, at A15, A18, col. 1., cited in R. A. Williams, Jr., Encounters on the Frontiers of International Human Rights Law: Redefining the Terms of Indigenous Peoples' Survival in the World, 1990 Duke L.J. 660, 692–93 n. 113; "In 1976 a GAO [General Accounting Office] study of four Indian Hospital Service facilities found that thousands of Indian women had been sterilized without their informed consent between 1973 and 1976": S. O'Brien, Federal Indian Policies and the International Protection of Human Rights, in American Indian Policy in the Twentieth Century 61 n. 46 (V. Deloria, Jr., ed. 1985).

21.

> [A]pproximately 25 to 35 percent of all American Indian children are separated from their families and placed in foster homes, adoptive homes, or institutions. In Minnesota, for example, one in every eight American Indian children under 18 years of age is living in an adopted home. Further, in 1971 to 1972, nearly one in every four American Indian children under one year of age was adopted.

G. McCartney, The American Indian Child-Welfare Crisis: Cultural Genocide or First Amendment Preservation? 7 Colum. Human Rights L. Rev. 529 (1975–76).

22. See *supra* text and notes, Chapter 3, note 29, and Chapter 6, note 177.

23. Declaration on Principles, at ch. 3 (R. Akkerman, P. Van Krieken & C. Pannenburg eds. 1977).

24. T. Wyckoff, The Navajo Nation Tomorrow—51st State, Commonwealth, or . . . ? 5 Am. Ind. L. Rev. 267 (1977); S. P. McSloy, American Indians and the Constitution: An Argument for Nationhood, 14 Am. Ind. L. Rev. 139 (1989); Native Power: The Quest for Autonomy and Nationhood of Indigenous Peoples (J. Brosted, J. Dahl, A. Gray, H. Gullov, G. Henriksen, J. Jorgensen & I. Kleivan eds. 1985); Indigenous Peoples and the Nation-State: "Fourth World" Politics in Canada, Australia, and Norway (N. Dyck ed. 1985). *See also* Y. Dinstein, Models of Autonomy (1981); H. M. Catudel, Jr., The Enclave Problem of Western Europe (1979) (found 255 enclaves to currently exist); Self-Determination—Two Views from the Front, On the Record, July 26, 1991, at 2 (This article by current working group member Danilo Türk contends that the preservation of the status quo by existing nation states has no intrinsic value and that the acceptance of the principle of self-determination of peoples provides the ideal means for peaceful and orderly change).

25. "In the United States today an estimated 300,000 to 2 million human remains of indigenous peoples[,] . . . including many remains of our South and Central American Indians are housed and put on display in the federal, state, and private museums of the United States": R. Snow Arrow Fausett, 19 Americans before Columbus, A Publication of the National Indian Youth Council, no. 1, at 1 (1991).

26. G. Bennett, The I.L.O. Convention on Indigenous and Tribal Populations—The Resolution of a Problem of Vires, 1972–1973 Brit. Y.B. Int'l. L. 382.

27. Pope John Paul II did not respond to a request by an indigenous organization that he publicly comment upon and clearly revoke the bull Inter Caetera of 1493: Letter of Tupac Enrique of ANASAZI (American Nations Alliance Sovereign Aztlan Indijena) (Spring 1984) to Pope John Paul II.

28. L. Kuper, Genocide 183 (1981).

Appendix 1

League of Nations Covenant, Article 23

Subject to and in accordance with the provisions of international conventions existing or hereafter to be agreed upon, the Members of the League:

(a) will endeavour to secure and maintain fair and humane conditions of labour for men, women, and children, both in their own countries and in all countries to which their commercial and industrial relations extend, and for that purpose will establish and maintain the necessary international organisations;

(b) undertake to secure *just treatment* of the native inhabitants of territories under their control;

(c) will entrust the League with the general supervision over the execution of agreements with regard to the traffic in women and children, and the traffic in opium and other dangerous drugs;

(d) will entrust the League with the general supervision of the trade in arms and ammunition with the countries in which the control of this traffic is necessary in the common interest;

(e) will make provision to secure and maintain freedom of communications and of transit and equitable treatment for the commerce of all Members of the League. In this connection, the special necessities of the regions devastated during the war of 1914–1918 shall be borne in mind;

(f) will endeavour to take steps in matters of international concern for the prevention and control of disease. [Emphasis added.]

Appendix 2

The Charter of the United Nations, Chapter XI, Declaration Regarding Non-Self-Governing Territories, Article 73

Members of the United Nations which have or assume responsibilities for the administration of territories whose peoples have not yet attained a full measure of self-government recognize the principle that the interests of the inhabitants of these territories are paramount, and accept as a sacred trust the obligation to promote to the utmost, within the system of international peace and security established by the present Charter, the well-being of the inhabitants of these territories, and, to this end:

a. to ensure, with due respect for the culture of the peoples concerned, their political, economic, social, and educational advancement, their *just treatment*, and their protection against abuses;

b. to develop self-government, to take due account of the political aspirations of the peoples, and to assist them in the progressive development of their free political institutions, according to the particular circumstances of each territory and its peoples and their varying stages of advancement;

c. to further international peace and security;

d. to promote constructive measures of development, to encourage research, and to cooperate with one another, and, when and where appropriate, with specialized international bodies with a view to the practical achievement of the social, economic and scientific purposes set forth in this Article; and

e. to transmit regularly to the Secretary-General for information purposes, subject to such limitation as security and constitutional considerations may require, statistical and other information of a technical nature relating to economic, social, and educational conditions in the territories for which they are respectively responsible other than those territories for which Chapters XII and XIII apply. [Emphasis added.]

Appendix 3

Draft Declaration of Principles for the Defence of the Indigenous Nations and Peoples of the Western Hemisphere

Preamble

Having considered the problems relating to the activities of the United Nations for the promotion and encouragement of respect for human rights and fundamental freedoms,

Noting that the Universal Declaration of Human Rights and related international covenants have the individual as their primary concern, and

Recognizing that individuals are the foundation of cultures, societies, and nations, and

Whereas, it is a fundamental right of any individual to practice and perpetuate the cultures, societies and nations into which they are born, and

Recognizing that conditions are imposed upon peoples that suppress, deny or destroy the cultures, societies, or nations in which they believe or of which they are members,

Be it affirmed, that,

1. Recognition of Indigenous Nations

Indigenous peoples shall be accorded recognition as nations, and proper subjects of international law, provided the people concerned desire to be recognized as a nation and meet the fundamental requirements of nationhood, namely:

(a) Having a permanent population

(b) Having a defined territory

(c) Having a government
(d) Having the ability to enter into relations with other States

2. Subjects of International Law

Indigenous groups not meeting the requirements of nationhood are hereby declared to be subjects of international law and are entitled to the protection of this Declaration, provided they are identifiable groups having bonds of language, heritage, tradition, or other common identity.

3. Guarantee of Rights

No indigenous nation or group shall be deemed to have fewer rights, or lesser status for the sole reason that the nation or group has not entered into recorded treaties or agreements with any State.

4. Accordance of Independence

Indigenous nations or groups shall be accorded such degree of independence as they may desire in accordance with international law.

5. Treaties and Agreements

Treaties and other agreements entered into by indigenous nations or groups with other States, whether denominated as treaties or otherwise, shall be recognized and applied in the same manner and according to the same international laws and principles as the treaties and agreements entered into by other States.

6. Abrogation of Treaties and Other Rights

Treaties and agreements made with indigenous nations or groups shall not be subject to unilateral abrogation. In no event may the municipal law of any State serve as a defence to the failure to adhere to and to perform the terms of treaties and agreements made with indigenous nations or groups. Nor shall any State refuse to recognize and adhere to treaties or other agreements due to changed circumstances where the change in circumstances has been substantially caused by the State asserting such change has occurred.

7. Jurisdiction

No States shall assert or claim or exercise any right of jurisdiction over any indigenous nation or group or territory of such indigenous nation or group unless pursuant to a valid treaty or other agreement freely made with the lawful representatives of the indigenous nation or group concerned. All actions on the part of any State which derogate from the indigenous nations' or groups' right to exercise self-determination shall be the proper concern of existing international bodies.

8. Claims to Territory

No State shall claim or retain, by right of discovery or otherwise, the territories of an indigenous nation or group, except such lands as may have been lawfully acquired by valid treaty or other cession freely made.

9. Settlement of Disputes

All States in the Western Hemisphere shall establish through negotiation or other appropriate means a procedure for the binding settlement of disputes, claims, or other matters relating to indigenous nations or groups. Such procedures shall be mutually acceptable to the parties, fundamentally fair, and consistent with international law. All procedures presently in existence which do not have the endorsement of the indigenous nations or groups concerned, shall be ended, and new procedures shall be instituted consistent with this Declaration.

10. National and Cultural Integrity

It shall be unlawful for any State to take or permit any action or course of conduct with respect to an indigenous nation or group which will directly or indirectly result in the destruction or disintegration of such indigenous nation or group or otherwise threaten the national or cultural integrity of such nation or group, including, but not limited to, the imposition and support of illegitimate governments and the introduction of non-indigenous religions to indigenous peoples by non-indigenous missionaries.

11. Environmental Protection

It shall be unlawful for any State to make or permit any action or course of conduct with respect to the territories of an indigenous nation or group which will directly or indirectly result in the destruction or deterioration of an indigenous nation or group through the effects of pollution of earth, air, water, or which in any way depletes, displaces or destroys any natural resource or other resources under the dominion of, or vital to the livelihood of an indigenous nation or group.

12. Indigenous Membership

No State, through legislation, regulation, or other means, shall take actions that interfere with the sovereign power of an indigenous nation or group to determine its own membership.

13. Conclusion

All of the rights and obligations declared herein shall be in addition to all rights and obligations existing under international law.

E/CN.4/Sub.2/476/Add.5/Annex IV.

Appendix 4

Draft Universal Declaration on the Rights of Indigenous Peoples

PREAMBULAR PARAGRAPHS TO THE DRAFT DECLARATION AS SUBMITTED BY THE MEMBERS OF THE WORKING GROUP ON 25 JULY 1991

1st Preambular Paragraph

Affirming that all indigenous peoples are free and equal in dignity and rights in accordance with international standards, while recognizing the right of all individuals and peoples to be different, to consider themselves different, and to be respected as such,

2nd Preambular Paragraph

Considering that all peoples contribute to the diversity and richness of civilizations and cultures, which constitute the common heritage of humankind,

3rd Preambular Paragraph

Convinced that all doctrines, policies and practices of racial, religious, ethnic or cultural superiority are scientifically false, legally invalid, morally condemnable and socially unjust,

4th Preambular Paragraph

Concerned that indigenous peoples have often been deprived of their human rights and fundamental freedoms, resulting in the dispossession of lands, territories and resources, as well as in poverty and marginalization,

5th Preambular Paragraph

Welcoming the fact that indigenous peoples are organizing themselves in order to bring to an end to all forms of discrimination and oppression wherever they occur,

6th Preambular Paragraph

Recognizing the urgent need to promote and respect the rights and characteristics of indigenous peoples which stem from their history, philosophy, cultures, spiritual and other traditions, as well as from their political, economic and social structures, especially their rights to lands, territories and resources,

7th Preambular Paragraph

Reaffirming that indigenous peoples, in the exercise of their rights, should be free from adverse discrimination of any kind,

8th Preambular Paragraph

Endorsing efforts to consolidate and strengthen the societies, cultures and traditions of indigenous peoples, through their control over development affecting them or their lands, territories and resources,

9th Preambular Paragraph

Emphasizing the need for demilitarization of the lands and territories of indigenous peoples, which will contribute to peace, understanding and friendly relations among all peoples of the world,

10th Preambular Paragraph

Emphasizing the importance of giving special attention to the rights and needs of indigenous women, youth and children,

11th Preambular Paragraph

Recognizing in particular that it is in the best interest of indigenous children for their family and community to retain shared responsibility for the upbringing of the children,

12th Preambular Paragraph

Believing that indigenous peoples have the right freely to determine their relationships with the States in which they live, in a spirit of co-existence with other citizens,

13th Preambular Paragraph

Noting that the International Covenants on Human Rights affirm the fundamental importance of the right to self-determination, as well as the right of all human beings to pursue their material, cultural and spiritual development in conditions of freedom and dignity,

14th Preambular Paragraph

Bearing in mind that nothing in this Declaration may be used as an excuse for denying to any people its right to self-determination,

15th Preambular Paragraph

Calling upon States to comply with and effectively implement all international instruments as they apply to indigenous peoples,

16th Preambular Paragraph

Solemnly proclaims the following Declaration of The Rights of Indigenous Peoples:

DRAFT OPERATIVE PARAGRAPHS AS SUBMITTED BY THE MEMBERS OF THE WORKING GROUP ON 26 JULY 1991

Part I

Operative Paragraph 1

Indigenous peoples have the right to self-determination, in accordance with international law. By virtue of this right, they freely determine their relationship with the States in which they live, in a spirit of co-existence with other citizens, and freely pursue their economic, social, cultural and spiritual development in conditions of freedom and dignity.

Operative Paragraph 2

Indigenous peoples have the right to the full and effective enjoyment of all of the human rights and fundamental freedoms which are recognized in the Charter of the United Nations and other international human rights instruments.

Operative Paragraph 3

Indigenous peoples have the right to be free and equal to all other human beings and peoples in dignity and rights, and to be free from adverse distinction or discrimination of any kind based on their indigenous identity.

Part II

Operative Paragraph 4

Indigenous peoples have the collective right to exist in peace and security as distinct peoples and to be protected against genocide, as well as the individual rights to life, physical and mental integrity, liberty and security of person.

Operative Paragraph 5

Indigenous peoples have the collective right individual right to maintain and develop their distinct ethnic and cultural characteristics and identities, including the right to self-identification.

Operative Paragraph 6

Indigenous peoples have the collective and individual right to be protected from cultural genocide, including the prevention of and redress for:

(a) any act which has the aim or effect of depriving them of their integrity as distinct societies, or of their cultural or ethnic characteristics or identities;

(b) any form of forced assimilation or integration;

(c) dispossession of their lands, territories or resources;

(d) imposition of other cultures or ways of life; and

(e) any propaganda directed against them.

Operative Paragraph 7

Indigenous peoples have the right to revive and practice their cultural identity and traditions, including the right to maintain, develop and protect the past, present and future manifestations of their cultures, such as archeological and historical sites and structures, artifacts, designs, ceremonies, technology and works of art, as well as the right to the restitution of cultural, religious and spiritual property taken from them without their free and informed consent or in violation of their own laws.

Operative Paragraph 8

Indigenous peoples have the right to manifest, practice and teach their own spiritual and religious traditions, customs and ceremonies; the right to maintain, protect, and have access in privacy to religious and cultural sites; the right to use and control of ceremonial objects; and the right to the repatriation of human remains.

Operative Paragraph 9

Indigenous peoples have the right to revive, use, develop, promote and transmit to future generations their own languages, writing systems and literature, and to designate and maintain the original names of communities, places and persons. States shall take measures to ensure that indigenous peoples can understand and be understood in political, legal and administrative proceedings, where necessary, through the provision of interpretation or by other effective means.

Operative Paragraph 10

Indigenous peoples have the right to all forms of education, including access to education in their own languages, and the right to establish and control their own educational systems and institutions. Resources shall be provided by the State for these purposes.

Operative Paragraph 11

Indigenous peoples have the right to have the dignity and diversity of their cultures, histories, traditions and aspirations reflected in all forms of education and public information. States shall take effective measures to eliminate prejudices and to foster tolerance, understanding and good relations.

Operative Paragraph 12

Indigenous peoples have the right to the use of and access to all forms of mass media in their own languages. States shall take effective measures to this end.

Operative Paragraph 13

Indigenous peoples have the right to adequate financial and technical assistance, from States and through international co-operation, to pursue freely their own economic, social and cultural development, and for the enjoyment of the rights contained in this Declaration.

Operative Paragraph (to be numbered)

Nothing in this Declaration may be interpreted as implying for any State, group or individual any right to engage in any activity or to perform any act contrary to the Charter of the United Nations or to the Declaration of Principles of International Law on Friendly Relations and Co-Operation among States in Accordance with the Charter of the United Nations.

DRAFT OPERATIVE PARAGRAPHS AS SUBMITTED BY THE MEMBERS OF THE WORKING GROUP ON 29 JULY 1991

Part III

Operative Paragraph 14

Indigenous peoples have the right to maintain their distinctive and profound relationship with their lands, territories, and resources, which include the total environment of the land, waters, air and sea, which they have traditionally occupied or otherwise used.

Operative Paragraph 15

Indigenous peoples have the collective and individual right to own, control, and use the lands and territories they have traditionally occupied or otherwise used. This includes the right to the full recognition of their own laws and customs, land-tenure systems and institutions for the management of resources, and the right to effective State measures to prevent any interference with or encroachment upon these rights.

Operative Paragraph 16

Indigenous peoples have the right to the restitution or, to the extent this is not possible, to just and fair compensation for lands and territories which have been confiscated, occupied, used or damaged without their free and informed consent. Unless otherwise freely agreed upon by the peoples concerned, compensation shall preferably take the form of lands and territories of quality, quantity and legal status at least equal to those that were lost.

Operative Paragraph 17

Indigenous peoples have the right to the protection of their environment and productivity of their lands and territories, and the right to adequate assistance including international co-operation to this end. Unless otherwise freely agreed upon by the peoples concerned, military activities and the storage or disposal of hazardous materials shall not take place in their land and territories.

Operative Paragraph 18

Indigenous peoples have the right to special measures for protection, as intellectual property, of their traditional cultural manifestations, such as literature, designs, visual and performing arts, cultigens, medicines and knowledge of the useful properties of fauna and flora.

Operative Paragraph (to be numbered)

In no case may any of the indigenous peoples be deprived of their means of subsistence.

Bibliography

BOOKS

Barsh, Russel Lawrence, and James Youngblood Henderson. The Road: Indian Tribes and Political Liberty. Berkeley: University of California Press, 1980.

Belgian Government Information Center. Sacred Mission of Civilization: To Which Peoples Should the Benefits Be Extended? The Belgian Thesis. New York: Belgian Government Information Center, 1953.

Bennett, Gordon. Aboriginal Rights in International Law. London: Anthropological Institute for Survival International, 1978.

Berkhofer, Robert F. Salvation and the Savage: An Analysis of Protestant Missions and American Indian Response. Lexington: University of Kentucky Press, 1965.

———. The White Man's Indian: Images of the American Indian from Columbus to the Present. New York: Knopf, 1978.

Betts, Raymond F. Assimilation and Association in French Colonial Theory, 1890–1914. New York: Columbia University Press, 1961.

———. The "Scramble" for Africa; Causes and Dimensions of Empire. Boston: Heath, 1966.

Brion, Marcel. Bartolome de Las Casas, "Father of the Indians." Trans. Coley R. Taylor. New York: E. P. Dutton & Co., 1929.

Buchheit, Lee C. Secession: The Legitimacy of Self-Determination. New Haven, CT: Yale University Press, 1978.

Cataudel, Honore Marc. The Enclave Problem of Western Europe. Tuscaloosa: University of Alabama Press, 1979.

Cohen, Felix S. Handbook of Federal Indian Law. Washington, DC: U.S. Government Printing Office, 1941.
———. The Legal Conscience: Selected Papers. Ed. Lucy Kramer Cohen. New Haven, CT: Yale University Press, 1960.
Davenport, Frances Gardiner, and Charles Paul Paullin, eds. European Treaties Bearing on the History of the United States and Its Dependencies. Carnegie Institution of Washington. Gloucester, MA: P. Smith, 1967.
Davis, Robert, and Zannis, Mark. The Genocide Machine in Canada: The Pacification of the North. Montreal: Black Rose Books, 1973.
Deloria, Vine, Jr. Behind the Trail of Broken Treaties: An Indian Declaration of Independence. New York: Delacorte Press, 1974.
———, ed. American Indian Policy in the Twentieth Century. Norman: University of Oklahoma Press, 1985.
Dippie, Brian W. The Vanishing American: White Attitudes and U.S. Indian Policy. Middletown, CT: Wesleyan University Press, 1982.
Dobyns, Henry F. Native American Historical Demography: A Critical Bibliography. Bloomington: Indiana University Press, 1976.
Dyck, Noel, ed. Indigenous Peoples and the Nation-State; 'Fourth World' Politics in Canada, Australia, and Norway. St. John's, Newfoundland, Canada: Institute of Social and Economic Research, 1985.
El-Ayouty, Yassin. The United Nations and Decolonization: The Role of Afro-Asia. The Hague: Martinus Nijhoff, 1971.
Getches, David H., Daniel M. Rosenfelt, and Charles F. Wilkinson. Cases and Materials of Federal Indian Law. St. Paul, MN: West Publishing Co., 1979.
Grotius, Hugo. The Freedom of the Seas; or, The Right Which Belongs to the Dutch to Take Part in the East Indian Trade. Trans. Ralph Van Deman Magoffin. New York: Arno Press, 1972.
Hall, Hessel Duncan. Mandates, Dependencies, and Trusteeship. New York: Kraus, 1977.
Hanke, Lewis. All Mankind is One: A Study of the Disputation between Bartolome de Las Casas and Juan Gines de Sepulveda in 1550 on the Intellectual and Religious Capacity of the American Indians. DeKalb: Northern Illinois University Press, 1974.
———. Bartolome de Las Casas, Bookman, Scholar & Propagandist. Philadelphia: University of Pennsylvania Press, 1952.
———. Pope Paul III and the American Indians. Cambridge, MA: Harvard University Press, 1937.
———. The Spanish Struggle for Justice in the Conquest of America. Philadelphia: University of Pennsylvania Press, 1949.
Indigenous Peoples: A Global Quest for Justice. A report for the Independent Commission on International Humanitarian Issues. London: Zed Books, 1987.
Jacobs, Wilbur R. Dispossessing the American Indian: Indians and Whites on the Colonial Frontier. New York: Scribner, 1972.
Jennings, Francis. The Invasion of America: Indians, Colonialism, and the Cant of Conquest. Chapel Hill: University of North Carolina Press, 1975.
Johansen, Bruce E. Forgotten Founders: Benjamin Franklin, the Iroquois, and the Rationale for the American Revolution. Ipswich, MA: Gambit, 1982.

Kinney, Jay P. A Continent Lost, A Civilization Won: Indian Land Tenure in America. New York: Octagon, 1975.
Kuper, Leo. Genocide: Its Political Use in the Twentieth Century. New Haven, CT: Yale University Press, 1981.
Las Casas, Bartolome de. Bartolome de Las Casas: A Selection of His Writings. Trans. and ed. George Sanderlin. New York: Knopf, 1971.
———. The Devastation of the Indies: A Brief Account. Trans. Herma Briffault. New York: Seabury Press, 1974.
Lindley, Mark Frank. The Acquisition and Government of Backward Territory in International Law; Being a Treatise on the Law and Practice Relating to Colonial Expansion. New York: Negro Universities Press, 1969.
Lugard, Frederick John Dealtry. The Dual Mandate in British Tropical Africa. London: F. Cass, 1965.
MacNutt, Francis Augustus. Bartholomew de Las Casas: His Life, His Apostolate, and His Writings. New York: G. P. Putnam's Sons, 1909.
Ortiz, Roxanne Dunbar. Indians of the Americas: Human Rights and Self-Determination. New York: Praeger, 1984.
Parry, John Horace. The Spanish Theory of Empire in the Sixteenth Century. Cambridge, England: Cambridge University Press, 1940.
Prucha, Francis Paul. A Bibliographical Guide to the History of Indian-White Relations in the United States. Chicago: University of Chicago Press, 1977.
———. United States Indian Policy: A Critical Bibliography. Bloomington: Indiana University Press, 1977.
Roy, Bernadette Kelly, and Dallas K. Miller. The Rights of Indigenous Peoples in International Law: An Annotated Bibliography. Saskatoon, Canada: University of Saskatchewan Native Law Centre, 1985.
Sady, Emil John. The United Nations and Dependent Peoples. Washington, DC: Brookings Institution, 1956.
Sanders, Ronald. Lost Tribes and Promised Lands: The Origins of American Racism. Boston: Little, Brown, 1978.
Savelle, Max. Empires to Nations: Expansion in America 1713–1824. Minneapolis: University of Minnesota Press, 1974.
———. The Foundations of American Civilization, A History of Colonial America. New York: H. Holt and Co., 1942.
———. The Origins of American Diplomacy: The International History of Angloamerica, 1492–1763. New York: Macmillan, 1967.
Scott, James Brown. The Spanish Origin of International Law. Oxford: Clarendon Press, 1934.
Simpson, Lesley Byrd. The Encomienda in New Spain: The Beginnings of Spanish Mexico. Berkeley: University of California Press, 1950.
Snow, Alpheus Henry. The Question of Aborigines in the Law and Practice of Nations, Including a Collection of Authorities and Documents. Northbrook, IL: Metro Books, 1972.
Thompson, Ruth, ed. Rights of Indigenous Peoples in International Law: Selected Essays on Self-Determination. Saskatoon, Canada: University of Saskatchewan Native Law Centre, 1987.
Toussaint, Charmian Edwards. The Trusteeship System of the United Nations. New York: Praeger, 1956.

Vattel, Emmerich de. The Law of Nations; or, Principles of the Law of Nature, Applied to the Conduct and Affairs of Nations and Sovereigns. Ed. Joseph Chitty. Philadelphia: T. & J. W. Johnson & Co., 1858.

Victoria, Franciscus de. De Indis Et De Ivre Belli Relectiones. Ed. E. Nys; trans. J. P. Bate. In J. B. Scott, The Classics of International Law. 1917. Reprint. New York: Oceana, 1964.

Washburn, Wilcomb E. The American Indian and the United States; A Documentary History. New York: Random House, 1973.

———. The Assault of Indian Tribalism: The General Allotment Law (Dawes Act) of 1887. Philadelphia: Lippincott, 1975.

———. Red Man's Land/White Man's Law: A Study of the Past and Present Status of the American Indian. New York: Scribner, 1971.

Weinberg, Albert Katz. Manifest Destiny: A Study of Nationalist Expansion in American History. Baltimore, MD: Johns Hopkins University Press, 1935.

Westlake, John. The Collected Papers of John Westlake on Public International Law. Ed. L. Oppenheim. Cambridge, England: Cambridge University Press, 1914.

Wheaton, Henry. Elements of International Law. Philadelphia: Lea and Blanchard, 1866. Reprint.

Williams, Robert A., Jr. The American Indian in Western Legal Thought: The Discourses of Conquest. New York: Oxford University Press, 1990.

Wise, Jennings C. The Red Man in the New World Drama: A Politico-Legal Study with a Pageantry of American Indian History. Ed. Vine Deloria, Jr. New York: Macmillan, 1971.

Wright, Quincy. Mandates under the League of Nations. New York: Greenwood Press, 1968.

Zavala, Silvio. New Viewpoints on the Spanish Colonization of America. Philadelphia: University of Pennsylvania Press, 1943.

LAW REVIEW ARTICLES

Andress, J. L., and J. E. Falkowski. Self-Determination: Indians and the United Nations—The Anomalous Status of America's "Domestic Dependent Nations," 8 Am. Ind. L. Rev. 97 (1980).

Barsh, R. An Advocate's Guide to the Convention on Indigenous and Tribal Peoples, 15 Okla. City U. L. Rev. 209 (1990).

———. Current Developments: Indigenous Peoples: An Emerging Object of International Law, 80 Am. J. Int'l. L. 369 (1980).

———. Indigenous North America and Contemporary International Law, 62 Ore. L. Rev. 73 (1983).

———. The IX Inter-American Indian Congress, 80 Am. J. Int'l. L. 682 (1986).

Bennett, G. Aboriginal Title in the Common Law: A Stony Path through Feudal Doctrine, 27 Buf. L. Rev. 617 (1978).

———. The Developing law of Aboriginal Rights, International commission of Jurists, *The Review*, no. 22, at 42 (June 1979).

———. The I.L.O. Convention on Indigenous and Tribal Populations—The Resolution of the Problem of Vires, 1972–73 Brit. Y.B. Int'l. L. 382.

Berman, H. The Concept of Aboriginal Rights in the Early Legal History of the United States, 27 Buf. L. Rev. 637 (1978).

Brewsaugh, G. Federal Indian Policy: A Violation of International Treaty Law, 4 W.S.U.L. Rev. 229 (1977).

Burke, J. The Cherokee Cases: A Study in Law, Politics, and Morality, 21 Stan. L. Rev. 500 (1969).

Cabranes, J. Human Rights and Non-Intervention in the Inter-American System, 65 Mich. L. Rev. 1147 (1967).

Carter, N. Race and Power Politics as Aspects of Federal Guardianship over American Indians: Land Related Cases, 1887–1924, 4 Am. Ind. L. Rev. 197 (1976).

Clinebell, J. H., and J. Thomson. Sovereignty and Self-Determination: The Rights of Native Americans under International Law, 27 Buf. L. Rev. 669 (1978).

Cohen, F. S. Original Indian Title, 32 Minn. L. Rev. 28 (1947).

———. The Spanish Origin of Indian Rights in the Law of the United States, 31 Geo. L. Rev. 1 (1942).

Coulter, R. T. The Denial of Legal Remedies to Indian Nations under U.S. Law, 3 Am. Ind. J., no. 9, at 5 (1977).

Daes, E. Native People's Rights, 27 C. de D. 123 (1986).

Elias, T. O. The Doctrine of Intertemporal Law, 74 Am. J. Int'l. L. 285 (1980).

Ericson, R. and D. R. Snow. The Indian Battle for Self-Determination, 58 Ca. L. Rev. 445 (1970).

Franck, T. Of Gnats and Camels: Is There a Double Standard at the United Nations? 78 Am. J. Int'l. L. 811 (1979).

———. The Stealing of the Sahara, 70 Am. J. Int'l. L. 694 (1976).

Galey, M. E. Indigenous Peoples, International Consciousness Raising and the Development of International Law on Human Rights, 8 H.R.J. 21 (1975).

Gunter, M. Liechtenstein and the League of Nations: A Precedent for the United Nation's Ministate Problem? 68 Am. J. Int'l. L. 496 (1974).

Hannum, H. New Developments in Indigenous Rights, 28 Va. J. Int'l. L. 649 (1988).

Harvey, I. Constitutional Law: Congressional Plenary Power over Indian Affairs—A Doctrine Rooted in Prejudice, 10 Am. Ind. L. Rev. 117 (1982).

Henderson, J. Youngblood. Unraveling the Riddle of Aboriginal Title, 5 Am. Ind. L. Rev. 75 (1977).

Johnson, D. The Quest of the Six Nations Confederacy for Self-Determination, 44 U. Toronto Fac. L. Rev. 1 (1986).

Lawrey, A. Contemporary Efforts to Guarantee Indigenous Rights under International Law, 23 Van. J. Transnat'l. L. 703 (1990).

Mandell, L. Indian Nations: Not Minorities, 27 C. de D. 101 (1986).

McCartney, G. The American Indian Child-Welfare Crisis: Cultural Genocide or First Amendment Preservation? 7 Colum. Human Rights L. Rev. 529 (1975).

McSloy, S. P. American Indians and the Constitution: An Argument for Nationhood, 14 Am. Ind. L. Rev. 139 (1989).

Narvey, K. The Royal Proclamation of 7 October 1763, The Common Law, and Native Rights to Land within the Territory Granted to the Hudson's Bay Company, 38 Sask. L. Rev. 123 (1974).

Newton, N. J. At the Whim of the Sovereign: Aboriginal Title Reconsidered, 31 Hast. L.J. 1215 (1980).

Norgren, J. Protection of What Rights They Have: Original Principles of Federal Indian Law, 64 N.D.L. Rev. 73 (1988).

Pomerance, M. The United States and Self-Determination: Perspectives on the Wilsonian Conception, 70 Am. J. Int'l. L. 1 (1976).

Rethinking the Trust Doctrine in Federal Indian Law, 98 Harv. L. Rev. 422 (1984).

Roper, D. M. In Quest of Judicial Objectivity: The Marshall Court and the Legitimation of Slavery, 21 Stan. L. Rev. 532 (1969).

Roy, B, and G. Alfredsson. Indigenous Rights, The Literature Explosion, 13 Transnational Perspectives 19 (1987).

Sanders, D. Another Step: The UN Seminar on Relations between Indigenous Peoples and States, 4 C.N.L.R. 37 (1989).

———. The UN Working Group on Indigenous Populations, 11 H.R.Q. 406 (1989).

Shaw, M. The Western Sahara Case, 49 Br. Y.B. Int'l. L. 119 (1978).

Strickland, R. Genocide at Law: An Historic and Contemporary View of the Native American Experience, 34 U. Kan. L. Rev. 713 (1986).

Thomas, A. and A. Thomas, Jr. The Organization of American States and the Monroe Doctrine—Legal Implications, 30 La. L. Rev. 541 (1970).

Williams, R. A., Jr. The Algebra of Federal Indian Law: The Hard Trail of Decolonizing and Americanizing the White Man's Indian Jurisprudence, 1986 Wis. L. Rev. 219 (1986).

———. Encounters on the Frontiers of International Human Rights Law: Redefining the Terms of Indigenous Peoples' Survival in the World, 1990 Duke L.J. 660.

———. The Medieval and Renaissance Origins of the Status of the American Indian in Western Legal Thought, 57 So. Cal. L. Rev. 1 (1983).

Wycoff, T. The Navajo Nation Tomorrow—51st State, Commonwealth, Or . . . ? 5 Am. Ind. L. Rev. 267 (1977).

Index

ABOUT THE AUTHOR

JAMES E. FALKOWSKI is a Fresno County Deputy District Attorney in Fresno, California. His degrees include a J.D. from the University of California at Davis and an LL.M. (International Human Rights Law) from the University of Essex.

www.ingramcontent.com/pod-product-compliance
Ingram Content Group UK Ltd.
Pitfield, Milton Keynes, MK11 3LW, UK
UKHW020820290926
15470UKWH00003B/1272

9 780275 943189